Praise for *Happy for No Reason*

"You can't depend on external circumstances for lasting happiness. It has to come from inside you. Based on scientific research and the experiences of truly happy people, *Happy for No Reason* shows you step-by-step how to raise your happiness set-point."

—Mehmet C. Oz, MD, coauthor of *YOU: On a Diet* and *YOU: Staying Young*

"As I read the book, I felt myself rejoicing in the liberation from my old belief that happiness is to be acquired."

—*Balance* magazine

"The personal stories of happy interviews prove enlightening, and the principles they support are sound and commonsensical."

—*Publishers Weekly*

"Marci Shimoff is one of the most compelling people I've ever known. I'm happy she's shared her wisdom with all of us in *Happy for No Reason*."

—Marianne Williamson, #1 *New York Times* bestselling author of *A Return to Love*

"*Happy for No Reason* offers seven clear, powerful, and effective steps you can practice to be happier right now!"

—John Gray, #1 *New York Times* bestselling author of *Men Are from Mars, Women Are from Venus*

"Tremendous! Marci Shimoff has produced a book that is practical, inspiring, and accessible. *Happy for No Reason* gives readers powerful ways to become happier in all dimensions of life: body, mind, heart, soul, personal power, purpose, and relationships. It's seven books holistically rolled into one."

—Stephen M. R. Covey, bestselling author of *The Speed of Trust: The One Thing That Changes Everything*

"I love this practical approach to true happiness. The real-life stories of people who are Happy for No Reason are extraordinarily moving and inspiring. Just reading this book made me happier!"

—Olivia Hussey, Golden Globe Award–winning actress

"If you want to be happy (and who doesn't?) Marci Shimoff has—amazingly—'cracked the code' for doing so. This isn't the latest pop-psychology craze. Instead, it's based on the latest scientific research about real and lasting happiness. What if you (or your loved ones) really could be happy, regardless of circumstances? *Happy for No*

Reason shows you how—and it's easier than you think. This remarkable book is sure to change a lot of lives, including yours."

—Bill Harris, Director of Centerpointe Research Institute

"*Happy for No Reason* offers an engaging, wise, and profound look at happiness that can change your life. Marci Shimoff has creatively crafted a purposeful guide to assist us in experiencing the gift of happiness."

—Chaka Khan, Grammy Award–winning singer and songwriter, author, and philanthropist

"Rule #1 for happiness: Read this book! Be Happy for No Reason, because everything else comes from that. If you want health, wealth, and wisdom, follow the Happiness Habits presented in these pages and transform your life."

—Phil Town, #1 *New York Times* bestselling author of *Rule #1*, host of CNBC show *Rebel Investor*

"In *Happy for No Reason*, Marci Shimoff shares a new paradigm of happiness, rooted in ancient wisdom, yet validated by cutting-edge research in the fields of both neuroscience and positive psychology. I was enthralled the whole way through."

—Candace B. Pert, PhD, Scientific Director of RAPID Pharmaceuticals, featured in the film *What the Bleep Do We Know!?*, and author of *Everything You Need to Know to Feel Go(o)d*

"*Happy for No Reason* is the most important book about happiness you'll ever read! A completely unique and life-changing approach to being happy 'no matter what.'"

—Raymond Aaron, Canada's #1 business and investment coach

"Marci Shimoff has opened a new era of inner peace for humanity with her brilliant work. The search for happiness now starts and ends inside us as we raise our happiness set-point using her insightful guidance. As an educator, I'm most impressed at how Marci presents a complex topic in an easy-to-read and easy-to-share book. I recommend it happily!"

—Paul R. Scheele, cofounder of Learning Strategies Corporation and author of *Natural Brilliance* and *PhotoReading*

"*Happy for No Reason* is a wonderful guide for how to be happier as individuals and how to share that happiness with our families, our communities, and our world. Everyone will benefit from the wisdom and coaching that this valuable book offers."

—Dr. Bill and Kathy Magee, CEO and President, cofounders of Operation Smile

"*Happy for No Reason* offers a practical and hopeful solution to fear, depression, anxiety, and stress. Here's the secret: Each of us has the ability to focus on joy and happiness—regardless of what is going on in the world. And therein lies our power—and ability to be healthy and happy. This book is a winner."

—Christiane Northrup, MD, author of *Women's Bodies, Women's Wisdom* and *The Wisdom of Menopause*

"Wonderful! This book provides a program that will bring you powerful results. Finding lasting happiness has never been as clear and easy."

—Bobbi DePorter, cofounder and president of Quantum Learning Network/SuperCamp

"*Happy for No Reason* not only reports on the lofty science of happiness, but the authors also wisely remember to include stories from the lives of everyday people."

—Robert Biswas-Diener, Program Director for Education and Learning, Center for Applied Positive Psychology (UK)

"Wealth and success are meaningless without happiness! *Happy for No Reason* shows you how to be happy wherever you are in life."

—Dr. Ivan Misner, Chairman and founder of BNI (Business Networks International)

"*Happy for No Reason* is *the* premier book for any person wanting to experience more happiness. Keep it by your bedstand! It's an important book to show you how you can be happy every day."

—Jill Lublin, international speaker and bestselling author of *Guerrilla Publicity, Networking Magic*, and *Get Noticed*

"This book will change the way you think about happiness. In *Happy for No Reason*, Marci Shimoff has plenty of reasons to share this wisdom. If you want more joy, peace, and well-being in life, this book is for you."

—Yakov Smirnoff, MAPP (master of applied positive psychology) and comedian

Happy for No Reason

7 Steps to Being Happy from the Inside Out

Marci Shimoff

With CAROL KLINE

Free Press
New York London Toronto Sydney

*f*P

Free Press
A Division of Simon & Schuster, Inc.
1230 Avenue of the Americas
New York, NY 10020

First Free Press trade paperback edition March 2009

FREE PRESS and colophon are trademarks of Simon & Schuster, Inc.

For information about special discounts for bulk purposes, please contact Simon & Schuster Special Sales at 1-800-456-6798 or business@simonandschuster.com

Designed by Nancy Singer Olaguera/Sarah Clarehart

Manufactured in the United States of America

10 9 8 7 6 5 4 3 2 1

The Library of Congress has cataloged the hardcover edition as follows:

Shimoff, Marci.
Happy for no reason : seven steps to being happy from the inside out / Marci Shimoff with Carol Kline.
p. cm.
Includes bibliographical references.
1. Happiness. I. Kline, Carol, 1957– II. Title.
BJ1481.S556 2008
158—dc22

2007029803

ISBN-13: 978-1-4165-4772-3
ISBN-10: 1-4165-4772-X
ISBN-13: 978-1-4165-4773-0 (pbk)
ISBN-10: 1-4165-4773-8 (pbk)

This book is dedicated to anyone who's ever wanted to be happy.

It's not just pie in the sky anymore.

And to Dad, my first Happy for No Reason role model.

I carry your joy in my heart.

CONTENTS

FOREWORD

by Jack Canfield

Money *can* buy happiness—you've just done it with the money you've spent on this book!

Or at least you've taken the first, most important step toward becoming what my colleague and dear friend, Marci Shimoff, calls "Happy for No Reason."

It's the perfect time for a book on this subject. Now that most of us have our basic survival needs met and some degree of material comfort, we're looking for more in life. Whether we're buying a great car, going on a dream vacation, getting a raise, or coaching Little League—what we're hoping these things will give us is the deeper experience of being happy. But we're coming up short. I can't think of a more universal need today than that of true happiness.

In *Happy for No Reason,* Marci offers a breakthrough approach to being happy. While most books focus on creating happiness from the outside, *Happy for No Reason* is about creating happiness from the inside—where it really counts. In these pages, you'll find simple, practical steps for experiencing a deeper, more permanent state of happiness, regardless of your external circumstances.

If you saw the film *The Secret,* you know that Marci and I are both great believers in the Law of Attraction, the idea that you have the power to attract into your life what you desire most deeply. With this book, Marci provides the crucial foundation for most effectively practicing this law, which is maintaining a vibrational state of joy and happiness at your core.

When I first met Marci almost twenty years ago at one of my self-esteem training courses, she immediately impressed me with her energy and desire to learn everything—right now! She later assisted with my programs and developed her own life-changing seminars on success and self-esteem. Then one day, this ball of fire called me to say that she had a great idea for a book: *Chicken Soup for the Woman's Soul.* (Only the original *Chicken Soup for the Soul* book had been published at the time.) "Sounds like a brilliant idea," I told her. "But why do I need you to do it?"

Marci and her business partner, Jennifer Hawthorne, didn't skip a beat: "Because we're both writers, we both speak to women's audiences, and we're both women," they told me.

"Well, you got me on that last one," I had to admit.

It was a great collaboration, and Marci and I have worked together closely ever since. When I decided to form the Transformational Leadership Council, an organization of 100 top transformational leaders in the world, I invited her to be a founding member and part of the executive committee.

Marci is the perfect person to write this book. She's been pursuing spiritual growth and the deepest values of happiness for as long as I've known her. I see her as the scout at the head of the pack, the point guard who surveys the territory up ahead and comes back with a road map of what's useful. Whenever Marci tells me I ought to check something out, I know it will be something good.

Marci's always had a unique talent for making deep spiritual concepts immediately accessible. With *Happy for No Reason,* she's hit a home run. This book presents a definitive, broad-based approach to becoming truly happy that combines great spiritual depth, top-notch research, and psychological practicality. It's also a pleasure to read. From our *Chicken Soup* experience, we learned that for a book to really work, it needs to include stories that Velcro its message to our memories. Since the days we humans sat around fires in our caves, our brains have been wired for stories—it's how we make sense of the world. In *Happy for No Reason,* Marci and her cowriter, Carol Kline, have captured moving and amazing real-life stories of people who've applied these principles to their own lives to establish a state of deep and lasting happiness.

I call Marci my sister in the pursuit of the secrets to fulfillment in life, the "ultimate magical manifester." I'm certain that if you follow the practices in her dazzling new book, you too will manifest a lifetime of happiness.

PART I

Happiness That's Here to Stay

This joy I have—the world didn't give it,
the world can't take it away.

—Shirley Caesar, gospel singer

INTRODUCTION

Welcome to a Happier Life!

I was crammed in the back of an ancient flatbed truck with thirty other Westerners, bumping down a rock-strewn dirt road heading toward the foothills of the Himalayas. We each had a bandana covering our nose and mouth to keep us from choking on the dust. We were on our way to a small, remote mountain village where we would provide humanitarian support for the villagers' educational, medical, and housing needs. I was tired, grumpy, and sore all over. After six hours, the driver stopped the truck, got out, and unceremoniously hauled all our luggage onto the dusty ground.

"You'll need to walk the rest of the way," he said. "It's another mile, and from here on, the road is too steep and narrow for my truck." As the truck rattled off, I looked at my ninety-one-pound suitcase with dread. Why had I packed all that unnecessary stuff? Ridiculous. I tried dragging it a few yards up the rough, mountainous trail, but it was hopeless; I wasn't strong enough. Dusk was falling; what could I do? Everyone else in the group was wrestling with their own bags; no one could help me. But they were managing to make their way up the hill and soon were nearly out of sight. I sat down and spent a couple of minutes fighting down a rising panic. Were there tigers here?

Then a tiny, barefoot old woman, her face seamed with wrinkles, came out of the forest and up the road toward me. She approached me with a warm smile, picked up my bag, and, astonishingly, hoisted it up onto her head as though it weighed no more than a basket of fruit. Then she headed up the hill, motioning for me to follow.

As we ventured up the path together, though we had no language in common, I was struck by the twinkle in her eyes and the simple happiness that she exuded. When we finally reached the top of the mountain, I was met with the huge smiles and enthusiastic greetings of her fellow villagers.

I spent the next two weeks working side-by-side with these people, attending to the children, preparing food, and helping administer medical care. Like them, I slept on the ground, bathed in the river, and drank milk fresh from the cow. To my surprise, I found that this no-frills lifestyle agreed with me. I felt clear, peaceful, and full of energy.

During my stay, I also spent a lot of time observing my mountain hosts. Here were people who had no electricity or running water, living on the bare minimum with no creature comforts. Yet there was a lightness of spirit, a sense of humor, and an easy friendliness about them that was remarkable. They were simply happy from the inside out.

Of course, I realized that their happiness wasn't a product of their poverty. I'd seen plenty of dirt-poor men, women, and children in all corners of the world who were utterly miserable. I'd also met people with every shiny, expensive toy money could buy who were ecstatic about their good fortune, as well as fabulously wealthy folks who were living proof of the saying "Money can't buy happiness."

The experience reinforced my conviction that happiness isn't about having everything you've ever dreamed of, nor is it simply negating the need for material pleasures in life. It goes deeper than that. What we're all really looking for is happiness from within that doesn't depend on external circumstances—the kind I call Happy for No Reason.

My time among the Himalayan villagers crystallized my goal: without giving up my regular life, I wanted to find a way to enjoy that kind of happiness, no matter where I was or what I was doing.

Chances are you picked up this book for the very same reason. If you're human, it comes with the package: everyone, everywhere, wants to be happy. You might already be pretty happy and just want to crank up the volume a notch or two. Or you may be seriously unhappy and wondering how others around you manage to find delight in their lives. Perhaps you've created your version of the American Dream, but still feel an emptiness inside that nothing on the outside seems to fill.

The good news is that it doesn't matter where you begin. Wherever you are right now, this book will show you how to be happier. You don't have to have happy genes, win the lottery, or become a saint. By the time you finish reading these pages, you will know how to experience an authentic state of sustained happiness for the rest of your life.

My Heart's Quest

This book was born of my own deep longing to be happy. The kind of happy that is solid, true, and anchored in my being, so that no matter what my external circumstances are, there is still a feeling of unshakable fulfillment, joy, and inner peace. Other people lived this way, so I knew it was possible. Yet for so many years, no matter what I did, it seemed to elude me.

As you'll read in my story in Chapter 1, I was unhappy from the get-go. As a young teen, I began a personal, and later professional, quest that lasted over thirty-five years and ultimately led me to the amazing findings in this book. During that time, I took every transformational seminar under the sun. For years I studied and taught success principles. I applied them in my own life and gained a good measure of success. I had plenty of *reasons* to be happy: I was a #1 *New York Times* best-selling author, I'd received national acclaim as an inspirational speaker, and I'd touched millions of people's lives. I was very familiar with what it meant to be "happy because . . ." The problem was it didn't bring me the happiness I wanted.

Looking around, I saw that the happiest people I knew weren't the most successful and famous. Some were married, some were single. Some had lots of money, and some didn't have a dime. Some of them even had health challenges. From where I stood, there seemed to be no rhyme or reason to what made people happy. The obvious question became *Could a person actually be happy for no reason?*

I had to find out.

The Study of Happiness

So I threw myself into the study of happiness. I interviewed scores of experts and delved into the research from the burgeoning field of positive psychology, the scientific study of the positive traits that enable people to enjoy meaningful, fulfilling, and happy lives. I soaked it up like a sponge and found a number of gems—fascinating, amazing, and useful information that's changed my life and will change yours too.

My first major discovery was that scientists have found that we each have a "happiness set-point," the genetic and learned tendency to remain at a certain level of happiness, similar to a thermostat setting on a furnace. Fortunately for those of us not born on the sunny side of the street, it's been shown that we can change our happiness set-points. I'll discuss this more in the next chapter and offer you specific exercises throughout the book to raise your happiness set-point.

I also learned that two of our greatest barriers to happiness, fear and anxiety, have been hardwired in us for millennia to ensure our survival as a species. In today's world, however, that old wiring has become more harmful than helpful. In the coming chapters, you'll discover ways to disconnect that internal alarm system so you can lead a happier life.

Research findings like these thrilled me, but I still wanted more. In my years studying success, I'd found that *success leaves clues.* You can look at the lives of successful people to learn how to become successful yourself. I figured that the same must be true of happiness, so I set out to interview 100 truly happy people.

The Happy 100

It turned out that it wasn't that easy to find 100 truly happy people, even in a nation of 280 million! I'd read about the epidemic of unhappiness in our country: one out of every five women in America is on antidepressants, and 6 million men start taking antidepressants every year. But I was still shocked to experience it firsthand. I asked everyone I met, "Who's the happiest person you know?" People really had to stop and think. Then, inevitably, the first person they'd name would be someone who was fabulously successful. "But wait," they'd say, "he (or she) isn't really *happy*." Many people couldn't think of anyone they considered truly happy. But I persisted in my search, and eventually I found over 100 deeply happy people to interview. I call them the Happy 100. They're men and women of all ages and backgrounds, from all different walks of life. Their stories are amazing and revealing. They've opened my eyes to a whole new way of living.

In addition to conducting interviews, I posted a very simple survey on my website, a single question asking "What do you think is the most important thing necessary to experience the Happy for No Reason state?" The responses were illuminating.

I was right. Like success, happiness does leave clues. I came away from my interviews and survey with clear evidence that happy people live their lives differently from unhappy people. I discovered 21 habits that happy people share—I call them the Happiness Habits—that anyone can practice to easily and effectively support the experience of deep and lasting happiness.

Then I came upon my most important discovery, one that sets this book apart from all the rest: the concept of Happy for No Reason. Other experts on happiness urge you to find the things in life that make you happy, and do more of those things. There's nothing wrong with that, but it won't bring you true and lasting happiness. *Happy for No Reason* takes a radically different approach, showing you breakthrough methods to consistently experience the deep, inner happiness that's at your core—a happiness that's beyond reasons and that's here to stay.

My research on happiness and my own experience have convinced me that becoming Happy for No Reason is entirely doable. Today we know so much more about everything in our world. We've used technology to explore many aspects of life, from our own bodies to the composition of the galaxy, and are finally using technology to explore happiness. In the past two decades, scientists in the field of positive psychology have made tremendous strides, identifying the happiness set-point, the neurotransmitters of happiness, and even where happiness is located in the brain. For the first time in history, we know that happiness isn't an abstract emotion; it's a physiological state that can be measured—and experienced more often in our everyday lives.

My discoveries were so remarkable I wanted to share them with as many people as possible, so I decided to write this book. I called my dear friend of over twenty-five years, Carol Kline, a writer who shared my enthusiasm for this topic, and I asked her to join me. Carol had seen me through everything, so she was the perfect person to embark on this journey with me. We both feel blessed by the thousands of hours spent researching and talking with experts and hearing the stories of happy people. And the result, *Happy for No Reason,* is a combination of the best knowledge and current research on happiness, practical methods gleaned from the happy people I interviewed, and the inspirational stories of their lives.

What You'll Find in This Book

Happy for No Reason is divided into three sections. In this first section, Part I, we'll continue to explore the paradigm of true happiness I call Happy for No Reason. Just understanding this idea can change the way you experience happiness in your own life. You'll find a Happy for No Reason questionnaire that will help you assess and understand your own present level of happiness. You'll also learn three guiding principles that will help you get past the common blocks to happiness in your life and speed your progress. Finally, I'll share with you how I've applied the Law of Attraction to being happier. I'm honored to be featured in the worldwide film phenomenon *The Secret,* which focuses on this law. I've seen how powerfully it can change lives.

Part II is the how-to section that shows you step-by-step how to raise your level of happiness. Through my research, I discovered that there are seven specific steps for becoming Happy for No Reason. I wanted to make these seven steps easy to remember, and because people's homes are so often a metaphor for their lives, I decided to present them in a simple, easy-to-remember analogy: building a Home for Happiness. The seven steps of building your Home for Happiness correspond to the seven main areas of your life: personal power, mind, heart, body, soul, purpose, and people.

This holistic approach is vital. Many books on happiness just focus on the mind, but if you don't also address your habitual behavior in the other areas of your life, you won't experience true happiness. Here's an overview of the steps (one per chapter):

1. The Foundation—Take Ownership of Your Happiness
2. The Pillar of the Mind—Don't Believe Everything You Think
3. The Pillar of the Heart—Let Love Lead
4. The Pillar of the Body—Make Your Cells Happy
5. The Pillar of the Soul—Plug Yourself In to Spirit
6. The Roof—Live a Life Inspired by Purpose
7. The Garden—Cultivate Nourishing Relationships

Each step has three Happiness Habits, with corresponding exercises based on the latest research and findings on how to raise your happiness set-point, as well as inspirational stories.

As a *Chicken Soup for the Soul* coauthor, I'd been deeply moved reading over 20,000 stories that had been submitted for my books. When the books were published, the overwhelming response from millions of readers confirmed for me that stories open people's hearts and affect them deeply. That's why I decided to include some of the inspiring first-person stories of transformation from the Happy 100 in this book. From my 100 interviews with these unconditionally happy people, I've selected twenty-one stories that clearly define what it means to be Happy for No Reason.

You'll read phenomenal tales from a variety of people, including a former drug dealer turned minister, a hit filmmaker, a political refugee, and a famous actress who escaped a "family curse," as well as stories from doctors, nurses, mothers, teachers, and business executives. You'll meet Zainab, who lived under Saddam Hussein's thumb and locked up her memories—and her happiness—in a box hidden deep inside. And Janet, who was living a ho-hum life and working at a dead-end job, until she discovered a simple yet profound way to be deeply happy every day. You'll hear Gay's story of losing 100 pounds, and gaining the life of his dreams, after finding the key to really nourishing himself. These stories are wonderful illustrations that there are many paths to Happy for No Reason, and that we're all capable of arriving at that destination no matter where we begin the journey.

Part III is about being Happy for No Reason—permanently. No more waiting for the other shoe to drop, wondering how long your happiness will last. In this section, you'll get clear direction about how to put the Happiness Habits into practice every day and find resources that can help you sustain being Happy for No Reason for the rest of your life.

Becoming Happy for No Reason may not happen overnight—though, as I found in some instances, it can! Having the vision that it exists and knowing the steps to achieve it will put you on the fast track to a complete transformation of your life. I know, because it's happened to me and to thousands of others. I've used the tools and techniques presented in this book myself and with my clients. Though I wasn't happy for many years, I've been able to move from a D+ to an A– on the happiness scale. Now, when life tosses my boat around, I return to an even keel more easily; I don't capsize anymore. I'm still on the journey, still a student as well as a teacher, but I am living proof that these steps can move you immediately in the right direction, no matter where you start. Believe me, if I can do it, so can you.

It is my deep prayer and wish that this book lead you to build a home for happiness inside yourself that is unshakable—and from that strong and peaceful place you create more happiness in the world.

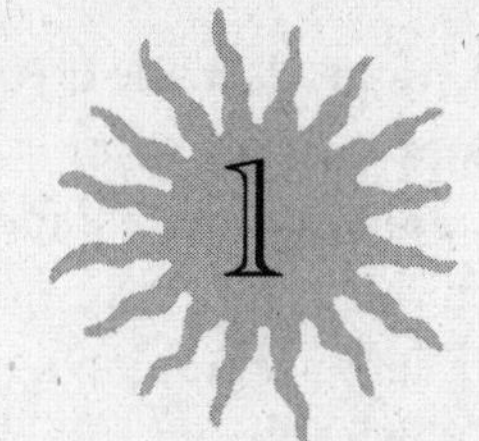

Happy for No Reason . . . Really?

Happiness is the meaning and the purpose of life, the whole aim and end of human existence.

—Aristotle

Years ago, I taught a success seminar in which I asked the participants to each take a big sheet of heavy paper and write across the top "100 THINGS TO BE, DO, HAVE." Then they made three long columns and began listing their dreams, big and small. When they shared their goals afterward, they were invariably all fired up: people wanted to go scuba diving in the Great Barrier Reef, own a Mercedes SL600 Roadster (cream white, with titanium silver alloy wheels), dance at the White House, fly a small plane around the world. They wanted to rise to the top of their field, end world hunger, create world peace, be on the cover of *Time* magazine.

Somewhere on the BE list a few people wrote "Be happy," but I was surprised at how often most people overlooked that. That's what the whole page was about, wasn't it? Didn't being, doing, and having all these things equal happiness?

Over time, I've come to look back on those lists as a great example of taking the long way around. Big and wonderful as those things are, they aren't the ultimate thing we all want. If you cut to the chase, what we really want is to be happy.

The truth is that happiness is so compelling, so attractive—so irresistible—that whether you realize it or not, everything you do is aimed at making yourself happy. Happiness has been called the holy grail of human existence, the be-all and end-all of life. Aristotle called it the goal of all goals.

Studies around the world show that when people are asked to rank what they want from life, they put the desire to be happy at the top of the list, more important than wealth, status, a good job, fame, and sex. This is true for people of all cultures, races, religions, ages, and lifestyles. And research also shows how vital happiness is: happy people live longer, are healthier, and have better relationships. In fact, happiness leads to more success in every area of your life.

Unfortunately, many people are not experiencing much sustained, authentic happiness. Consider these sad statistics:

- Less than 30 percent of people report being deeply happy.
- Twenty-five percent of Americans and 27 percent of Europeans claim they are depressed.
- The World Health Organization predicts that by 2020, depression will be second only to heart disease in terms of the global burden of illness.

Although our lifestyles are better than ever, we're unhappier than ever. It seems the more gadgets and goods we gather, the worse we feel.

In this book, I'm not going to show you directly how to make more money, be more successful, or have better relationships. I leave that to my friends and colleagues in the transformational world who do that all so well. What I *am* going to do is tell you what I would most want to know. This book answers the question I've spent the past thirty-five years studying and researching, the one that is most important to me—and that I believe is also most important to you: **How can I be truly happy?**

Although this question absorbed me for most of my life, for years I didn't have much luck answering it. In fact, I spent most of that time barking up the wrong tree.

One Unhappy Camper

I had imagined it all as a child: I would grow up, live in a beautiful house, have a wonderful husband and a great career. My body would be perfect and my social life fun and exciting. I would be *HAPPY*!

To live that life of my dreams, I knew I'd have to work hard to get all my ducks in a row. And although I was clear about what I wanted, I wasn't sure how I'd get it. The only thing I knew for sure was that I wasn't happy. I came out of the womb filled with existential angst. I was the brooding five-year-old who was worrying about the condition of the world while everyone else was watching *Romper Room.* At age seven, I was grilling my wonderful, loving parents about God and spirituality and becoming frustrated that they couldn't answer my questions. When I look through family albums, I see my brother and sister beaming at the camera while I always look as though I've just lost my best friend.

Even though I wasn't a naturally happy person, something deep within me knew that I didn't have to accept that way of being. It was as if I had some kind of antenna tuned to whatever I needed to learn most. When I was eleven, I slathered myself in suntan oil and snuck into my sister's room to steal a book to read while sunbathing. I grabbed the skinniest one, since I'd always been a slow reader, and headed outside. By the time I was halfway through the book, Hermann Hesse's *Siddhartha,* the story of a young Indian man on a quest for enlightenment thousands of years ago, I was in tears. I recognized that I wasn't alone; someone else on the planet understood my search and shared my longing for connection and joy. That book put me on the path of seeking.

While other girls were perfecting their stag leap for cheerleading tryouts, I was taking self-development courses. When I was thirteen, I heard my first motivational speaker, Zig Ziglar. As I watched him walk back and forth across the stage, revealing the secrets of success and telling stories that gave me goosebumps, lightning struck. I realized that being a professional speaker was what I wanted to do. It was a strange career goal for a young teenage girl in the early 1970s. Even so, I pictured myself speaking in front of large audiences all over the world, inspiring people to change their lives for the better. My parents were supportive, even though my father was a dentist and they really wanted me to be a dental hygienist. Mom said, "You sure talk enough, so you might as well get paid for it."

I moved my Nancy Drew mysteries to the side to make room for every humanistic psychology book I could lay my hands on. I devoured them. At the age of sixteen, I began meditating every day, and by the time I turned twenty, I was a teacher of meditation. Though meditating had a profound impact on my life, I was still searching.

As time passed, I never lost sight of my goal of becoming a speaker. I immersed myself in success principles and did my best to put every one into practice. I tithed a percentage of my income and visualized my goals. I made vision boards to help me picture those goals and discovered I had a gift for manifesting my desires. For example, after earning my MBA, I drew to myself a wonderful job that included many qualities I had always yearned for in a career. As vice president of marketing for a company that sold Austrian crystal, I was responsible for training and inspiring employees. I loved it! I taught them everything I'd studied in my own life: the principles of the Law of Attraction, being clear about what you want, and knowing how to harness your intuition, overcome obstacles, and achieve your goals.

From there, I moved on to teaching those same principles of success as a corporate trainer for Fortune 500 companies and then for a national seminar company speaking to large audiences of women all over the country. With every new position came a bigger paycheck and more kudos. But I wasn't exactly happy. I knew there was something still missing. I just couldn't tell you what it was.

Maybe it was my subject matter, I decided. So instead of teaching success seminars, I began to teach self-esteem seminars for women. Jack Canfield, the nation's top expert on self-esteem, became my amazing mentor—years before he created the mega-best-selling book series *Chicken Soup for the Soul*—and soon I was giving keynotes to two or three hundred women a day on self-esteem. I taught on my high heels from 7:00 in the morning until late afternoon, then jumped in a car and drove three hours to the next city, day after day after day. It was exhausting but exhilarating. I loved standing in front of my audiences and watching their faces light up. Yet I still felt it wasn't quite enough—I wanted to reach more people.

Then came my big break. It began with a decision to take care of myself. Burned out from all my traveling, I signed up for a seven-day silence retreat, a real challenge for a Chatty Cathy like me. On the fourth day, in the middle of meditation, the proverbial lightbulb clicked on. I flashed on a title: *Chicken Soup for the Woman's Soul.* Up to this point, only the original *Chicken Soup* book had been published, and I knew this idea was a colossal winner. I was so excited; I'd just had the epiphany of my career. The only problem was I had to stay silent for three more days! The minute the retreat ended, I ran to the nearest payphone and called Jack. A year and a half later, *Chicken Soup for the Woman's Soul* became a #1 *New York Times* best-seller and I went on to write five more *Chicken Soup for the Soul* books that have sold over 13 million copies.

There I was, on national TV and radio shows, giving speeches to huge audiences, being treated like a queen and living the whirlwind life of success. At one conference, I was picked up in a white stretch limo to speak to a crowd of 8,000. Throughout the three-day event, thousands of women stood in a line that stretched around the entire convention center waiting for me to sign their books. A massage therapist rubbed my hands every hour as I autographed copy after copy after copy—so many they had to be airlifted from every corner of the country to meet the demand. Many women in the autograph line told me my books had changed, or even saved, their lives. I was deeply moved by their stories and felt good that I had done something that made a difference. But when I went to my hotel room each night, I flopped on the bed, feeling drained and strangely flat.

You'd think I'd have been on top of the world. But I wasn't. Sure, my ego had gotten a boost, but I still had the same worries, tensions, complaints, and bad hair days as everyone else. At each step of the way, I was excited about the successes I'd achieved, but I noticed that the high never lasted. I was happy about the *things* in my life, but not really *happy*.

Yes, I know how this sounds. Cry me a river, you're thinking. Well, I too have sat through many an *E! True Hollywood Story* and rolled my eyes over the sad story of the celeb whose rise to fame and fortune brought only tears. *Oh please,* I'd tell myself, if I were in their shoes, I'd be so happy you'd have to tie me down so I wouldn't float away. But now I was having a taste of that life, and the deep happiness I craved just wasn't happening. I was meeting famous people and seeing that many of them weren't happy either.

Maybe the problem wasn't my career, but my love life. If I just found the right partner, I told myself, *then* I'd be happy. I approached this challenge with the same single-mindedness I'd given to pursuing success. I dated enthusiastically and had a few relationships that were close but not *it.* Then, one weekend, I attended a seminar at a large retreat center in upstate New York. There, in the gravel parking lot, we were introduced by friends—and before we'd even said hello, he took me in his arms and waltzed me around, sweeping me off my feet with his European flair. Sergio, my Italian Prince Charming, had arrived. Like most romances, it had its ups and downs, but eventually we settled down together, bought a lovely house, and moved in.

Finally, I had the life I'd imagined: the house, the man, the career, and a great social life. (Okay, so I didn't have Halle Berry's body—but four out of five isn't bad.) Still, I couldn't shoo away the thoughts of dissatisfaction that kept popping up in my head or escape the gnawing pain I felt in my heart.

I realized I had a big problem. I couldn't continue to acquire or accomplish any more thinking that would make me happy. My life until that point had proven the futility of that approach. I'd come to the end of the line. Something had to change.

I had to admit the awful truth to myself: I still felt empty. I had *every* reason to be happy and yet I wasn't.

Although it seems obvious in hindsight, I had believed for so long that happiness would come from what I owned, achieved, or experienced that it took me a while to finally get it. Maybe happiness didn't come from the reasons I had imagined. Maybe happiness didn't come from any reason at all.

That's when I shifted my focus to the idea of Happy for No Reason and started applying the principles I discovered through my research and interviews. As a result, my own happiness level took a quantum leap. I felt a greater sense of peace and well-being that came from deep inside. I found myself singing throughout the day and appreciating the people around me more. I knew I'd made real progress when about five years ago my friends started calling me the "joy bunny." I was as thrilled as if I had won the Nobel Prize.

Of my findings, one piece of information stood out. It completely transformed my approach to being happy and explained why, for so many years, true happiness had always been just outside my grasp.

Why Some People Are Happier Than Others

If you and I were sitting over some tea at a sidewalk café and I asked you, "Are you happy?," what would your answer be?

A few of you might say, "Absolutely—if I were any happier, I'd be twins!" (Okay, that would be a *very* few of you.)

A lot of you would probably reply, "Sometimes."

But I'd bet dollars to doughnuts that at least half of you would say, "No, not really."

Some people enjoy their lives no matter what happens, while others can't find happiness no matter how hard they try. Most of us fall somewhere in between.

The reason for this puzzling disparity is the happiness set-point I mentioned in the introduction. Researchers have found that *no matter what happens to you in life*, you tend to return to a fixed range of happiness. Like your weight set-point, which keeps the scale hovering around the same number, your happiness set-point will remain the same **unless you make a concerted effort to change it.**

In fact, there was a famous study conducted that tracked people who'd won the lottery—what many people think of as the ticket to the magic kingdom of joy. Within a year, these lucky winners returned to approximately the same level of happiness they'd experienced before their windfall. Surprisingly, the same was true for people who became paraplegic. Within a year or so of being disabled, they also returned to their original happiness level.

Whatever the experience—positive or negative—people return to their happiness set-point. Further research has shown only three exceptions to this phenomenon: losing a spouse, which can take more time to recover from; chronic unemployment; and extreme poverty.

Okay, you may be thinking, *if my happiness level is set—how did it get there?* Dr. David Lykken, a scientist at the University of Minnesota, had the same question. To determine how much of a person's happiness comes from nature and how much from nurture, Lykken and his team, in the late 1980s, began studying thousands of sets of twins, including a number of identical twins who had been raised apart. After extensive testing they found that approximately 50 percent of our happiness set-point is genetic and the other 50 percent is learned. Half of the reason you walk around generally cheery or perennially dreary is that you were *born* that way, the other half is determined by your thoughts, feelings, and beliefs formed in response to your life experiences.

THE TESTS SHOW YOU HAVE AN OVERACTIVE GRUMPY GENE.

In a recent review of the literature and studies on happiness, positive psychology researchers Sonja Lyubomirsky, Kennon Sheldon, and David Schkade confirmed Lykken's earlier findings that 50 percent of our happiness comes from our genetics. But more exciting was the new information they uncovered about the remaining 50 percent. It appears that only 10 percent of our happiness set-point is determined by circumstances such as our level of wealth, marital status, and job.

The other 40 percent is determined by our habitual thoughts, feelings, words, and actions. This is why it's possible to raise your happiness set-point. In the same way you'd crank up the thermostat to get comfortable on a chilly day, you actually have the power to reprogram your happiness set-point to a higher level of peace and well-being.

The discovery of the happiness set-point and our ability to change it turns everything we've all believed about being happy *upside down.* We spend our entire lives searching for happiness, yearning for it, trying to get the things we are sure will make us happy: wealth, beauty, relationships, career, and so on. But the truth is, to be truly happy, all you have to do is raise your happiness set-point.

I sure wish I'd known I was just one of those people who had a low happiness set-point before spending so much time and energy chasing after reasons to be happy. From my interviews with the Happy 100, I've come to see that genuinely happy people are Happy for *No* Reason.

Let's look at this phenomenon.

The Happiness Continuum

Happiness for any reason is just another form of misery.

—The Upanishads

One day, as I sat down to compile my findings, all the pieces of the puzzle fell into place. I had a simple, but profound "a-ha"—there's a *continuum* of happiness:

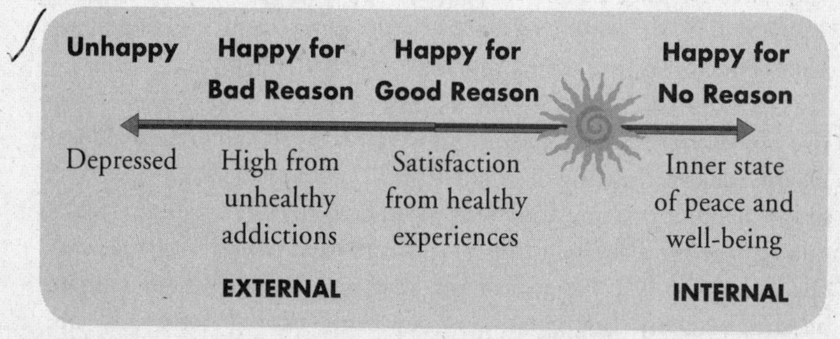

Unhappy: We all know what this means: Life is a bummer. Some of the signs are anxiety, fatigue, feeling blue or low—your garden-variety unhappiness. This isn't the same as clinical depression, which is characterized by deep despair and hopelessness that dramatically interferes with your ability to live a normal life, and for which professional help is absolutely necessary.

Happy for Bad Reason: When people are unhappy, they often try to make themselves feel better by indulging in addictions or behaviors that may feel good in the moment but are ultimately detrimental. They seek the highs that come from drugs, alcohol, excessive sex, "retail therapy," compulsive gambling, overeating, and too much television watching, to name a few. This kind of happiness is hardly happiness at all. It is only a temporary way to numb or escape our *un*happiness through fleeting experiences of pleasure.

Happy for Good Reason: This is what people usually mean by happiness: having good relationships with our family and friends, success in our career, financial security, a nice house or car, or using our talents and strengths well. It's the pleasure we derive from having the healthy things in our lives that we want.

Don't get me wrong. I'm all for this kind of happiness! It's just that it's only half the story. Being Happy for Good Reason depends on the *external* conditions of our lives. If these conditions change or are lost, our happiness usually goes too.

Deep inside, you know that life isn't meant to be about getting by, numbing your pain, or having everything "under control." True happiness doesn't come from merely collecting an assortment of happy experiences. At your core, you know there's something more than this.

You're right. There is one more level on the happiness continuum: Happy for No Reason.

Happy for No Reason: This is true happiness—a neurophysiological state of peace and well-being that *isn't* dependent on external circumstances.

Happy for No Reason isn't elation, euphoria, mood spikes, or peak experiences that don't last. It doesn't mean grinning like a fool 24/7 or experiencing a superficial high. Happy for No Reason isn't an emotion. In fact, when you are Happy for No Reason, you can have *any* emotion—including sadness, fear, anger, or hurt—but you still experience that underlying state of peace and well-being.

When you're Happy for No Reason, you *bring* happiness to your outer experiences rather than trying to *extract* happiness from them. You don't need to manipulate the world around you to try to make yourself happy. You live *from* happiness, rather than *for* happiness.

This is a revolutionary concept. Most of us focus on being Happy for Good Reason, stringing together as many happy experiences as we can, like beads in a necklace, to create a happy life. We have to spend a lot of time and energy trying to find just the right beads so we can have a "happy necklace."

Being Happy for No Reason, in our necklace analogy, is like having a happy string. No matter what beads we put on our necklace—good, bad, or indifferent—our inner experience, which is the string that runs through them all, is happy, creating a happy life.

When you're Happy for No Reason you're unconditionally happy. It's not that your life always looks perfect—it's just that however it looks, you'll still be happy.

As the thirteenth-century poet Rumi described it, "Happy, not from anything that happens. Warm, not from fire or a hot bath. Light, I register zero on a scale." Whenever I asked the Happy 100 to describe the qualities of being Happy for No Reason, I got the same answers over and over:

- Having a sense of lightness or buoyancy
- Feeling alive, vital, energetic
- Having a sense of flow, openness
- Feeling love and compassion for yourself and others
- Having passion about your life and purpose
- Feeling gratitude, forgiveness
- Being at peace with life
- Being fully present in the moment

Matthieu Ricard, a French scientist who became a Buddhist monk over thirty years ago, is often called "the happiest man in the world" by researchers who've measured his brain's functioning both in and out of meditation. (More about monks in the laboratory in Chapter 7.) Ricard's book, *Happiness: A Guide to Developing Life's Most Important Skill,* gives one of the clearest descriptions of Happy for No Reason I've ever heard. He writes, "By happiness I mean a deep sense of flourishing that arises from an exceptionally healthy mind. This is not a mere pleasurable feeling, a fleeting emotion, or a mood, but an optimal state of being."

How Happy for No Reason Are You?

The following Happy for No Reason questionnaire will give you a snapshot of how Happy for No Reason you are in your life right now. Though you may have filled out happiness questionnaires before, you may not have noticed that they're usually state-dependent; that is, they ask you to rate your happiness according to what's going on in your life (job, career, relationships, and so on) and how satisfied you are with your life circumstances. Those questionnaires measure Happy for Good Reason. This questionnaire is different; it measures Happy for *No* Reason.

The Happy for No Reason questionnaire is modeled after the Well-Being Scale that is part of the Multidimensional Personality Questionnaire, a tool developed by Auke Tellegen, a professor of psychology at the University of Minnesota, to help researchers determine happiness set-points. As you answer these questions, think about how they apply to you in general.

The Happy for No Reason Questionnaire

Rate each statement on a scale of 1 to 5:

1 = Not at all true
2 = Slightly true
3 = Moderately true
4 = Mostly true
5 = Absolutely true

1. I often feel happy and satisfied for no particular reason.

1 2 3 4 5

2. I live in the moment.

1 2 3 4 5

3. I feel alive, vital, and energetic.

1 2 3 4 5

4. I experience a deep sense of inner peace and well-being.

1 2 3 4 5

5. Life is a great adventure for me.

1 2 3 4 5

6. I don't let bad situations keep me down.

1 2 3 4 5

7. I am enthusiastic about the things I do.

1 2 3 4 5

8. Most days I have an experience of laughter or joy.

1 2 3 4 5

9. I trust that this is a friendly universe.

1 2 3 4 5

10. I look for the gift or the lesson in everything that happens.

1 2 3 4 5

11. I am able to let go and forgive.

1 2 3 4 5

12. I feel love for myself.

1 2 3 4 5

13. I look for the good in every person.

1 2 3 4 5

14. I change the things I can and accept the things I can't change.

1 2 3 4 5

15. I surround myself with people who support me.

1 2 3 4 5

16. I don't blame others or complain.

1 2 3 4 5

17. My negative thoughts don't overshadow me.

1 2 3 4 5

18. I feel a general sense of gratitude.

1 2 3 4 5

19. I feel connected to something bigger than myself.

1 2 3 4 5

20. I feel inspired by a sense of purpose in my life.

1 2 3 4 5

Scoring section:

If your score is 80–100: To a great degree, you are Happy for No Reason.

If your score is 60–79: You have a good measure of being Happy for No Reason.

If your score is 40–59: You have glimpses of being Happy for No Reason.

If your score is under 40: You have little experience of being Happy for No Reason.

Whatever your score, you can *always* move toward being more Happy for No Reason. As I said earlier, it doesn't matter where you begin; what matters is that you *do* begin. Once you've finished reading the book and have begun practicing the seven steps and the Happiness Habits, take the questionnaire again. After that, assessing your Happy for No Reason score on a regular basis will help you chart your progress.

Happy for No Reason: Your Natural State

Happy for No Reason isn't just a nice idea. As I'll explain in later chapters, it's **a specific, measurable physiological state characterized by distinct brain activity, heart rhythms, and body chemistry.**

Scientists tell us that every subjective experience we have has a corresponding state of functioning in our bodies. People who are Happy for No Reason tend to have greater activity in the left prefrontal cortex, orderly heart wave patterns, and more of the specific neurotransmitters associated with well-being and happiness: oxytocin, serotonin, dopamine, and endorphins.

Although modern science gives us new insight into the physiology of Happy for No Reason, it's a state that's been spoken of in virtually all spiritual and religious traditions throughout history. The concept is universal. In Buddhism, it is called causeless joy, in Christianity, the kingdom of Heaven within, and in Judaism it is called *ashrei,* an inner sense of holiness and health. In Islam it is called *falah,* happiness and well-being, and in Hinduism it is called *ananda,* or pure bliss. Some traditions refer to it as an enlightened or awakened state.

I've noticed the widespread recognition of this concept around the world. No matter where I go, when people hear the expression Happy for No Reason, it strikes a deep chord in them. We seem to know intuitively that our innermost essence is happiness. You don't have to create it; it's who you are. The rest of this book is devoted to showing you how to get back to that natural state.

Practicing Happiness

Things do not change; we change.

—Henry David Thoreau,
writer and philosopher

Think of people you know who are Happy for No Reason. Often, these people affect us like small suns, radiating warmth and positive energy to everyone who comes into their field of influence. They are certainly optimists, who not only see the glass as half-full, but who carry a pitcher to fill the glass all the way up—and top off others' while they're at it. They're not always rah-rah cheerleaders; sometimes they're simply a quiet presence of inner peace and contentment, centers of calm in the chaos where many of us live. These are the people you love to spend time with because they have a way of raising your spirits even on your grumpiest gray days.

I was blessed to grow up with one of these Happy for No Reason people: my father, Marc. He'd clearly hit the happiness set-point jackpot. No matter what he did or where he went, there was a perpetual sparkle about him. Yet, my dad's happiness didn't stem from his outer circumstances. He grew up quite poor during the Depression, struggled to pay for his education, had his share of personal losses, and stood a whopping 5'4" on a good day. But none of that seemed to matter to him. He loved *everything.*

After working his way through dental school, including a one-year stint in a chocolate factory (perhaps ensuring future patients), he went on to serve four years during World War II as an army dentist in the South Pacific. Though he certainly didn't relish being in the midst of battle, he never lost his inner sense of happiness. He was so devoted to my mother that he wrote her a letter every single day he was overseas—858 letters total—some of which have survived to this day. While in the army, he saved enough money from his poker earnings to finance his first dental practice when he returned home. He loved his career as a dentist, and when he retired, he did some amazing things that you'll hear about in a later chapter.

Although he continued to face challenges after the war—sometimes money was tight, we kids didn't exactly pop out of a Norman Rockwell painting, and his health eventually failed—my dad still felt happy all the time, passing away peacefully at age ninety-one, having spent his ninetieth birthday playing golf.

My father woke up every morning excited and grateful to be on this adventure called life. He was my first Happy for No Reason role model and the inspiration for this book. One day when I was about nineteen, I asked him his advice for life. He answered with two words: Be happy!

"Great, Dad," I said, "but how?"

He had no answer for me. Being happy was so natural to him that he couldn't understand why everyone didn't feel that way and why they were so busy pursuing happiness.

What Thomas Jefferson Really Meant

When I talk to people about happiness, they often quote Thomas Jefferson's famous line from the Declaration of Independence. "Sure, I want to be happy," they tell me. "After all, isn't everyone entitled to the right to life, liberty, and the pursuit of happiness?"

We've been conditioned to believe that happiness is something for us to *pursue*. So, like a dog going after a stick, we chase after happiness, grabbing at all the things we think will bring it to us.

Then, one day, I discovered what Thomas Jefferson really meant.

I was on an airplane going to a conference with my good friends, Stewart and Joan Emery, leading lights in the human potential movement. We were talking about the concept of happiness—something I do a lot—when Stewart turned to me and said in his charming Australian accent, "Marci, do you know what Thomas Jefferson really meant by the pursuit of happiness?"

Stewart, the coauthor of *Success Built to Last,* knows many fascinating and often obscure facts. Back in Jefferson's day, he explained, the common usage of the word "pursue" was not "to chase after." In 1776, to pursue something meant to practice that activity, to do it regularly, to make a habit of it.

What a difference a definition makes! Thomas Jefferson, our wise Founding Father, meant that we all had the right to **practice** happiness, not chase after it—which isn't very productive anyway.

So let's stop pursuing happiness and start practicing it. We do that by practicing new habits.

The Habits of Happy People

People with high happiness set-points are human just like the rest of us. They don't have special powers, an extra heart, or X-ray vision. They just have different habits. It's that simple. Psychologists say that at least 90 percent of all behavior is habitual. So, to become happier, you need to look to your habits.

Some books and programs will tell you that you can simply decide to be happy. Just make up your mind to be happy, and you will be.

I don't agree.

You can't just decide to be happy, any more than you can decide to be fit or to be a great piano virtuoso and expect instant mastery. You *can,* however, decide to take the necessary steps, like exercising or taking piano lessons, and by practicing those skills, you can get in shape or give recitals. In the same way, you can become Happy for No Reason through practicing the habits of happy people.

All of your habitual thoughts and behaviors in the past have created specific neural pathways in the wiring in your brain, like grooves in a record. When we think or behave a certain way over and over, the neural pathway is strengthened and the groove becomes deeper, in the way that a well-traveled route through a field eventually becomes a clear-cut path. Unhappy people tend to have more negative neural pathways. This is why you can't just ignore the realities of your brain's wiring and *decide* to be happy! To raise your happiness set-point, you have to create new grooves.

Scientists used to think that once a person reached adulthood, the brain was fairly well set in stone and there wasn't much you could do to change it. But new research is revealing exciting information about the brain's neuroplasticity: when you think, feel, and act in different ways, the brain changes and actually rewires itself. You aren't doomed to the same negative neural pathways for your whole life. Leading brain researcher Dr. Richard Davidson of the University of Wisconsin says, "Based on what we know of the plasticity of the brain, we can think of things like happiness and compassion as skills that are no different from learning to play a musical instrument or tennis . . . it is possible to train our brains to be happy."

While a few of the Happy 100 I interviewed were born happy, most of them *learned* to be happy by practicing habits that supported their happiness.

According to the Dalai Lama, one of my happiness heroes (I can't help but smile when I think of him), it's important to know which habits support happiness in your life and which don't. In his book, *The Art of Happiness,* he writes:

> *One begins identifying those factors which lead to happiness and those factors which lead to suffering. Having done this, one then sets about gradually eliminating those factors which lead to suffering and cultivating those which lead to happiness. That is the way.*

Throughout the book, I'll be identifying the factors that lead to happiness. But what are those "factors that lead to suffering" and block our happiness? Two of these Happiness Blockers, the Myth of More and the Myth of I'll-Be-Happy-When, are so prevalent in our culture, they have almost everyone hooked.

The Myth of More

Who is rich? He who is happy with his lot.

—The Talmud

Most of us fall prey to what I call the Myth of More: the more you have, the better you'll feel. Our society's collective trance of wanting more and more stuff, or "bright, shiny objects," as my friend Stewart calls them, is based on a shared, insidious, and often unconscious belief: more toys, success, and money mean more happiness. But as these statistics show, it just isn't true:

- Americans' personal income has increased more than two and a half times over the past fifty years, but their happiness level has remained the same.
- Nearly 40 percent of the people on the *Forbes* list of wealthiest Americans are less happy than the average American.
- Once personal wealth exceeds $12,000 a year, more money produces virtually no increase in happiness.

It's obvious that the happiest people aren't the ones with all the goodies. (If they were, there'd be a lot more happy people in Hollywood!) Yet we are seduced by the deep-seated belief that money will buy happiness—at least we think it will for us. A recent survey showed that at all income levels people think more money would definitely increase their level of happiness.

I heard that a reporter once asked Andrew Carnegie, the famous industrialist who'd amassed a fortune in steel, "You're the richest man in the world. How much is enough?" He thought for a moment and replied, "Just a little more."

This shows that our "desire to acquire" won't bring us true joy. So why is it so hard to escape wanting more?

Because Madison Avenue doesn't want us to. Advertising exists to perpetuate the Myth of More; it's the engine that drives our economy. Billions

"All I want is a chance to <u>prove</u> money can't make me happy."

of dollars are spent every year to convince you that you're not okay the way you are and that you need *things*—lots and lots of them—to make you happy. One night I did an experiment. I counted how many times and ways I was told this over the course of that night's television watching.

It was shocking. In just three hours, I was bombarded by sixty-eight messages telling me that I was doomed to misery if I didn't have what that company was selling. In the most entertaining, compelling, and creative ways possible, advertisers tried to convince me that I needed to have the right car (five different companies claimed theirs was the right one), the sexiest bra (like the one decorated with diamonds that cost $2 million—that's one million per boob!), the magic pills (we'll talk about those later), and the best skin care product (God forbid I should look my age).

I know what you're thinking: *But I don't pay attention to those commercials. They don't affect me*. Sorry to burst your bubble, but they do.

You can't help it: the messages we see and hear repeatedly go into our brain on a subconscious level and become beliefs. If they didn't, advertisers wouldn't be spending oodles of money to make sure you view their ads over and over again.

With children watching an average of five hours of television a day, is it any surprise that we have a bunch of unhappy kids who are in a frenzy to get the next toy, video game, or designer-label jeans? If you've been around children at Christmas, you'll know why I was so touched by the following story told to me by a young father I interviewed:

> When my oldest daughter, Victoria, was almost three, we read Dr. Seuss's *How the Grinch Stole Christmas* every night to her before the holiday.
>
> She'd curl up beside me as I'd read: *Every Who down in Who-ville liked Christmas a lot. . . .*
>
> Victoria followed along as the Grinch unveils his plans to ruin the Christmas of the Whos. Disguising himself as Santa and his dog as a reindeer, the Grinch steals into the Whos' homes and takes everything, leaving only the hooks and wires on the bare walls. But to his surprise, the Whos remain happy despite the loss of the presents and trees and trimmings and trappings. He hadn't stopped Christmas from coming; "it came just the same."
>
> On that Christmas morning, we woke just ahead of Victoria so that we could watch her three-year-old enthusiasm as she saw the presents under the tree. She first ran to the kitchen table where she had left a snack for Santa and his reindeer. She looked at the evidence of Santa's visit: the cookie crumbs on the plate and the empty milk glass and the missing carrots. My wife, pregnant with our second child, and I beamed seeing our daughter so wide-eyed and excited at the thought that Santa himself had been in our home. Next, she ran into the living room and saw the presents under the tree.
>
> We expected her to dive into them—but she didn't. She held up her little hand and she said, "Stop. Let's pretend.

> Let's pretend the Grinch has been here and took everything and left just hooks and wires and we'd still be happy."
>
> So we stopped, and were happy. And like the Grinch, my heart grew three sizes that day.

What would our lives be like if we could all be happy no matter what?

When you experience your inner, innate happiness and are Happy for No Reason, you still enjoy the things in your life, but you don't look to them to make you happy. You're able to banish the Myth of More.

The Myth of I'll-Be-Happy-When

A close cousin to the Myth of More is the Myth of I'll-Be-Happy-When. How many of the following statements sound familiar to you?

- I'll be happy when I have the perfect mate.
- I'll be happy when I have a better job.
- I'll be happy when I have a baby (or another baby).
- I'll be happy when the kids are in school.
- I'll be happy when I get more recognition or appreciation.
- I'll be happy when I can retire.

And the ever so popular:

- I'll be happy when I lose 5 (10, 15, 20) pounds.

No matter how many I'll-be-happy-whens you reach, it's never quite enough. With each one, you experience either fleeting satisfaction or outright disappointment. Think about the last five goals you achieved. How much happiness did they bring? And how long did that happiness last?

Yet you ignore the feeling that something is missing, and you keep trying: you work harder and harder, telling yourself, *Just a little more and I'll be there. If I could just get this handled, then I'd have it.* You're like a hamster on a wheel. Round and round you go, madly trying to control and manipulate your external circumstances—and always feeling scared of losing whatever it is that you already have. When you're caught up in I'll-be-happy-when, happiness is always off in the future, while in truth, the only time you can actually experience happiness is right here in this moment.

Recent studies by Daniel Gilbert, a well-respected Harvard psychology professor, have proven the utter futility of I'll-be-happy-when thinking. Gilbert, the author of *Stumbling on Happiness,* has done some fascinating research that shows we humans aren't very good at predicting what will make us happy in the future. He's concluded that time and time again, we overestimate the happiness we'll receive from getting the stuff we want. We imagine how great we'll feel when we go on a certain vacation or get a promotion or have a particular relationship, but when we actually get them, we are usually far less happy than we thought we'd be. Moreover, we habituate to whatever we thought would make us happy, so the thrill diminishes every time we experience the magical *it* that was supposed to make us happy forever.

"I've got the bowl, the bone, the big yard. I know I should be happy."

To become happier we have to snap out of the trance that our happiness rests in "more and better" which we'll get "someday." No matter what we have, Happy for No Reason exists only now, not later.

The Guiding Three: Principles to Live By

Over time, as I listened to the Happy 100 describe their lives, I began to see certain clear patterns emerging. They'd all managed to banish the Myth of More and jump off the hamster wheel of I'll-Be-Happy-When. And they all seemed to live by the same three guiding principles, or universal laws. No matter what words the Happy 100 used to describe them, these principles played a significant role in helping them become, or remain, Happy for No Reason. I call these principles the Guiding Three:

1. What expands you makes you happier. (The Law of Expansion)
2. The universe is out to support you. (The Law of Universal Support)
3. What you appreciate, appreciates. (The Law of Attraction)

As you practice the Happiness Habits you'll learn in Part II, there may be moments you find yourself stuck in old behaviors and ways of thinking and feeling. It's at times like these that you can call on the Guiding Three to help you through.

Guiding Principle #1: What Expands You Makes You Happier

Science has shown that everything in the universe, including you, is composed of energy. Everything you say, think, or do, everything you're around, either expands your energy or contracts it.

When your energy expands, you experience greater happiness; when your energy contracts, you experience less happiness.

> You can experience this yourself by doing this simple exercise: Sit up straight right now. Throw back your shoulders, open your arms wide, take a deep breath, and smile. Close your eyes and notice how you feel.

You'd probably describe your experience something like this:

Free
Open
Joyful
There's a feeling of lightness and space—that's expansion.

Now think of someone you love, admire, and enjoy being around. How does your body feel when you think of that person?

Again, you probably feel expanded, open, light. Whenever you're happy, you're in a state of expansion. In fact, scientists can tell you how happy you are just by looking at the level of expansion in your body's functioning. If you were hooked up to scientific measuring instruments during moments of happiness, you'd be able to see the increase in oxygen absorption, dilation of blood vessels, muscle relaxation, the smoothness of your heart rhythms, and the increased integration of your brain's functioning—all signs that you've expanded your energy.

Now hunch your shoulders, make fists, take short, quick breaths, and put a frown on your face. Notice how you feel.

Anxious
Tight
Agitated
There's a feeling of heaviness—that's contraction.

Think of someone you fear or are angry at. What do you feel? That same heavy, contracted energy.

This is our basic experience of unhappiness. All of our negative emotions—anger, fear, sadness, jealousy—contract us and literally constrict the flow of our life energy. When we feel them, our muscles tighten, our breathing becomes shallow, and our circulation is hampered. If you were hooked up to those same measuring instruments, you'd be able to see the level of your stress hormones rise. This crashes your immune system and raises the risk of infection and illness.

The Happy 100 choose the thoughts, feelings, and behaviors that expand them, rather than the ones that contract them. Raising your happiness set-point is a matter of developing those habits that expand your energy. Here's what makes us feel expanded or contracted:

Contraction	Expansion
unhappiness	happiness
fear	love
pessimism	optimism
constriction	flow
resistance	acceptance
low energy	vitality
disease	ease
malaise	well-being
separation	connection
feeling bad	feeling good

Expansion is your highway to happiness. You can use this guiding principle to see if you are moving toward happiness by being aware of how contracted or expanded you feel throughout the day.

Your Inner Guidance System, or the Hot/Cold Game

Have you been in one of the newer cars that have the built-in global positioning systems (GPS)? No matter where you are, the GPS can direct you to where you want to go. (You can even program the type of voice they speak to you in. My friend's GPS sounds like a well-bred British butler! She says it makes her feel like a queen.)

It turns out that we each have our own built-in GPS that leads us toward happiness in the form of an expansion/contraction feedback system. If you feel more expanded, you're going in the right direction;

if you feel contracted, it's time for a course correction. It's like the game you probably played as a kid, when you were looking for something. As you got closer to your target, your friends would say, "Warm, warmer, hot!" Or if you were getting farther away, "Cold, colder, freezing." The only difference is your inner GPS says "expanded" or "contracted."

I rely on my inner GPS often. When I'm faced with a choice, I stop, take a deep breath, and feel which option brings more lightness, openness, and expansion. I do this for simple decisions, like choosing an entrée on a menu, and for bigger decisions, like deciding which business opportunities to pursue. I'm always happier with the choice that makes me feel expanded.

To see how much of your life you're living in either expansion or contraction, do the following exercise:

Expansion/Contraction List

1. Write two headings at the top of a piece of paper. Put "Contraction" on the left and "Expansion" on the right.
2. Think about your life: your job, your house, your body, your relationships, and so on. As you consider each item, close your eyes, take a deep breath, and feel whether it expands or contracts your energy and list it under the appropriate heading.
3. Review the lists and notice which areas of your life are contributing to your happiness and which are dragging you down. The items on the contraction list are areas for course correction.

All of the Happiness Habits that I recommend practicing in Part II are based on this first guiding principle: Everything that expands you makes you happier. In each chapter you'll find an expansion/contraction chart relating to that step. Paying attention to what contracts you and what expands you—listening to your inner GPS—will reinforce the behaviors that raise your happiness set-point and help you experience being Happy for No Reason.

Guiding Principle #2:
The Universe Is Out to Support You

Einstein once said that the most important question a person can ask himself is "Is this a friendly universe?" The Happy 100 answer this question with a resounding "Yes!" Rather than thinking the universe is out to *get* them, they believe the universe is out to *support* them.

What's striking is that they don't believe the universe is benevolent only when good things happen to them—they take this approach all the time. When something bad occurs, they don't moan and groan, "Why me? It's not fair." They see all the events in their lives through the lens of "Ultimately, this is happening for my good. There are no mistakes. Let me look for the blessing in this." This belief in a friendly universe is the root of their relaxed and trusting attitude in life.

There's even research showing that belief in a friendly universe can impact a person's health. A recent study conducted by Gail Ironson, PhD, MD, professor of psychology and psychiatry at the University of Miami, found that people with HIV who believed in a universal power that was loving remained healthier longer than people who believed in a universal power that was punishing.

This may be a hard concept for you to swallow. Certainly there are many horrible things that happen in this world: war, persecution, famine, and suffering. It's easy to think that we don't live in a friendly universe. The one thing that's helped me embrace the idea that the universe is always out to support me is the knowledge that all the wise men and women who have ever lived—the sages and saints of the past and present—have shared this belief. So when I'm having a hard time seeing how the universe is supporting me in a particular situation, I'm willing to admit that my thinking and understanding may be limited and to remind myself of their enlightened and clearer vision.

But we don't have to get into the philosophical or religious implications of this belief; that's not the purpose of this discussion. I'm just reporting that people who are Happy for No Reason use it as a guiding principle, and you can use it yourself to raise your own happiness level.

Rather than trying to decide whether this principle is true or not, I suggest that you adopt this perspective for the next week or two, and see how different your life feels at the end of that period. That means that whatever happens, assume that the universe is on your side—even if it isn't obvious to you on the face of it.

When I first began doing this myself, I noticed that although I wasn't jumping up and down with joy and loving everything that I had to face in my life, I definitely felt a lot more ease and peace inside. At times, when I was particularly sad or knocked off-center—when a romantic relationship ended, for example—believing that the universe was always supporting me and that there was a bigger plan helped me get beyond my usual broken record of "It's so unfair" and "I'll never find true love." It helped me maintain an open heart that ultimately led me to Sergio.

When you believe that the universe is out to support you, you're able to stop resisting what is happening. This doesn't mean being passive or complacent about the events in the world or in your own life. It simply means not fighting or bemoaning *what has already happened* and can't be changed. Many of us spend a tremendous amount of energy being upset and resisting life. When you take the view that there are no mistakes and accept what is, you can use your energy instead to deal effectively with the situation *now.*

Trusting that the universe is always providing ways to support you and your best growth is a great tool to keep you feeling expanded.

Guiding Principle #3: What You Appreciate, Appreciates

This principle is based on the Law of Attraction, which, simply stated, is *Like attracts like:* whatever you think, feel, say, and act on, you draw to yourself like a magnet. Whenever you appreciate the happiness that already exists in your life, like money in the bank, it appreciates!

There's been a lot of buzz about the Law of Attraction in recent years, thanks in great part to the hit film and book phenomenon *The Secret.* I am honored that creator and producer Rhonda Byrne chose me to be part of this transformative film and book. Rhonda truly walks her talk: she used the Law of Attraction to create *The Secret*'s megasuccess. Her intention and vision has always been to spread joy and see the world transformed by using the Law of Attraction. The first time I met Rhonda, I was struck by how radiantly happy she was. Although she went through a period of great despair in her life, today she exudes a joyful enthusiasm combined with a deep peace. You'll find her remarkable story in Chapter 8 of this book.

Many people focus on using the Law of Attraction to draw in the things they think will make them happy. But that's backwards. Being happy is what draws in the things we want—it's the basis of the Law of Attraction. In Rhonda's book, *The Secret,* she writes:

> *I want to let you in on a secret to The Secret. The shortcut to anything you want in your life is to* BE *and* FEEL *happy now! It is the fastest way to bring money and anything else you want into your life. Focus on radiating out into the Universe those feelings of joy and happiness . . . Everything you want is an inside job! The outside world is the world of effects; it's just the result of thoughts. Set your thoughts and frequency on happiness.*

When you feel good, your energy creates a powerful vibrational field that draws to you what you want more easily. While it's fine to manifest your ideal car, home, or job, as we've already seen, the key to happiness in life isn't manipulating the world to give us what we want. The highest use of the Law of Attraction is applying it to the goal that underlies all goals: becoming Happy for No Reason. Though the Law of Attraction has worked like a charm for me in the material realm, I've received far greater rewards whenever I've applied it on the spiritual level, to heal myself from heartbreaks by focusing on gratitude, and to create transformation in my life by appreciating any step of progress, no matter how small. Using the Law of Attraction in this way leads to being Happy for No Reason.

My Secret Formula

My favorite tool for using the Law of Attraction is what I refer to as my Secret Formula: Intention, Attention, No Tension. I first learned this simple three-part process from my friend, performance consultant Bill Levacy. Here's how you can apply it to becoming Happy for No Reason.

1. Intention: Be clear about what you want—in this case, your desire for greater happiness.
2. Attention: What you put your attention on grows stronger in your life. Put your attention on happiness by practicing the Happiness Habits each day.
3. No Tension: Let go and relax. As you practice the habits, be easy with yourself and trust that you are removing the blocks to experiencing greater happiness.

Setting Your Intention and Envisioning Your Ideal

All conscious change begins with intention. Before you can raise your happiness set-point, it's important to set your intention to be Happy for No Reason. Start by writing down a declaration of your intention. Begin with "I'm grateful that I am . . ." and complete the sentence with what Happy for No Reason feels like to you.

I want you to use the phrase "I am" because these are the two most powerful words in the English language; they help call your intention into being. Please note that I'm asking you to declare this intention in the present tense, as though you are already experiencing being Happy for No Reason. The power and immediacy of the present tense magnetizes your heart's desire to you. For example, my personal Happy for No Reason intention is "I'm grateful that I am experiencing a deep state of inner peace and happiness."

Your Happy for No Reason Intention

____

Now picture yourself being Happy for No Reason. What would your life be like if you were experiencing that state of unshakable inner peace and well-being? What would you feel and do? How would you interact with others?

Imagining how you want to feel may seem fanciful or silly, but it's actually a very powerful exercise. The more clearly you can experience what Happy for No Reason feels like to you, the more easily you will bring it into being.

Just doing this process puts you in the vibrational field of Happy for No Reason. You probably began to feel happier just from intending and imagining it.

I also recommend that you create a vision board to look at as you practice the Happiness Habits. A vision board is a visual representation of whatever you want to create in your life. Many people use these boards to focus on the things they want to get: a car, a relationship, a home. I suggest you create a board that focuses on images that represent states of feeling happy. You might choose a picture of a beautiful spot in nature or an image of someone laughing or dancing. Perhaps you'll use pictures of yourself with people that you love or admire. Choose images that make you feel expanded, open, and uplifted, even if you can't put your finger on exactly why, and include your Happy for No Reason intention statement. Just as with your intention, it's important to focus on the things on the board as if they already exist.

My own board has pictures of me at my happiest, in nature and with people I love, and images, colors, and quotes that inspire joy in me. It's hanging on the wall across from my desk and I look at it throughout the day. Spend some time each day looking at your vision board and feeling the happiness it inspires in you.

Building Your Inner Home for Happiness

Now you're ready to begin putting your intentions into practice. In Part II, you'll learn the seven steps to build your Home for Happiness. After reading the book, I suggest you spend a week on each of these steps, practicing the Happiness Habits, doing the exercises, and taking the actions steps listed at the end of each chapter. You may find that some habits come easily, while others will present more of a challenge. When that happens, take the time you need to make the new practice easy.

As you work with these ideas and techniques, keep the Guiding Three in mind. Use your inner GPS to move you in the direction of expansion. See what happens when you choose to believe the universe is out to support you. And keep working with the Law of Attraction to raise your happiness set-point by deeply appreciating the happiness you're already experiencing.

With these tools in hand, it's time to begin building your Home for Happiness. Let's get started.

PART II

Building Your Home for Happiness

We first make our habits, and then our habits make us.

—John Dryden, seventeenth-century English poet and dramatist

3

The Foundation—Take Ownership of Your Happiness

Most of the shadows of this life are caused by standing in one's own sunshine.

—Ralph Waldo Emerson, writer and philosopher

Though building a house isn't at the top of my list of skills, I do know that the first step is to lay the foundation. It's the basis of a sturdy home.

Building your Home for Happiness starts with the same important first step: you lay the foundation by taking ownership of your happiness. That means first believing you can be happy, then becoming aware of the habits that are standing in your way, and, finally, gently and persistently shifting to new habits of thinking, feeling, and acting that will serve you better.

One of the things that struck me most about the Happy 100 was that in interview after interview no one questioned their ability to be happy. They knew that it was possible—and that their happiness was up to them. They didn't put off being happy for the future, waiting for the conditions of their life to be exactly right or hoping that someday they'd get lucky. And they didn't get stuck in the past, saying, "I can't be happy because of where I came from or what's happened to me." They were proactive about their lives, focusing on the possibilities for their future, rather than being victimized by their past or present circumstances.

This link between happiness and taking responsibility was demonstrated in an important study published in 2005 in the *International Journal of Behavioral Medicine.* The study, led by Dr. Gail Ironson, whose research I introduced in the previous chapter, showed that subjects diagnosed with HIV who were optimistic were more proactive in their behavior, coped better, and showed slower progression of the disease. According to Dr. Ironson, proactivity is highly correlated with optimism, a trait associated with increased happiness.

The good news is, no matter where you start, when you're proactive and take total responsibility for experiencing happiness, you put yourself in the driver's seat in life. Then you can take quantum leaps in raising your happiness set-point.

At our core, we are all already Happy for No Reason. An inner sun of peace and well-being is shining brightly in each of us, though it is often covered over with clouds. In this chapter, we'll shine a light on those clouds—our patterns of victimhood—the old ingrained habits that are blocking our ability to experience our essential happiness all the time.

Taking Ownership

What I've noticed in my work is that more and more people are waking up to the power they have to create their future through everything they think, feel, say, and do. They're recognizing that their choices determine their lives. When you understand the Law of Attraction, you know that you're responsible for the experience of happiness (or unhappiness) in your life.

Taking ownership of your happiness has two aspects:

1. Accepting that being happy is up to you and that you have the ability and power to be happier by changing your habits.

2. Taking "response-ability": responding to all the events in your life in a way that supports your happiness.

By reading this book, you've already begun. This isn't just "inspiring talk." It's been proven that simply putting your attention on becoming happier has a powerful effect. In fact, one of the very first happiness experiments ever conducted demonstrated this. In 1977, Dr. Michael Fordyce, a psychologist and the author of *The Psychology of Happiness,* published the groundbreaking results of his experiment showing that students asked to study the habits of happy people actually increased their happiness and life satisfaction by just learning about the subject.

Yet, as Dr. Sonja Lyubomirsky, psychology professor at UC Riverside, whose research I discussed in Chapter 1, points out, investing time and attention to become happier is like diet and exercise: you can't do it for just a day or two, it has to be continued over time. Unfortunately, most people put more energy into planning which car they're going to buy than into raising their level of happiness.

Response-ability: The Ability to Respond

Our ability to respond to what happens to us—our response-ability—dramatically affects our happiness. The Happy 100 respond to the events in their lives in a way that supports their inner peace and well-being.

Years ago, my mentor, Jack Canfield, taught me the following simple equation that explains this concept:

E + R = O (Events + Response = Outcome)

People who are Happy for no Reason orchestrate the events in their lives when they're able to. When they're not able to change the events, they *change their responses.*

Next time you're in a traffic jam, look around you. You'll probably see someone scowling, yelling at the other cars, and clutching the steering wheel in a death grip. Someone in another car may be shimmying in her seat to the radio, singing at the top of her lungs and boogeying down. Same event, different responses.

Every single time you make a choice to respond in a way that expands you and creates more peace and well-being, you're strengthening your ability to make that same positive choice in the future. This is true empowerment; it moves you from being a victim to being a victor.

The Ultimate Victor

I was first introduced to this life-changing idea in high school, when my English teacher gave the class an assignment to read *Man's Search for Meaning* by Viktor Frankl, a Holocaust survivor who wrote with incredible eloquence about how he and others rose above despair while enduring the daily atrocities of being prisoners in a Nazi concentration camp. At first, I resisted, afraid I'd be too horrified by his account, but with each page, I felt my heart lift as I became more and more inspired. One particular passage shook me to my core:

> *We who lived in concentration camps can remember the men who walked through the huts comforting others, giving away their last piece of bread. They may have been few in number, but they offer sufficient proof that everything can be taken from a man but one thing: the last of the human freedoms—to choose one's attitude in any given set of circumstances, to choose one's own way.*

If Viktor Frankl could find meaning—even experience love—in the worst circumstances imaginable, then I have to believe that we can all find the courage each day to change how we respond to whatever happens in our lives.

His name says it all. He is the ultimate Victor!

The Happiness Robbers

When we're stuck in old patterns of victimhood, we draw the same situations to ourselves again and again (there's that Law of Attraction at work). You see this all the time—for example, the woman who ends up in the same type of unhealthy relationship over and over. Different man, same problems.

Author Eckhart Tolle is someone I look to as a Happy for No Reason role model. In his book *The Power of Now,* he says we can shift the energy of victimhood that perpetuates our old problems by becoming aware of our own power in the present:

> *A victim identity is the belief that the past is more powerful than the present, which is the opposite of the truth. It is the belief that other people and what they did to you are responsible for who you are now, for your emotional pain or your inability to be your true self. The truth is that the only power there is, is contained within this moment. Once you know that . . . you realize that you are responsible for your inner space now—nobody else is—and that the past cannot prevail against the power of the Now.*

We're always free in the present moment to break our old habits and to establish Happiness Habits that will create a different future. Here are some of the old habits of victimhood that rob us of our happiness: complaining, blaming, and feeling shame.

Complaining: Complaining, feeling sorry for ourselves, trying to garner sympathy, or being a martyr or "overgiver" are all dead giveaways that we're the guest of honor at our very own pity-party. We know from the Law of Attraction that if we focus on what we don't want, constantly kvetching about how bad our relationships are or how much money we owe, we're drawing more of that to us—cementing the energy of bad relationships or debt in our lives. Complaining is like putting an order in to the universe for more of what we *don't* want!

The complainer's motto: Poor me!

Blaming: Blaming our circumstances by making excuses or blaming others for our pain or problems weakens us. We give our power away, and the energy we need to deal with the situation isn't available because we're directing it at someone or something else.

The blamer's motto: It's not my fault!

Feeling Shame: When we turn blame onto ourselves, feel ashamed about things that have happened to us, or feel guilty about some-

"You think I *want* to be unhappy?! I'm *carved* this way!"

thing we've done (or not done), we often try to suppress the pain or bury these uncomfortable feelings deep inside. This uses up a lot of energy and blocks our happiness.

The shamer's motto: It's all my fault!

Think of the unhappy people you know. They probably spend a lot of time blaming, complaining, and feeling shame, which robs them of the experience of their innate happiness. Shifting out of the victim game is a sure way to expand your energy and be happier:

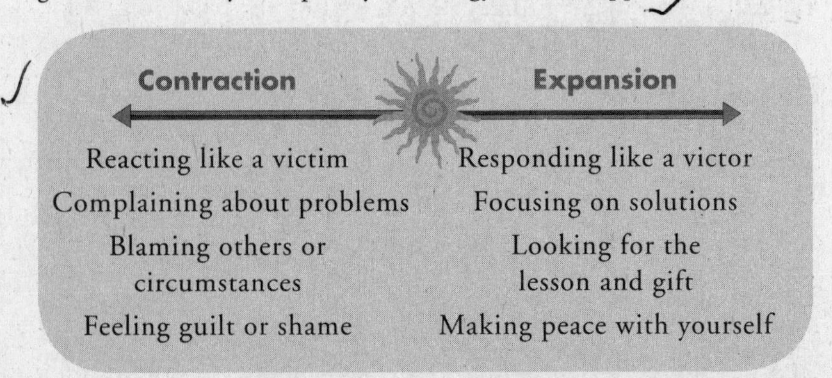

Contraction	Expansion
Reacting like a victim	Responding like a victor
Complaining about problems	Focusing on solutions
Blaming others or circumstances	Looking for the lesson and gift
Feeling guilt or shame	Making peace with yourself

Nabbing the Happiness Robbers

The habit of feeling like a victim can be very subtle and deeply ingrained. I first became aware of people's victim patterns in my days as a corporate trainer. I used to teach classes on the importance of taking personal responsibility, and at the beginning of class, I'd ask everyone if they'd agree to come back from our breaks on time. They all said yes. Whoever was late would have to stand in front of the class and sing their high school fight song or a song I chose if they couldn't remember back to their alma mater days. I can't tell you how many successful, hot-shot Fortune 500 executives were late and then made excuses, blamed others, or complained about our agreement! It was amazing to see how hard it was for people to take responsibility, even in small ways. But I held steady, and by the end of the three-day class, we'd all been treated to numerous renditions of my favorite choice, "Stop in the Name of Love," performed by top executives wearing name tags and sheepish expressions.

Then, a few years ago, I went to a three-day seminar where the tables were turned on me. The seminar leader had a rule that any time my seminar mates or I acted like a victim—any time we blamed anyone, made an excuse, complained, indulged in self-pity, or beat ourselves up—we had to put $2 into a bucket.

I couldn't get over how many times I did every one of those things in the course of a day! When I was late, I blamed the line at breakfast. Oops! There went $2 (at least I didn't have to sing). When I complained that I was too cold, it cost me another $2. (After all the seminars I've taken where the rooms are like iceboxes, you'd think I'd know to bring a sweater.) Blaming, feeling shame, and complaining had become so automatic that I was unconscious of doing them. I spent the whole day emptying my wallet, but the $2 fine was a small price to pay for learning how often I played the victim.

I wasn't alone. By the end of the three days, our bucket was full to the brim. (We gave it to a local charity.) And we were playing the victim game a lot less—just by paying attention to our habits.

I recommend you try this exercise for one week with your family, coworkers, or friends and see what happens. My guess is that you'll end up having collected some big bucks for charity too. Your new awareness will benefit you as well, providing clear cues for switching to the habits that support being Happy for No Reason.

It's Never Too Late

No matter when you start, it's always possible to change your habits. I've seen my own mother go through a wonderful transformation later in her life. Like so many women of her generation, Mom has always been a very loving woman with the tendency to "overgive"—so much so that she often neglected her own needs and became drained and exhausted. But over time, she's learned to overcome her old patterns and take greater responsibility for bringing more joy and satisfaction into her life. When she was in her fifties, she began meditating, which allowed her to go off certain medications and take her health back. In her late seventies, she started exercising regularly, something she'd never done before. At eighty-five, she now walks twice a day and is the oldest person in her senior aerobics class—the first exercise class she's ever taken! When my father died after their marriage of sixty-three years, she found the courage to do many things alone for the first time: travel, join various clubs, even get weekly massages. Mom is so much more empowered now at eighty-five than she was at fifty or even twenty-five—proof that it's never too late to take responsibility for your happiness.

In my interviews with the Happy 100, I found that they had three primary ways to overcome old patterns, be more empowered, and take responsibility for happiness in their lives:

Happiness Habits for Empowerment

1. Focus on the Solution
2. Look for the Lesson and the Gift
3. Make Peace with Yourself

Happiness Habit for Empowerment #1
Focus on the Solution

If you don't like something, change it. If you can't change it, change your attitude. Don't complain.

—Maya Angelou, author and poet

Have you heard that old saying: Worrying is like a rocking chair; it takes a lot of energy and doesn't get you anywhere. The same goes for complaining. I'm sure that at one time or another you've complained about a situation or problem that's bothered you, and gotten quite worked up over it.

Imagine taking that same energy and applying it to *solving* the problem—using your creativity, intelligence, and imagination to see the possibilities.

Which one makes you feel happier?

There's no contest: focusing on the problem contracts your energy, while focusing on what you can do to solve it expands your energy and makes you happier—à la Guiding Principle #1. Victors focus on solutions, while victims complain about problems.

When I read stories submitted for my *Chicken Soup for the Soul* books, I noticed that the most inspiring ones were about people who'd transformed their lives by moving from victim to victor.

The following story from my interview with Happy 100 member Aerial Gilbert is the first of the twenty-one amazing stories I'll be sharing with you throughout the book. I've selected her story to illustrate this Happiness Habit because it stands out as one of the most memorable examples of making the transition to victorhood.

I first heard about Aerial from my friend Paul. We were sitting at my dining room table having lunch as he described the happiest person he knew, Aerial, a lovely young woman who'd worked as a nurse at the local hospital before her life had been turned upside down. When Paul finished telling me about Aerial, I sat in silence, reflecting on what I'd heard. What secret did Aerial have that made her so happy? Read on to find out.

Aerial's Story

A New Vision

It was June 1988, the end of just another day. I had finished my shift as a pediatric nurse and was on my way home. My eyes felt irritated, so I stopped at the corner drugstore to get some over-the-counter eye drops. When I got home, the first thing I did was to put the drops in my eyes. Immediately, I felt a searing pain and could barely see.

I was still in my nurse's whites when I was rushed to the emergency room, where they did everything they could to help me, but with no success. The eye drops had been tampered with—laced with lye—and within an hour of putting them in my eyes, I was blind.

Suddenly I was a toddler in a thirty-four-year-old body. For months, I mostly lay in bed, sleeping fitfully and at odd hours. The damage to my eyes caused frequent migraines, which left me exhausted. If the phone rang, I rarely answered it. I didn't want any visitors. My self-pity was like a huge wall around me, holding me prisoner and keeping the rest of the world away. Although my husband and the few friends I talked to tried to comfort me, they couldn't get through.

Before I lost my sight, like most people I simply took my life for granted. It was enough to do my job, socialize with my friends, and pursue my interests and hobbies. In that life, my *real* life, I had been an intensely sight-oriented person. Besides being a nurse, I was an artist, a jeweler, a photographer, and a pilot. I loved astronomy. I had also been very athletic and loved being outdoors. I swam, played tennis, rowed regularly with a local team, and took long hikes with binoculars and bird-watching guide in hand.

From the time I was five, my grandfather and I would often go out birding together. The highly visual activity of scanning a landscape for signs of birdlife and then noting a bird's markings, plumage, and bill shape to identify species had heightened my powers of observation as well as my connection with the natural world. Now, bird-watching and all of the other things I had been good at and had loved seemed lost—completely out of reach for the new, blind me.

Almost a year passed like this. Then, one day, as I lay in bed, I asked myself, *What is the quality of my life?* I was wallowing in my misery, slipping further each day into a dark hole inside of me that was far worse than the absence of sight. I projected out for the next twenty, thirty, forty years. *Is this what you want?*

My spirit rebelled. *No!* I thought. *I can't live this way.* I felt the first spark of energy and interest in life revive within me. *Okay, I want my life back,* I thought, *so what do I do now?* All the blind people I'd ever seen either had guide dogs or a long white cane. I'd always been a dog person, so the choice for me was obvious. I wanted a guide dog.

For the first time in months, instead of complaining to myself about what had happened to me, I had a purpose and a direction. I needed to call Guide Dogs for the Blind. I felt my heart beat faster. Where was the phone? Would I be able to dial information to get the number? I sat up in bed and eagerly began running my hands over the nightstand, looking for the phone. It felt so good to be excited about something.

Fumbling but determined, I managed to call Guide Dogs for the Blind. They told me I needed to master basic living skills before I could get a dog. Another goal. As I made the arrangements to attend a training program for that purpose, I finally felt I was alive again.

Over the next six months, as I went through the program, I sometimes wanted to give up. It had been so much easier to lie around and feel sorry for myself. But soon I experienced that taking the plunge and doing something to change things, though scary, was actually exhilarating. Little bubbles of hope began welling up in me. The bubbles merged into one buoyant balloon of joy inside my chest the first time I took my guide dog Webster's leash in my hand and we walked together. Using a cane, I'd had to poke along at a slow pace, evaluating each step, worrying that I was going to bump into things. Now, as I walked with Webster at a fairly brisk clip, I could move through space in a completely comfortable and functional way. Suddenly everything felt fluid—I was myself again: at ease, confident, and competent.

Over time, with Webster as my guide, I even began to hike again. One day when I was hiking with my husband in Tucson, I heard a bird singing. I said, "Oh! Do you hear that bird? Can you see the color of its wings?"

My husband located the bird and told me the color. Excited, I began peppering him with questions. "Does it have black bars across its tail? Is it about this big?"

Equally excited, my husband described the bird to me. "Yes! And it has a white throat! And its beak is shaped like . . ." He gave me the details.

I was giddy. "Oh, it's a canyon wren!"

We laughed at our new bird-watching technique. For the rest of the hike, between the two of us, me hearing the bird, my husband giving me the visual information, and then me doing the identification, I was able to experience a joy I thought had been lost forever. In fact, this new form of bird-watching was even more enjoyable because I could share it with my husband in this wonderfully cooperative way.

Webster also allowed me to once more enter the working world. I got a job at the same hospital where I'd worked as a nurse, first developing X-rays in a darkroom and then as a medical transcriber. Now that I could function independently, I soon began volunteering for Guide Dogs for the Blind, giving talks and leading tours of the Guide Dogs campus near my home. Eventually I began working full time for Guide Dogs.

I loved my new job. Being a part of the transformation process for others was a wonderful feeling. I remember one man who came with his sighted wife for a tour of the Guide Dogs campus. This visit was probably his wife's idea. He was very quiet on the tour, almost withdrawn. One of the sighted volunteers told me that he wore a hat, had long hair and a big beard; he was still hiding from the world, just as I had for so long. But he ended up attending a one-month in-residence class. About halfway through, at the point when he was matched with his dog, he told the instructor that he wanted to get a haircut and to shave off his beard. He went out and bought new clothes. As he continued to connect with his dog and the world, he really blossomed, physically and emotionally. The change was stunning. When he walked across the stage during the graduation ceremony, his wife, who was sitting in the audience and hadn't seen him for the entire month, didn't even recognize him.

I can relate. I sometimes don't recognize myself. Before I lost my sight, I considered myself a fairly happy person. Yet today I am happier and more empowered than I was before—on a more consistent basis and from a more meaning-filled place. There is a deeper sense of contentment and peace in my life now. For although I lost my sight, my vision has become greater.

The Solutions Focus

Though most of us haven't experienced something as sudden and extreme as Aerial's blindness, we all have our own version of being a victim. The minor disappointments, betrayals, and frustrations of life can pile up, and before you know it, you're complaining about feeling burdened and unhappy. I recently heard that the average person complains seventy times per day!

Will Bowen, a pastor from Kansas City, came up with an innovative way to take on the complaining syndrome. He handed out purple wristbands to his congregation and asked them to participate in an experiment. Each time they caught themselves complaining, they were to move the wristband to the other arm. The goal was to go twenty-one days without moving the band. His challenge spread quickly, and now millions of people around the world are wearing purple wristbands as part of Will's effort to create "a complaint-free world."

Aerial's transformation began the moment she stopped thinking of herself as a victim and started looking for a way to solve her problem. Anyone can make this shift using a powerful technique called the Solutions Focus, developed by Paul Z. Jackson, a business consultant and coach, and Mark McKergow, a brilliant physicist turned corporate consultant, who wrote a book of the same title. I've used this process with great success, both professionally and personally. I remember one morning, right after we learned Solutions Focus, Sergio and I were in a bit of a funk about our relationship, so we decided to give it a try. (This is one of the major perks of living with a psychotherapist: he's willing to talk about our relationship!)

The first step of Solutions Focus is to rate how you feel about your situation on a scale of 1 to 10, with 10 meaning "I'm the most satisfied. Sergio led me through the process. "How satisfied are you with our relationship right now?" he asked me.

It was a particularly off day, so I said, "Hmmm, about a 6."

Now the next step is what really sets this technique apart and demonstrates Mark's genius. Before we learned Solutions Focus, Sergio and I would have spent the next three days talking about why our relationship didn't rate a 10. We'd have focused on all the reasons we were dissatisfied and the things we wanted to change.

Instead, Sergio said, "Wow, we're a 6!" (Sergio can be maddeningly positive at times.) "What do we do that makes us a 6—and not a 1?"

"Well," I said, after I'd thought about it, "we're a 6 because we have fun together, because we deeply love and trust each other. We're a 6 because we do the Appreciation Practice together every day (you'll hear more about that in Chapter 9). We're a 6 because we like going on bike rides and taking hikes together in nature." I went on to list all the reasons I felt our relationship worked.

Sergio agreed and added his own reasons for why we weren't a 1, including that we were honest with each other, we made time for each other, and we shared the same values.

That afternoon, we decided to go for a hike. We laughed and had fun; we listened to each other, and by the time we got home, our relationship was an 11!

Solutions Focus keeps you focused on what's working, so you can stop using your energy to complain and start creating more happiness in your life. Here are the simple steps for using the Solutions Focus technique in your life.

✓ Exercise

Solutions Focus Technique

Write down your answers to the questions below on a separate piece of paper:

1. Think of a situation that you've been complaining about. Rate how you feel about it on a scale of 1 to 10, where 1 is "I'm the least satisfied about the situation" and 10 is "I'm the most satisfied." ______________

(If you rated your situation a 1, please skip to question 3.)

2. Great, you didn't score a 1. Write down what you're doing (as many things as you can think of) that cause you to rate your level of satisfaction at the number you scored and not lower.
3. What would be the first *tiny* signs that your satisfaction has increased by one point? Think carefully and write down as many things as you can.
4. In light of what you've written above, what are the first small steps you could take in the next day to increase your satisfaction with this situation?
5. Begin to take some of the actions you've listed in number 4. Start to notice times when you are a little more satisfied, and build on whatever you're doing that helps you.

Adapted from Solutions Focus Technique. *Used with permission of Paul Z. Jackson and Mark McKergow.*

To download a free 26-page Happy for No Reason Workbook *containing all 21 Happiness Habit Exercises, go to www.HappyforNoReason.com/bookgifts.*

Happiness Habit for Empowerment #2

Look for the Lesson and the Gift

The best years of your life are the ones in which you decide your problems are your own. You do not blame them on your mother, the ecology, or the president. You realize that you control your own destiny.

—Dr. Albert Ellis, psychologist

Research confirms that blaming is a happiness robber. A 1999 study conducted by Shane Frederick of MIT and George Loewenstein of Carnegie Mellon University showed that subjects who blamed others for severe accidents they had been involved in eight to twelve months earlier "displayed especially low coping scores." The sad truth is that as long as you say "It's my mother's fault, my husband's fault, the government's fault, my sixth-grade piano teacher's fault . . ." you won't be happy.

The Happy 100 have a secret that allows them to stop blaming. They believe that the universe is out to support them (Guiding Principle #2), and they feel that whatever is happening has a gift or a lesson in it for them.

If blame is one of the clouds obscuring your inner happiness, try it yourself. Rather than asking *Who's to blame?* start asking *What can I learn from this? What is the gift in this for me?*

Author and motivational speaker Chellie Campbell is a shining member of the Happy 100. But she wasn't always like that. In the following story, Chellie describes how every woman's nightmare finally helped her wake up to her blame habit.

Chellie's Story

The End of the Whine

"I can't go through with it," said my fiancé, Stan.

I was sure I didn't hear him correctly. It was early evening and we had both just arrived home from work. I handed him a couple of shirts I'd bought him at a department store, but he barely looked at them and threw them on the table.

"I just can't go through with it," he repeated.

A black wave engulfed me and I closed my eyes. I stopped breathing. *No, no, no, no, no.*

He hung his head and looked at the floor. "I'm sorry," he said. "I can't marry you."

The wedding was in three weeks.

I gaped at him. *Don't cry, don't cry, don't cry.*

"Why?" I finally gasped. "What's happened?"

He couldn't answer. For the next few hours, we argued, I pleaded, he withdrew, I yelled, he yelled, I whined, I struggled to find the answer.

Cold feet? He didn't like the church, the cake, his tux, the DJ, what? Give me some answer, any answer, just please not "I don't love you."

It wasn't even that good. It was, "I don't feel that close to you."

I fled then. It was three o'clock in the morning, and I called my best friend, Gaye. She and I had always joked that a best friend was someone who would take you in at three in the morning. Take me in, I said. Stan doesn't want to marry me.

Over the next few weeks, Stan and I canceled our happy life. Canceled the dress, canceled the church, canceled the flowers, canceled the bridesmaids, the photographer, the reception hall, the honeymoon. Returned the gifts, recalled the invitations. My parents cried. My friends hugged me. I moved out.

Ten weeks later, Stan married someone else.

I went through at least two boxes of Kleenex a day for a week. In an effort to cope, I did individual therapy. I did group. I ranted, I railed, I whined, I spit, I beat the couch to death with a tennis racket. At every meeting I sobbed, "Our relationship was *sooo* beautiful! It was the best relationship in the *wooorld*!"

"Oh, yeah?" my long-suffering therapist finally said one day during group therapy. "How beautiful was it? If it was that great, it wouldn't be over."

The hideousness of that bald truth hit me like a hard punch from a champion prizefighter. A collective gasp rose from the group in concert with mine. I stared at my therapist wide-eyed. How could she say that to me? Whose side was she on?

I didn't want to stop blaming, stop making Stan wrong, stop posturing as the innocent victim. Victimhood feels so cushy when all your friends hug you and love you and soothe your many wounds. You get to blame everyone else but yourself for your miserable life: the guy, your parents, your therapist, your job, even God. Now I called all my friends to tell them of this latest betrayal. Not only was I used and abused by my bad boyfriend, but my bad therapist thought it was my fault! I reveled in the safe cocoon of martyrdom.

I shut myself behind my office door at work and everyone walked on eggshells around me. Until one morning, a coworker of mine walked into my office unannounced and looked me straight in the eye.

"When I was eighteen and pregnant, my fiancé left town the week before the wedding and joined the army," she said.

I stared at her for a long moment. She sat there, waiting calmly for it to sink into my consciousness that someone else had suffered—as much as or more than I had—and survived. She was fun-loving, accomplished, and happy. Somehow she had recovered, regained her sense of self-worth, and prospered. She had not let one unhappy incident in her life cast her forever in the role of victim.

Her disclosure threw down a challenge: What was I going to do about my life now? Live it as Miss Havisham, frozen in time with a tattered wedding dress and moldy cake? Or take responsibility, learn what I had done to create the situation, and grow?

The angel that bends over me, whispering "Grow," won the day. I went back to therapy. Now the work of recovery could truly begin.

I began to see my part in what had happened. Why had Stan's unhappiness come as such a big surprise? I ran through the little alarms, the blinking warning lights that signaled the big sign that said "Road Closed!" He complained that I was controlling when I wanted to set an agenda. I wanted to spend when he wanted to save. He even told me when he went to his brother's wedding that they seemed in love in a special way, different from us. In hindsight, the signs were so clear. I should have been paying attention. Stan wasn't bad or wrong—and I wasn't either. We were just different. Our time of walking the same road had come to an end, and now I could see that our highest good lay in different directions. I wanted to be a winner, but I couldn't do it by making him a loser. I had to stop thinking like a victim, stop blaming other people for my misfortunes, stop telling victim stories.

Taking responsibility was a whole new ballgame. Though I'd made some bad choices in the past, I decided to adopt new thoughts and behaviors in order to change my experiences.

I found role models who lived the kind of life I wanted to live and connected with them. I read the biographies of famous people I wanted to emulate and followed their suggestions. I celebrated every success as evidence that I was a winner. I found happy, joyful, successful people, kept them close, and learned their ways. When my next boyfriend complained about my behavior in an argument, I stopped and listened. I looked at myself from his perspective, and said, "Steve, you are right. I don't even like my behavior. I don't know why I did that. I think it was just an old pattern of mine."

"Wow," he said quietly. "I'm impressed not only that you could see it that way, but that you would tell me so. Thank you."

Along with better relationships came better clients, better jobs, better wins. I started teaching workshops and helping others. I wrote two books. In seminars and speeches, I shared my stories and hard-won lessons and helped others become winners in their lives too.

I've discovered that what looks like bad news isn't always bad news. Who could have predicted that being left at the altar three weeks before my wedding would help me break the most damaging habit I had—the one that was keeping me from happiness? Blaming is a no-win proposition and I've got better things to do—like being peaceful, content, and happy.

Rejection Is God's Protection

Choosing to look for the gift and lesson in the situation instead of getting stuck in blame frees us from our old pattern of pointing the finger and from re-creating the same situation over and over again.

Looking for the lesson may seem challenging at first. Believe me, I get it. When I'm going through a hard time, it's not easy to listen when someone tells me, "Just wait. This will turn out to be a good thing for you." But I've come to see they're right.

One of my friends often reminds me that "rejection is God's protection." Though I'm not always able to recognize this as it's happening, when I look at my disappointments of the years past, I can see how so many of the things I set my heart on wouldn't have made me happy anyway (personal confirmation of Daniel Gilbert's research!). And often the things I thought were bad ended up being the greatest blessings in my life.

This occurs so frequently that a number of years ago, I started using a phrase that has served me well. Whenever I begin to blame a person or circumstance, I stop and ask myself: If this were happening for a higher purpose, what would that be?

The Happy 100 recognize that it isn't useful to label events as "good" or "bad" in the first place. Instead, they choose to trust that everything contains a gift or a lesson, though they may not always be able to see it in the moment.

There is an ancient Chinese story that illustrates this point beautifully:

> An old farmer used a horse to till his fields. One day, the horse ran away, and when the farmer's neighbors sympathized with the old man over his bad luck, the farmer shrugged his shoulders and replied, "Bad luck? Good luck? Who knows?"
>
> A week later, the horse returned with a herd of wild mares, and this time the neighbors congratulated the farmer on his good luck. His reply was, "Good luck? Bad luck? Who knows?"
>
> Then, when the farmer's son was attempting to tame one of the wild horses, he fell and broke his leg. Everyone agreed this was very bad luck. But the farmer's only reaction was, "Bad luck? Good luck? Who knows?"
>
> A week later, the army marched into the village and drafted all the young men they could find. When they saw the farmer's son with his broken leg, they let him stay behind. Good luck? Bad luck?

As you see, we can never know.

When things don't work out the way you want them to, try believing that what's happened is for the best. Remember: the universe is out to support you. This will instantly expand your energy. And with practice this process gets easier and easier.

Here's an exercise that will help you break the blame habit by looking for the lesson and the gift:

Exercise

Look for the Lesson and the Gift

1. Sit quietly by yourself. Close your eyes and take a few deep breaths.
2. Recall a specific situation that has caused you to feel

wronged or to blame others. Picture the person or people involved, the setting, and what was said or done.

3. Imagine taking several steps back and observing the situation from a distance, as though you were watching a movie on a screen.
4. What part of what happened can you take responsibility for? Did you ignore signs that should have clued you in that there was a problem? Did you act in a way that might have provoked the situation? Did your thoughts or actions escalate the situation?
5. What's your lesson to learn from what happened? Do you need more patience or better boundaries? Do you need to listen more, say less?
6. Ask yourself: If this were happening for a higher purpose, what would that be? Can you find the gift?
7. Write down the most important thing you can do differently as a result of finding the lesson or the gift.

Happiness Habit for Empowerment #3

Make Peace with Yourself

We can never obtain peace in the outer world until we make peace with ourselves.

—His Holiness the Dalai Lama

Let me guess. Like most people, there are things in your life that haven't gone so well, right? And you blame yourself. Maybe it's a failed marriage or business, or your children are having difficulties. Maybe you hurt someone or let someone hurt you. Blaming ourselves is as big a happiness robber as blaming others; it causes feelings of shame and guilt. When we try to stuff down those unpleasant feelings, we use a lot of energy keeping them there. And they slowly eat away at us, undermining our ability to experience lasting happiness.

To make peace with yourself, it's important to free up your energy by accepting any feelings you've been avoiding, and by letting go of the past. When you do, you'll be able to move your life forward and experience greater expansion and happiness.

The following remarkable story from my interview with Happy 100 member Zainab Salbi, an author, activist, and the founder and CEO of the humanitarian organization Women for Women International, describes one way to do this.

Zainab's Story

Telling My Story

I grew up in a suburb of Baghdad during the 1970s. My father was a pilot for Iraqi Airlines, and as a child I traveled all over the world. I played with sports cars and Barbie dolls equally, and there were no limits to my dreams for the future. Things changed when I turned eleven and the Iran-Iraq War started. That was when I first saw military planes and antiaircraft fire in the sky, soldiers and their guns filling the streets, and even missiles falling on people's homes. I remember my parents discussing whether it would be better for the whole family (my two brothers, my parents, and me) to sleep together in one bed, so we would all die together if a bomb hit our house, or to continue to sleep in our bedrooms and live our lives normally. Life was definitely not normal, and at times felt terrifying and perilous. Then, overnight, it became infinitely more dangerous: my father became Saddam Hussein's private pilot.

When my father was offered the job, he couldn't refuse; it would have meant prison, even execution. So we tried to avoid the relationship. But like a poisonous gas, Saddam leaked his way into my family's home. He took over our lives as we breathed him in slowly. Everything about us eventually became associated with my father's job. My family's home was referred to as the pilot's home, the street I lived on was referred to as the pilot's street, and, worst of all, I was always referred to as the pilot's daughter.

Like all Iraqi kids, I was instructed to call Saddam "Amo" (Arabic for "uncle"). But unlike the other Iraqi kids, I was often invited with my family to his palace parties. Being in Saddam's inner circle was fraught with danger. My mother instructed me never to relax or let down my guard. Many times we'd be sitting in his living room having a conversation and he would casually mention killing a member of his family or a friend or colleague. Then he'd watch us very carefully. Offending Saddam with the wrong remark or facial expression could be fatal, so I learned to match my responses to his. If he was serious, I was serious. If he smiled, I'd smile. For years, my family and I lived in fear of this man and his craziness.

Then, when I was almost twenty, my mother asked me to accept a marriage proposal from a man I'd never met, an Iraqi expatriate who lived in Chicago. I was horrified. Marrying someone I didn't know and definitely didn't love went against everything my parents had said they wanted for me: love, passion, and the freedom to choose my own life. At first I refused, but my mother cried and pleaded with me so desperately, I finally agreed, more to make my mother happy than anything else. What I didn't know then, and my mother wouldn't tell me for another ten years, was that she was worried that Saddam might have begun to have amorous intentions toward me and she was frantic to get me out of Iraq and out of his reach.

Our family flew to Chicago for the wedding, and at the first sight of my prospective husband, my stomach sank. I had absolutely no attraction to him. But he told me that he would try to be a good husband; I would have the freedom to finish the university study that I'd left in Iraq and pursue a career, and, in time, we would learn to love each other.

Within a few short weeks I discovered that my new husband had no intention of honoring the promises he'd made to me. He gave me almost no money and no access to a car, and wouldn't allow me to attend the university. For months, I felt trapped, victimized and violated, an indentured domestic servant in a home where I was disrespected and verbally and emotionally abused. I kept telling myself that things would get better, but they didn't. The last straw was a violent sexual encounter with my husband that left me as bruised in spirit as I was in body. Afterward, I dragged myself to the shower and stood with the hot water pounding over me as I sobbed. It didn't matter that I was married to this man; he had raped me. I packed my things and all the money I had, about $400, and called a friend of my mother's in the area who helped me escape.

Things began to look up after that. I moved to a new city, started going to school, and made new friends. I put everything that had happened—my war-scarred childhood, my years living in Saddam's shadow, and my abusive marriage—behind me. I took all the pain, fear, and trauma I'd gone through and stuffed it in a box deep inside of me. I never wanted to look at it or think of it again. During this period, although I often had happy moments, there was always a part of me that was profoundly sad.

In 1992, I married again, this time to a wonderful man I'd met and fallen in love with while in school. We were saving our money to go on a honeymoon when I read a magazine article about the thousands and thousands of Bosnian and Croatian women being imprisoned in "rape camps" during the war. Something in the pictures of the women's faces touched the deep pain I held inside of me and I began to sob. My husband raced into the room to find out what was wrong. When I explained what I was crying about, he took me in his arms and we both cried. We wanted to do something to help but couldn't find any organizations that were assisting these particular women, so we decided to take action ourselves. We took our honeymoon savings and, with the aid of the Unitarian church who supported our efforts, traveled to Croatia to help.

The response overwhelmed us. Very quickly I knew that this was what I was supposed to do. Our trip to Croatia was the start of Women for Women International, an organization that today helps women survivors of war worldwide to rebuild their lives by connecting them to women in the United States who each month send a small amount of money, as well as a personal letter. I began to travel all over the world, speaking with thousands of women who had been victims of unspeakable violence and rape, and encouraging them to tell their stories. I experienced over and over that sharing their stories started the healing process and helped them make the transition from victim to survivor and eventually to active citizen.

Then, in 2003, when Saddam was captured, I decided to write a book about what the women of Iraq had gone through and were still going through. I had no intention of delving into my own trauma, but one day my agent called me and said, "You really need to make this book about you. You *are* the story."

I cried, "No! This is not about me, this is about other women." I made every single excuse, but there was a deep anger and fear inside as I battled with myself about exposing the pain and trauma I'd distanced myself from for so long. Telling my story would ruin the image of the strong woman, feminist, and women's rights advocate that I projected to the world—and that I believed myself. But more than anything, I was truly convinced that if I told anybody that I knew Saddam Hussein, my own identity, beliefs, and accomplishments would disappear and Saddam would take over everything, just as he had when I'd lived in Iraq.

A few days after that phone call, in Congo on a Women for Women International mission, I came to a turning point. For two hours, I had been sitting in a room with a woman named Nabito and a translator as Nabito described what had happened to her during the fighting in her country. It was a terrible story—and a common one. Soldiers had gang-raped this woman and her daughters; the soldiers had ordered one of her sons to rape his mother, and when he refused, they shot him in the leg. I found myself shaking as I listened to the details. When she finished she looked at me and said, "I have never told anybody but you my story."

Her statement triggered so many things in me. She was telling me her truth, and I was too afraid to tell mine. So I asked her, "What do you want me to do? My job is to write about your story and tell the world about it. Should I keep it a secret? Should I not tell anybody about it?"

She looked me in the eye and, with a smile, said, "If I can tell the whole world about my story, maybe that will stop other women from going through what I've gone through. Yes, you go ahead and tell the world—just not the neighbors."

It was one of the most humbling moments of my life. I got in my car and cried for the entire five hours it took me to drive from Congo to Rwanda. I couldn't stop thinking about Nabito. She was illiterate, homeless; she had nothing, only one dress that someone had given her and shoes she'd made out of garbage, but she had so much more compassion and courage than I did. Not only was she willing to own her story and open the box that held all the pain and trauma inside, but if it could help even one woman avoid going through what she had suffered, she was willing to tell the world.

Though there were still many reasons to hold on to my fear, I knew that my mother had died in her silence and so had my grandmother. I didn't want to be one more woman who dies in her silence. So when I arrived at the hotel in Rwanda, I emailed my cowriter and my agent and told them, "I'll do it."

I began writing my own story, peeling away layer after painful layer of truth and emotion. In the end, it was the most liberating experience of my life. I truly believe that opening that box inside of me and taking ownership of the feelings I'd stuffed inside was the way to my healing and my peace.

Today, I no longer have that pain inside me. It's like crystal in there now. When I take a breath, it goes all the way through me. I have a deep sense of comfort with myself, and the joy I've always had for life is much more intense.

I've seen so much death and so much life. And life's just so gorgeous; it's like an apple when you take the first bite—that cracking sound and the juice and the sweetness. Oh, I love it!

I really believe that every misfortune I have gone through has led me to my fortune, the happy life I have today. If people are afraid to tell their stories, I tell them from my own experience, it will only lead you to a great fortune—of inner peace, and the joy and lightness that come with it.

A Fresh Start

There are many ways to make peace with yourself. If, like Zainab, you've been traumatized by earlier events in your life, you may need to unbury your suppressed feelings and learn to accept your past. Research shows that people who bury their traumas live shorter, unhealthier, unhappier lives than those who tell their stories.

Still, it's important not to get stuck in those feelings either. According to the cultural anthropologist Angeles Arrien, in many indigenous cultures, people are encouraged to "tell their story" when they've had a painful or traumatic experience, but no more than three times. These cultures recognize that it's important to share the story with loving and supportive people in order to release the pain, but repeating it more than three times only keeps the person trapped in the energy of victimhood. Making peace with yourself is about healing yourself and freeing yourself to move forward.

Sometimes people feel victimized by shame, not because of anything that's happened to them, but because of regret or guilt about their own actions in the past. It's hard to feel good when a little voice inside is always piping up to remind you that "after what you did," you don't deserve to be happy. When we continue to judge ourselves about our past, it's like dragging around a heavy weight—it takes up a lot of our energy. As Harriet Goslins, the developer of Cortical Field Reeducation, told me, "When you can differentiate between taking responsibility and blaming yourself, then you are free to make new choices. This opens the possibility of true self-forgivness."

In situations like these, making peace with yourself may mean making amends. Although you can't change what happened in the past, with a little creativity you can usually find a way to make things right. For example, if you borrowed money from someone and never repaid him, you could pay him back now, either in a lump sum or in installments—and anonymously if you prefer. Or if you can't locate that person, you could donate the same amount of money to a worthy charity. You'll be amazed at the lightness and energy you feel after making amends.

Mind-Body Magic

In the past ten years, I've become very interested in the rapidly growing field of energy psychology, which includes a variety of cutting-edge mind-body techniques that release old patterns of victimhood and judgment. These techniques, practiced by therapists, doctors, and laypeople, consist of postures and actions that act as switches to restore our proper energetic balance. They clear blockages in the subtle energy field of the body through the energy meridians, energy channels that have been recognized by ancient health systems for thousands of years. The techniques also reprogram the subconscious mind, which controls 90 percent of our behavior, and establish new patterns in the central nervous system that promote well-being. A number of them can be done in just a few minutes and can be self-applied without formal training.

There are now thousands of documented cases of people benefiting from energy psychology techniques, with hundreds of new studies underway. In my interview with Dawson Church, PhD, the author of *The Genie in Your Genes* and founder of the Soul Medicine Institute, he told me about a recently completed National Institutes of Health study conducted by Kaiser Permanente in which they found an energy psychology technique to be very useful in helping people successfully manage their weight. When people eliminate their limiting patterns and beliefs, they're more connected to their vibrant, energetic, and empowered selves.

Some easy and effective energy psychology practices include the Bio Energetic Synchronization Technique (B.E.S.T.), Emotional Freedom Technique (EFT), Tapas Acupressure Technique (TAT), and Psych K. (You can find more information about these in the resource section of this book.)

I recently learned about the B.E.S.T. system from its developer, Happy 100 member Dr. M. T. (Ted) Morter, a doctor of chiropractic and pioneer in the field of mind-body health. One of my liveliest interviews was with Dr. Morter, who at seventy-two is as bright, energetic, and vital as any thirty-five-year-old. I sat with him over a wonderful

Italian dinner one evening as he told me fascinating tales of his life and his philosophy of happiness. He had clearly mastered being happy in his own life, so I was thrilled when he offered to teach me the M-Power March, a specific B.E.S.T. exercise he developed to help people remove their blocks to happiness. (I share it with you below.)

According to Dr. Morter, the M-Power March resets the central nervous system, clears subconscious blocks, and activates forgiveness. The exercise, which involves simultaneous movements of the upper and lower body and left and right sides, puts the central nervous system into a more balanced state so it can process thoughts and emotions more efficiently and effectively. It "clears the computer" so we can reprogram the way we process subconscious information such as old hurts and regrets. It's a great tool to help shift any of the victim and judgment patterns we've talked about in this chapter. This simple three-minute exercise, as well as other B.E.S.T. procedures and exercises, have been remarkably effective in helping me feel more empowered in my own life, and are all very easy to do.

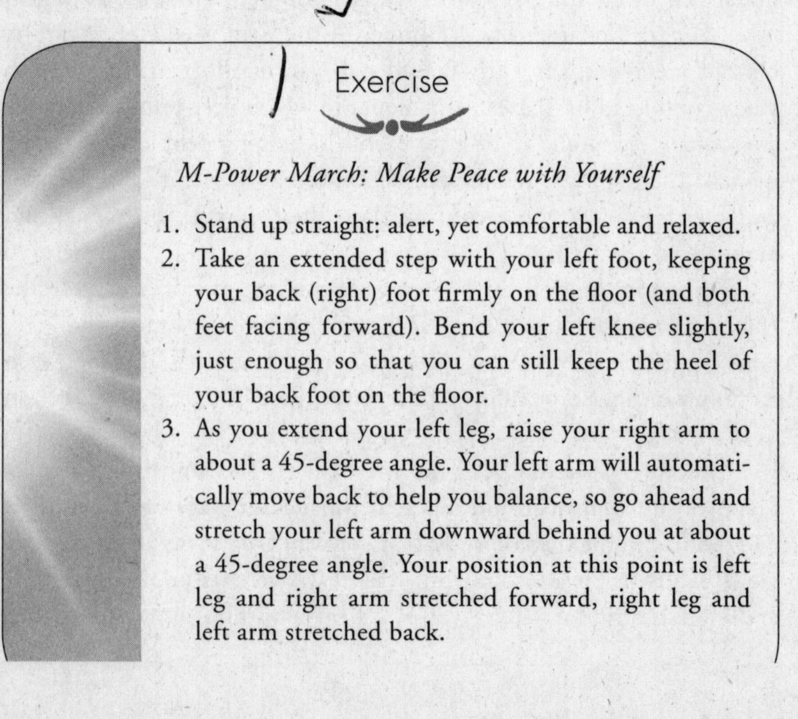

Exercise

M-Power March: Make Peace with Yourself

1. Stand up straight: alert, yet comfortable and relaxed.
2. Take an extended step with your left foot, keeping your back (right) foot firmly on the floor (and both feet facing forward). Bend your left knee slightly, just enough so that you can still keep the heel of your back foot on the floor.
3. As you extend your left leg, raise your right arm to about a 45-degree angle. Your left arm will automatically move back to help you balance, so go ahead and stretch your left arm downward behind you at about a 45-degree angle. Your position at this point is left leg and right arm stretched forward, right leg and left arm stretched back.

4. Now, turn your head toward the side of the extended right arm; look up; close your eyes and s-t-r-e-t-c-h.

5. While you are in your extended position, think of something about which you feel regret, shame, or guilt. Take a deep breath and focus on feeling "forgiveness." Hold both your breath and position for five to ten seconds.
6. Exhale and repeat the maneuver with the opposite leg and arm. Repeat the sequence three times.

Summary and Happiness Action Steps

You lay the foundation of your Home for Happiness by taking ownership of your happiness: you let go of being a victim, focus on solutions, look for the lesson and gift in situations, and make peace with yourself. Use the following action steps to practice the Happiness Habits for Empowerment:

1. For one week, put $2 in a basket each time you blame, shame, or complain. Keep track of how much money you collect each day, and see if you make progress during the week. Use the money for a family outing or make a donation to the charity of your choice.
2. Do an experiment: go cold turkey. See if you can spend one entire day without blaming, complaining, or feeling shame.
3. Use the Solutions Focus technique when you find yourself complaining.
4. To break the habit of blame, find one experience each day that didn't go the way you wanted and use the "Look for the Lesson and the Gift" exercise. (If you can't find something, congratulations—you're well on your way to being Happy for No Reason!)
5. To make peace with yourself or to shift any patterns of victimhood, practice the M-Power March for three minutes every day.

The next four steps in building your Home for Happiness are raising the pillars: learning the Happiness Habits that relate to your mind, heart, body, and soul. Just as the pillars or cornerposts of your home are connected by walls, your mind, heart, body, and soul are inextricably linked: your thoughts affect your physiology, your feelings affect your thinking, and so on. I've separated these four aspects of our lives into four different chapters for ease of explanation, but I recognize that this creates somewhat arbitrary distinctions. As you read through each chapter, you'll see that sometimes the steps overlap. Because these areas of our life are so interconnected, improving one will strengthen them all.

The Pillar of the Mind—Don't Believe Everything You Think

The mind is its own place, and in itself can make
a heaven of Hell, a hell of Heaven.
—John Milton, English poet

I once heard a revered sage speak. He took a question from a man dressed in a $3,000 suit, wearing classy shoes, and dripping with gold jewelry. The man asked, "What do I need to give up to experience true happiness and inner peace?"

The sage replied, "There's good news and there's bad news. The good news is that you don't have to give up any of your stuff. Poverty isn't the way to happiness. The bad news is that you have to do something that may be even harder for you. You have to give up the way you think."

Give up the way I think? Isn't that like saying I have to stop breathing? Well, it's not as hard as it may sound. From my research, my own experience, and my interviews with the Happy 100, I've learned some powerful techniques for changing the way we think. In this chapter, I'll show you ways that allow your mind to support your happiness rather than sabotage it. This strengthens the pillar of the mind, the next step in building your Home for Happiness.

Scary Mind Math

How many times a day are you ambushed by negative thoughts?

"I'm not good enough."

"My husband (or wife) doesn't love me."

"I hate the way I look."

"I'm worried I won't be able to pay my bills."

"My daughter doesn't respect me"

"I'm so stupid."

"I can't stand this job."

If you're like most people, it's probably a lot. With all those negative thoughts running through our heads, it's hard to stay happy.

Our minds—made up of our thoughts, beliefs, and self-talk—are always "on." According to scientists, we have about 60,000 thoughts a day. That's *one thought per second during every waking hour.* No wonder we're so tired at the end of the day!

And what's even more startling is that of those 60,000 thoughts, 95 percent are the same thoughts you had yesterday, and the day before, and the day before that. Your mind is like a record player playing the same record over and over again. (Okay, an iPod for all of you under thirty.) Talk about being stuck in a rut . . .

Still, that wouldn't be so bad if it weren't for the next statistic: for the average person, 80 percent of these habitual thoughts are *negative.* That means that every day most people have more than 45,000 negative thoughts like the ones above! Dr. Daniel Amen, a world-renowned psychiatrist and brain imaging specialist, calls them automatic negative thoughts, or ANTs.

Not surprisingly, when your mind is swarming with these ANTs, it has a profound physiological effect on you. Researchers at the National Institutes of Health, among others, have measured the flow of blood and activity patterns in the brain and have found that having negative thoughts stimulates the areas of the brain involved in depression and anxiety. On the other hand, positive thoughts have a calming, beneficial effect on the brain. Our negative thoughts are like poison in our system, and positive thoughts are like medicine. In the following chart, you can see how our thinking contracts or expands us, affecting our happiness:

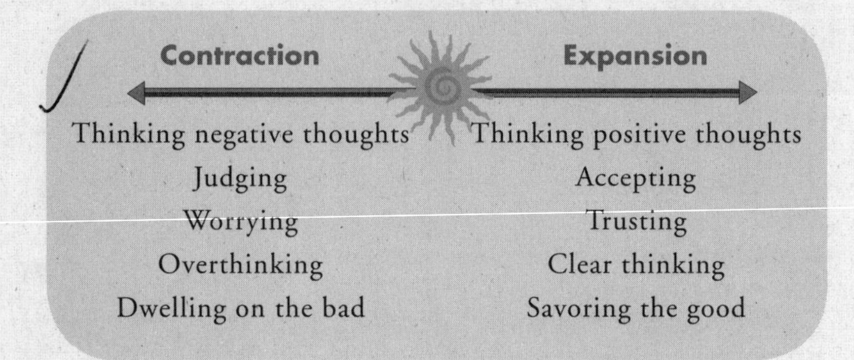

The Truth about Your Thoughts

The good news is that to keep the thousands of negative thoughts we have each day from dragging us down, we don't have to try to get rid of each one of them. There's a simpler way. The secret is in accepting an astonishing fact:

Your thoughts aren't always true.

It sounds simple enough, but in fact, this revolutionary idea requires a major shift in our perspective. We're so accustomed to believing that our thoughts are true and automatically reacting to them, that we're hardly aware we're doing it. I can remember the time many years ago I first made this discovery.

I was well into my presentation in front of 450 people packed into a hotel ballroom. My palms were clammy and my heart had started to pound—I was bombing big-time. How was I so sure? Because the man in the third row was letting me know in no uncertain terms. He sat rigidly, arms crossed. He hadn't laughed at a single one of my jokes. Not even a small nod of comprehension. Was that an eye roll I detected? My stomach churned. He hated what I was doing. He hated me.

I was horrified when the man made a beeline for the stage the second I wrapped up my presentation. I braced myself for his scathing critique of my lousy talk.

Instead, he came right up to me and thrust out his hand. "Thank you so much," he said, in a voice husky with emotion. "That talk changed my life."

I almost fell over—he hadn't hated it at all! It was my own negative thoughts that had been freaking me out. That's when I realized that my mind—my constant companion through the thick and thin and ups and downs of life—doesn't always tell the truth. It's the same for all of us. Until we become aware of this, our path to Happy for No Reason is blocked.

You don't believe everything you hear, do you? Of course not. You don't believe everything you read either. And in this age of special effects and Photoshop, you certainly can't believe everything you see. So . . .

Don't believe everything you think!

Thoughts are just packets of energy formed by neurochemical events in your brain, which can be measured in terms of electrical impulses and wave frequencies. Your thoughts don't always give you an accurate picture of reality, yet your mind goes on broadcasting them anyway. When you shine a light on your negative thoughts—and see that you don't have to believe them—it takes away much of their power to create misery.

Have you ever wondered why our negative thoughts have such a strong grip on us in the first place? We're simply wired that way. The problem stems from our primitive survival mechanisms that have run amok.

Velcro vs. Teflon

In the days when caveman Ugh and his wife, Mrs. Ugh, were trying to survive long enough to raise the baby Ughs, they had to pay more attention to potential threats than to positive events to avoid prehistoric dangers like being eaten by a saber-toothed tiger.

This selective attention to negativity is what allowed Mr. and Mrs. Ugh and all the baby Ughs to survive. If you wanted to live a long life, it was better to react to every single thing that might be life-threatening, even if it turned out to be harmless, than to ignore something truly lethal. Our ancestors were the "Nervous Nellies" and "Fearful Franks" of the tribe; the people who were more relaxed about these possibly dangerous situations usually weren't around long enough to have kids and pass on their genes!

Today, even though we don't have to be on the lookout for tigers anymore—well, at least not in my neighborhood—we're still hard-wired the same way: we pay more attention to the negative than to the positive. As the psychologist and brain researcher Dr. Rick Hanson explained to me during our interview, our brains are "Velcro for negativity and Teflon for positivity." Our negative experiences stick to us like Velcro, while our positive experiences slide right off us like Teflon. In fact, researchers have found it takes numerous positive experiences to overcome a single negative one! Unfortunately, this wiring turns out to be disastrous for our happiness.

"No, I don't think you're crazy. Like most of us, you're just a victim of bad programming."

Remember what happened in my mind during that talk? You have to admit, it takes a special talent to tune out the 449 people who'd spent my entire presentation laughing, smiling, and nodding so I could focus exclusively on the one guy I thought—wrongly—didn't like what I was saying. I'm sure you've noticed this yourself. If you receive ten compliments and one insult, which do you remember? If you're like most people, you'll make yourself miserable by stewing on the insult for hours, overlooking the larger number of positive messages. Psychologists call this tendency to respond more intensely to disturbing thoughts and experiences our "negativity bias."

Psychologist Dr. John Cacioppo, at the University of Chicago, demonstrated this tendency in a study in which he measured the electrical activity in the area of subjects' brains that processes incoming information. He showed each subject three types of pictures. One set inspired positive feelings (sporty cars, delicious food), another provoked negative feelings (gruesome and disturbing images), and one produced only neutral feelings (everyday objects like plates and dryers). The surge in electrical activity was dramatically higher when people looked at the images they found negative. Negativity simply makes a greater impression on the brain.

Researchers are beginning to understand the physiological reasons why our negative experiences are so "sticky." The amygdala, the part of our brain's alarm system that triggers the fight-or-flight response, is involved. To learn more about this process, let's put on our white coats and step into the lab to take a closer look at the brain and how it works.

Adrenaline and the Hot Amygdala

What follows here should be a detailed explanation in precise scientific language using lots of terms that require frequent trips to the dictionary. I don't know about you, but those kinds of explanations make my eyes glaze over and my mind want to take an extended vacation to the Bahamas. Instead, let me offer a very brief overview of the brain's alarm system and its impact on our bodies.

Whenever the amygdala signals fight or flight, your body immediately jacks up your heart rate, releases floods of adrenaline, and sends other stress hormones cascading into your bloodstream. That adrenaline, according to a recent study conducted by Dr. Jim McGaugh of the University of California–Irvine, creates stronger memories in the brain than pleasure hormones do. This means that your disturbing experiences are "chemically supercharged" to stay with you far longer than your happy ones.

What makes this an even bigger problem is that many of us have amygdalas that are overreactive: they trigger the release of adrenaline too easily and often. Scientists call this having a "hot" amygdala and say that it's a major obstacle to being happy. It's behind the tendency to have a short fuse, panic easily, and generally make mountains out of molehills. People with the hottest amygdalas are the drama queens, rage-a-holics, worrywarts, and chronic complainers among us.

When the amygdala gets stuck in overdrive, it widens the negative neural pathways in our brain. Our minds become overrun with negative thoughts, and we worry, picturing over and over what we don't want to happen, creating anxiety and unhappiness in our lives. We tell ourselves stories based on our Stuck Old Beliefs, what I call our S.O.B. stories.

Having a hot amygdala has negative health implications as well: when your amygdala is constantly pushing the fight-or-flight button, the stress chemicals released into the body build up. In today's world, the saber-tooth tigers of our ancestors have been replaced by such things as near-accidents on the highway, confrontations with a boss or coworker, and arguments with a spouse. Although these everyday situations trigger the release of fight-or-flight hormones, they don't require you to sprint to safety or punch someone out, physical activities that once used up those powerful stress chemicals. Instead, the chemicals hang around and accumulate, creating fatigue and disease in your body.

Having an overreactive alarm system can damage your health and dramatically lower your happiness set-point—unless you learn to override it.

Teaching an Old Brain New Tricks

Though your brain is hardwired to be Velcro for negativity and to have a highly sensitive alarm system, there's hope for increasing your happiness: your brain's neuroplasticity. Unlike an old dog, your brain really can learn new tricks. Changing your thoughts produces changes in your brain, and perhaps even in your DNA.

Studies done by Dr. Richard Davidson, director of the Laboratory for Affective Neuroscience at the University of Wisconsin–Madison, whom you met in Chapter 1, demonstrate that thinking new and different thoughts creates new neural pathways. When we change our thinking to support our happiness, the negative neural pathways shrink and the positive neural pathways widen. This makes it easier and more automatic for us to think more positively.

For years, it's been commonly accepted that the genetic component of our happiness set-point—the 50 percent determined by our DNA—can't be changed. But according to Bruce Lipton, a molecular biologist and author of *The Biology of Belief*, our DNA may not be as immutable as we think. His intriguing research suggests that our DNA is influenced by our positive and negative thoughts—one more indication that our thinking can reprogram our happiness set-point.

I'm not talking about wishful thinking, or simply deciding to be happier. That's like pasting a smiley face over our pain or spreading a layer of icing over cake that's burned to a cinder. The bad stuff is still there. What I'm talking about is accessing the higher center of your brain, your neocortex, to reverse the negativity bias and override your primitive alarm system.

Crank up the Neocortex

According to the latest research, the neocortex is where happiness lives in the brain—in the left prefrontal area, to be exact. Studies have shown that happy people have a high level of activity in this area, while those who have a tendency toward anxiety, fear, and depression have higher activity in the right prefrontal cortex.

When it comes to happiness, you can't fool the brain. Psychologist Dr. James Hardt, one of the world's experts on brain waves, explained to me that the brain wave activity of a happy person is different from the brain wave activity of someone who is unhappy. His research shows that people who are less reactive to the fearful messages of their amygdala have more alpha wave activity—the sign of a happy brain.

Instead of being overrun with negative thoughts or constantly going into fight-or-flight mode, happy people have habits that allow them to respond more easily from their higher brain center, the neocortex. From my interviews with the Happy 100, I've found that they don't believe everything they think. They:

- Are more skeptical of their negative thoughts. They question the alarms and override them when necessary.
- Don't fight with their negative thoughts. They know that these are often just by-products of their negativity bias and that they can go beyond the mind and let them go.
- Register their positive thoughts more deeply and savor their positive experiences.

Here are three Happiness Habits to help you create new brain pathways and respond more readily from your neocortex:

Happiness Habits for the Mind

1. Question Your Thoughts
2. Go Beyond the Mind and Let Go
3. Incline Your Mind Toward Joy

Happiness Habit for the Mind #1
Question Your Thoughts

There is only one cause of unhappiness; the false beliefs you have in your head, beliefs so widespread, so commonly held, that it never occurs to you to question them.

—Anthony de Mello, Jesuit priest and psychotherapist

Sergio and I recently had the great privilege of meeting privately with the State Oracle of Tibet, a man who has served as the advisor to His Holiness the Dalai Lama and to the Tibetan government for the past twenty years. Deeply impressed by the joy and serenity he radiated, I asked the Oracle to comment on the topic of happiness. This is what he told me: "The real enemy of happiness is the mind's fixations and delusions. Look at the situation differently, see the truth and the suffering is less. If you have the right mind, you can overcome anything—you can be happy, no matter what."

How can you tell if your mind is telling you the truth? By asking! When you take your upsets with a grain of salt and don't buy the underlying premise, it's amazing how a storm of emotion simply evaporates.

The next story powerfully illustrates the benefits of not believing everything you think. In our interview, Happy 100 member, Bruce Fraser (a pseudonym), described his journey out of suffering as he learned to question his thoughts about what was happening in his life.

Bruce's Story

Nothing but the Truth

My wife and I had been married for over twenty years. We had a nineteen-year-old daughter and what I'd always thought was a rock-solid commitment—if not to stay married, then at least to talk everything through. If we ever split up, I was certain it would be a decision we would come to after a long period of trying to work things out—together.

I was aware that things had been difficult for the past two years. My work had temporarily taken me to another city, so we were doing the long-distance thing, seeing each other two or three times a month. It wasn't ideal, but I really thought we could weather it.

We couldn't.

One weekend when I was home, my wife told me she needed to talk to me. "I've been doing a lot of thinking," she began, "and I don't want to be married anymore."

I stared at her, unbelieving. *What was she saying?*

She continued, "Of course, I still love you and want us to be friends, but I want a divorce."

Divorce. The word hit me like a ton of bricks, knocking the wind out of me. Yet even through the haze of my shock, I understood that she wasn't saying we needed to *talk* about a divorce; her mind was made up. She was informing me that our marriage was over.

I couldn't believe that she wouldn't include me in this life-changing decision. Over the course of the weekend, I tried everything to get her to change her mind. I begged. I bargained. I cried.

Then, over the course of the next week, things went from bad to worse. My wife, immovable in her decision to leave the marriage, finally admitted that she had met someone else. This explained why she wasn't interested in trying to save our relationship. She just wanted out so she could be with him.

I went into a tailspin. I felt betrayed, rejected, unloved, and unlovable. *How could she do this to me?* My despair began coloring my job, my health, and especially my mind. In desperation, I signed up for a nine-day seminar that was supposed to help me change the way I dealt with my thoughts.

At the beginning of the seminar we were asked, "On a scale of 1 to 10, how happy are you?" My happiness level was at an all-time low. I was a 1.

For the next two days, I just sat and listened. The premise of the seminar was that when events happen to us, we react by creating a story in our head about those events. It's not actually the events that make us suffer; it's our story *about* the events that produces the suffering. So when we find ourselves unhappy about something that's happened, it's important to question our story to see if it's true. This made sense, but I felt so paralyzed by my grief, I couldn't do it.

On the third day, when things seemed utterly hopeless, I finally began to question my story using the process the seminar leader had recommended.

"What," I asked myself, "do I really think about this whole sorry mess?"

The answer came quickly: "My wife should not be behaving the way she is. Her betrayal has caused me to lose my home and my family, I can never be happy again."

I don't know why, but at that moment, I had just enough breathing room from the grip of my intense pain to continue the process by asking, "Are those things true?"

They felt true, but I dug deeper. "Can I absolutely *know* that she shouldn't be acting like that? Can I absolutely *know* that I won't ever be happy again?"

Surprisingly, the answer was "No" to both questions.

For a moment, I was stunned. I'd interrupted the endless loop of thought/pain/thought/pain/thought/pain that had been playing in my head for the past few weeks. I almost laughed. Without the constant drumbeat of my tragic thoughts, I felt quiet and calm.

I realized that if I took a larger view of the situation, I had no idea if what was happening was "good" or "bad." It simply wasn't in my power to know if she should be acting that way. Suddenly, everything I had been thinking about the situation seemed suspect. The dread of facing my "ruined" future disappeared, and in its place, I felt an excitement. "Maybe," I thought, "things will be even *better* than they were in the past!"

This moment of light and possibility lasted for a few minutes—until I thought about my wife being with another man. An explosion of pain and anger went through my heart. *How could she do this to me?*

But the relief I'd felt for those few minutes had loosened my story's hold on me. I looked at my story and saw another layer of it: I believed that my wife loved someone else more than she loved me.

I took a deep breath and asked myself the same simple question: "Is that true?"

Again, it certainly felt true, so once more I asked the deeper question: "Can I absolutely know for sure that she loves this guy more than she loves me?"

"No, I can't." The thought that she loved someone else more than me had been causing me to double over with pain, yet I couldn't be absolutely sure it was true. It floored me that one thought—how I answered this question—had the power to determine my happiness.

It was an "aha!" moment. Everything I had been hearing at the seminar suddenly clicked into place. It was really pretty simple: my story about the situation appeared as powerful statements of fact in my head and caused knee-jerk responses of suffering and sadness. Yet when I investigated those "statements of fact," they were usually pretty flimsy. It was shocking—and comforting—to realize that the situation itself was not the source of my pain.

I was so excited with this revelation that I eagerly continued to question my thoughts and beliefs for the next week.

By the end of the nine days, I was not the same desperate and victimized person that had arrived at the seminar. I was at peace, filled with a serenity and a sense of acceptance. I'd learned that my misery always came from my story about what had happened in the past. Now I was interested only in being in the present moment. What freedom!

When I returned from the seminar, I called my wife and told her I was ready to let her go. I offered to do anything I could to make this transition easier. I even told her that if she had found something better than our relationship, she should go for it. And I sincerely meant it.

A year later, that sense of freedom is still here. There's still some residual grieving that wells up from time to time. But as soon as I catch myself telling stories to myself about what I've lost and what it means, I stop right there. I look at my story and ask myself: What's the belief behind this pain? Then, once I've identified the belief, I explore the even more crucial question: Is it true? At first it took some conscious effort, but with practice, it's becoming more and more automatic.

I remember the time, just a few weeks after the seminar, when I came across a favorite picture of my wife and me that had always been on my desk. As I looked at our smiling faces and thought of all the happy times we'd had together, I felt a wave of sadness. I stopped and asked myself, "Okay, what's the belief here?" It was my old favorite: "I'll never be that happy again." So I asked myself the all-important question: Could I really know that was true? Suddenly I laughed as I remembered the day the photo was taken. It hadn't been all roses; we had been bickering on and off all afternoon. The truth was, I was happier the minute before I picked up that photo than I had been the day the photo was taken.

The bottom line is this: thoughts come and go, relationships come and go, pain comes and goes. I've discovered that clinging to my stories about what I think I want and need is a surefire recipe for suffering.

Today I've come to a place of real peacefulness, of letting go and accepting things as being just what they are and nothing more. This one simple change has made me happier than I could ever have imagined. On a scale of 1 to 10, count me as a 9—heading toward 10—and not looking back.

Doing The Work

We are disturbed not by what happens to us, but by our thoughts about what happens.

—Epictetus, Greek philosopher

I too have been helped tremendously by the technique for self-inquiry (referred to as The Work) Bruce describes in his story. Developed by a woman named Byron Katie (everyone calls her Katie), The Work consists of asking yourself four simple questions about your painful thoughts and beliefs:

1. Is it true?
2. Can you absolutely know that it's true?
3. How do you react when you believe that thought?
4. Who would you be without the thought?

Then you apply a "turnaround" statement, a sentence expressing the reverse of your thought or belief. The turnaround is a way to experience the truth of the opposite of what you believe.

Katie discovered The Work as a result of her own life transformation. She went from being as unhappy as a person can be to experiencing what I can only call a moment of grace, which left her in a permanent state of bliss and peace. Before her transformation, Katie, a mother of three and a self-employed businesswoman, described herself as "completely depressed, suicidal, stuck in total pain and self-loathing." Sometimes she couldn't get up for days or weeks to bathe or brush her teeth. Eventually, her self-esteem became so low that she didn't feel she deserved to sleep in a bed and began sleeping on the floor.

One morning, she awoke on the floor when something crawled across her ankle. She opened her eyes and saw a cockroach—and in that exact same moment, something else awakened in her. She realized that all of her suffering came from her thoughts about her situation—*my life is horrible, I don't deserve happiness*—not from the situation itself. She began to laugh. It suddenly seemed so clear: when she believed her thoughts, she suffered, and when she didn't, she was happy. And she saw that it was the same for everybody. **All suffering comes from believing our thoughts.**

Although I don't come from Missouri, I have a "show me" kind of attitude about things. I wanted to know if Katie was really Happy for No Reason. Every time I saw her in a seminar, she certainly seemed happy enough. But that was in public. What was she like out of the spotlight? I decided to meet her and interview her for this book.

Katie is absolutely amazing, one of the most present, genuinely loving people I've ever known. She is the perfect example of what it means to be Happy for No Reason. Though she's been threatened at gunpoint, gone through a divorce, and faced losing her eyesight, she still remains anchored to a deep inner state of happiness. Listening to Katie and doing The Work has completely changed the way I "think about my thinking."

Since I've always had an inquisitive mind and a tendency to interrogate everyone I know, questioning my own mind came easily to me. Today I'm interested in, as they used to say on *Dragnet,* "just the facts, ma'am."

Once, for example, after a mild spat, I caught myself thinking, "Sergio should be less judgmental of me."

Wait a second, I wondered, *is that true?* Hmmm, not sure.

Can I absolutely know it's true? No, the evidence certainly wouldn't stand up in a court of law.

How do I feel when I think that thought? Contracted. Definitely an energy-killing thought.

Who would I be without that thought? Freer. More expanded. Happier.

Then I did the turnaround. I wrote down my initial thought: *Sergio should be less judgmental of me.* Then I played around with it, trying different versions to see if any rang true:

Sergio should not be less judgmental of me.

I should be less judgmental of Sergio.

I should be less judgmental of me.

As I went along, I found myself feeling compassion instead of judgment, and my initial thought—Sergio should be less judgmental of me—simply disappeared.

When you get into the habit of questioning your thoughts, you'll find that you don't have to try to control your mind or push out your painful thoughts. As time goes by, they simply lose the power to upset you. Your mind becomes peaceful, strong, and expanded, which automatically raises your happiness set-point. The following exercise is an opportunity to use The Work yourself.

Exercise

The Work Mini-Worksheet

Enter a belief or a judgment on the line below and then question it in writing using the following questions and turnaround:

Belief: ____________________________________

1. Is it true?
2. Can you absolutely know that it's true? (Can you really know what is best in the long run for your path or another person's path?)

3. How do you react when you believe that thought? What happens? (How do you treat yourself and others when you believe that thought?)
4. Who would you be without that thought? (How would you live life differently if you didn't believe that thought?)

Then turn the thought around.

___

(Is that as true or truer?)

For each turnaround, find three genuine examples of how the turnaround is true in your life. This is not about blaming yourself or feeling guilty. It's about discovering alternatives that can bring you peace.

When we do The Work, we free ourselves from the effects of believing stressful thoughts such as "I'm not good enough," "He doesn't love me," "She doesn't understand me," "I'm too fat," "I need more money," and "Something terrible is going to happen." We can turn our stress, frustration, and anger into a freedom that we never dreamed possible.

For a more complete description of how to use The Work, go to www.thework.com.

Used by permission of Byron Katie.

Happiness Habit for the Mind #2

Go Beyond the Mind and Let Go

If you let go a little, you will have a little peace. If you let go a lot, you will have a lot of peace. If you let go completely, you will have complete peace.

—The Venerable Ajahn Chah, twentieth-century Buddhist monk

In Borneo, the natives have an ingenious technique for capturing the wild monkeys that raid their crops and stores of food. They take an empty coconut shell and make a small hole in it, just large enough for a monkey's hand. They put some rice into the coconut for bait and tie the coconut to the ground. The thieving monkey, smelling the food, comes to investigate. He sticks his hand inside the coconut to grab the rice but when he tries to pull his hand out, because it's clasped in a fist around the rice it won't fit through the hole anymore. To escape, the monkey must let go of the rice. Because they won't let go, the monkeys of Borneo remain trapped!

A lot of us are like those monkeys: trapped by our negative thoughts because we just won't let go of them. And the more we resist them, the more they stick around. It doesn't help to try pushing them away—they'll just keep coming back.

Another way to address our troubling thoughts is to go beyond our minds and connect with the feelings associated with the negative thoughts. It's the feeling that keeps the thought glued to the mind. When we welcome the feeling, accept it and then let it go, the thought will quite miraculously dissolve. An effective way to do this is through a simple, yet powerful technique called the Sedona Method.

Lester's Miracle

The Sedona Method was discovered over fifty years ago by a man named Lester Levenson. In 1952, Lester, a physicist and successful entrepreneur, was forty-two years old. Although he was at the pinnacle of worldly success, he was very unhappy and unhealthy. He suffered from depression, an enlarged liver, kidney stones, spleen trouble, hyperacidity, and ulcers that had perforated his stomach and formed lesions. After having his second coronary, Lester's doctors sent him home to his Central Park South penthouse apartment in New York City to die.

But Lester was a man who loved challenges. So, instead of giving up, he decided to find some answers. He holed himself up in his apartment and did some serious soul searching. He found what he considered the ultimate tool for personal growth, a way of letting go of all inner limitations, that is the basis of the Sedona Method still taught today. He was so excited by his discovery that he used it intensively for a period of three months. By the end of that period, his body had become totally healthy again. What's more, he entered a state of profound peace and happiness that never left him. Instead of dying in just a few weeks as the doctors predicted, he lived to the age of eighty-four—another forty-two years.

Dropping the Pen

I first learned about the Sedona Method from my dear friend Hale Dwoskin, who was one of Lester's students and today carries on Lester's work all over the world. Hale is amazing! He's like a laughing Buddha, and it's contagious. I can't be around him without wanting to giggle. He's definitely one of my Happy for No Reason mentors.

When I met Hale, letting go was not my strong suit. Sometimes I fought my negative thoughts and feelings, but mostly I was the queen of holding on to them, doggedly determined to figure them out, to understand where they came from and what they meant. Hale kept telling me, "Marci, just do the process." But I didn't think I could just let my thoughts and feelings go. It seemed too ridiculously simple.

What helped me finally get it was a little demonstration Hale showed me of how letting go works. Try it for yourself.

First, get a pen. Now hold the pen tightly in your hand. The pen represents your thoughts and feelings, and your hand is your awareness.

Notice that although gripping the pen is uncomfortable, after a little time it begins to feel familiar or "normal." Are you feeling that yet? In this same way, your awareness holds on tightly to your thoughts and feelings, and eventually you get used to holding on and don't even realize you're doing it.

Now open your hand and roll the pen around on your palm. Notice that your pen and your hand are not attached to each other. The same is true of your thoughts and feelings. Your thoughts and feelings are no more attached to you than the pen is attached to your hand. *You are not your thoughts or feelings.*

Now turn your hand over and let the pen go.

What happened? The pen dropped to the floor.

Was that hard? No—you simply stopped holding on!

That's what it means to let go.

Mariel Hemingway, the actress and granddaughter of writer Ernest Hemingway, has found the Sedona Method very helpful too. A week before our interview, I arranged to meet Mariel at a local bookstore where she was doing a signing for her most recent book, *Healthy Living from the Inside Out*. Mariel is lovely, funny, and authentic on all levels, a member in good standing of the Happy 100. In our interview Mariel told me the following story, which describes the freedom and happiness she's experienced as a result of going beyond her mind and letting go.

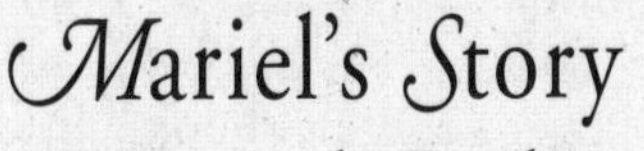

Mariel's Story

It Runs in the Family

I come from a family famous for its creative genius, beauty, love of the great outdoors—and problems. My grandfather, the writer Ernest Hemingway, struggled with depression for years and was also a notorious drinker. People are always telling me, "I once had a drink with your grandfather." This has happened so many times, in so many places, that I am convinced my grandfather had a drink with a significant percentage of the world's population.

In the end, his depression and drinking drove him over the edge. Four months before I was born, he killed himself, the fourth member of his immediate family to commit suicide. Since then, alcoholism, drug abuse, mental illness, and depression have continued to plague my family.

Although I escaped the "Hemingway curse" in most ways, my biggest struggle in life has been overcoming my self-hatred. For years, a nasty voice in my head was always saying, *You're just not good enough*. If a friend had talked to me in that horrible voice, I'd have certainly stopped being her friend.

I was especially hard on myself about how I looked. I was terribly self-conscious about my wide face, my flat chest, and my long, skinny legs. I thought I was ugly and detested my high-pitched voice. I was obsessed with my body.

This obsession also seems to run in the family. It's a little known fact that my grandfather Ernest used to weigh himself every day and write his weight on the side of the toilet in the bathroom of every house he lived in: *March 8, 1945–185 pounds,* and so on. My sister Margaux's body issues, including her bulimia, were better known, and most likely contributed to her depression and eventual suicide. It isn't hard to see the disastrous behavior pattern: either go crazy or kill yourself. Sometimes both. It was a grim prospect for a young girl growing up.

For a long time, I worried that I'd wake up one morning and have lost my mind like so many people in my family. So I became a control freak—especially around food. For years all I thought about was what I was going to eat next. It was so embarrassing. *What a waste of time,* I'd tell myself. But it was where my head would go because I couldn't face the deeper pain of being afraid to die or go crazy. My body and the food I ate were easier issues to deal with; at least they were controllable.

Of course, I knew better than to drink or do drugs—I'm a Hemingway, for heaven's sake!—but I was incredibly strict about exercise and what I put in my mouth. One positive side effect of my intense need for control was that I was afraid of throwing up, which kept me from being bulimic. What I mostly felt was an overriding negativity about myself that I never, ever, ever thought would go away. Like a black cloud obscuring my happiness, it was just a part of my life.

For many years I existed on a steady diet of espressos—the air and caffeine diet—and it damaged my health. I eventually cleaned up my act and started eating healthier and being gentler with myself about exercise, but I still felt the fear inside. If anything went wrong in my life, my need for control would rear its ugly head again.

I thought if I could control my body and my world, then that voice inside that was so filled with judgment would go away. And to top it off, I would judge myself for being so judgmental. Trying to get rid of my negative thoughts never worked; it only made me feel worse.

Then I learned a method for letting go of my thoughts and feelings called the Sedona Method. By asking myself some very simple questions, I could simply let go of even the stickiest feeling and thought. I suddenly understood that a major part of the problem was my conviction that my thoughts and feelings were attached to me. They aren't! My thoughts stick around because I resist and fight them, and hold on to the feelings that come along with them. What if I stopped holding on and simply let go?

Could it really be that easy?

At first I was resistant. Every flippin' second of my life, I was thinking I should be better. But right away, I found letting go helped lighten the intensity of my negative thoughts and feelings. The simple process of asking myself the Sedona Method questions—"Could I let go of this feeling?" "Would I let it go?" "When?"—seemed to pop the bubble of tension I felt around whatever problem I was facing. As I continued to practice, something loosened up inside. It was a relief to stop fighting my need for control and begin to accept myself the way I was. Though I'm not sure why it works, I know it does, and that's all that matters.

My favorite time to practice letting go is while I am out hiking. Like my father and grandfather, I've always loved being out in nature. When I find myself feeling unhappy about anything, I usually go outside.

I remember one time when something had set me off and I felt terrible about myself; I was convinced that I was unattractive—a huge, oversized blob. It was a gorgeous day, so I took off into the mountains. As I walked along the path that started in our backyard in Sun Valley, Idaho, I went through the letting-go process out loud. There I was, striding along the path, talking to myself. Thank God, no one was in earshot; they'd have thought I was a crazy woman.

When I got home, I looked at myself in the mirror and couldn't believe I was the same person that had set off on the walk. I was wearing the exact same shirt and shorts. I hadn't lost a pound, but I thought, *You look fine. Just fine.* Nothing was different physically; the only thing that had changed was that I'd let go of those feelings associated with self-judgment. I saw so clearly the power of my thoughts and feelings and how they had controlled me.

Although I still beat myself up at times, I forget how it once ruled my life. I used to beat myself up every six minutes; now it's only every six months. I've gone from being painfully obsessed with my body image to not even thinking about it. Though I still take good care of myself, it's because I want to, not out of a need to control my life.

Today, at age forty-five, I no longer have that nasty voice in my head. I'm kind to myself and talk to myself as a friend. When I finally saw that my thoughts, my feelings, and that horrible voice weren't nailed into me, I let them go—and found my true essence, the happiness I was born with. Now, most of the time, I feel the way I felt as a small child: as if I am floating through my life, not being *judged,* but just *being*.

Dropping the Excess Baggage

Most of us can identify to some degree with Mariel's struggle with her negative self-worth. For some people this struggle plays out in body image, for others, relationships or career. No matter the area, the underlying feeling of *not being enough* destroys our happiness. We free ourselves when we stop fighting our thoughts and learn to drop them.

Like Mariel, I used to think it was my duty to wrestle to the ground every negative thought I had. It was on the trip to the Himalayas I described in the beginning of the book that I finally saw what I was doing to myself. As I watched that small Indian woman carrying my ninety-one-pound suitcase up the mountain on top of her head, I realized what a potent metaphor she'd given me. It was time to let go of all that unnecessary junk I was carrying around in my head! It was a burden for me and for the people around me. Learning to go beyond my mind and let go of my thoughts and feelings has been an easy and effective way for me to get rid of that dead weight.

Putting the Sedona Method into Practice

The Sedona Method is based on two main premises:

1. Thoughts and feelings aren't facts and they're not you.
2. You can let them go.

At your core you already have the happiness you're seeking and all you need to do is uncover this natural happiness by letting go of the unhappiness or limitation that appears to be covering or obstructing it.

The tendency to hold on and attach ourselves to our unhappy thoughts and feelings is so strong it appears even in the way we use language. When we feel sad, we usually say, "I'm sad." When we feel unhappy, we usually say, "I'm unhappy." We are constantly reinforcing the belief of our being attached to our thoughts and feelings. The Sedona Method helps break that attachment.

The following exercise is an introduction to the Sedona Method and will show you how to use the questions that Mariel mentioned in her story.

Exercise

The Letting Go Process

Make yourself comfortable and focus inwardly. Your eyes may be open or closed.

Step 1: Focus on an issue that you would like to feel better about, and then allow yourself to feel whatever you are feeling in this moment. This doesn't have to be a strong feeling. In fact, if you are feeling numb, flat, cut off, or empty inside, those are feelings that can be let go of just as easily as the more recognizable ones. Just welcome the feeling and allow it to be as fully as you can.

This instruction may seem simplistic, but it needs to be. Most of us live in our thoughts, pictures, and stories about the past and the future, rather than being aware of how we actually feel in this moment. The only time that we can actually do anything about the way we feel (and, for that matter, about our businesses or our lives) is NOW.

Step 2: Ask yourself: *Could I let this feeling go?*
This question is merely asking you if it is possible to take this action. "Yes" and "No" are both acceptable answers. You will often let go even if you say "No." All the questions used in this process are deliberately simple. They are not important in and of themselves but are designed to point you to the experience of letting go.

Step 3: Ask yourself this simple question: *Would I let this go?* In other words: *Am I willing to let go?*

If the answer is "No," or if you are not sure, ask yourself: "Would I rather have this feeling, or would I rather be free?" Even if the answer is still "No," go on to Step 4.

Step 4: Ask yourself this simpler question: *When?* This is an invitation to just let it go NOW. You may find yourself easily letting go. Remember that letting go is a decision you can make any time you choose.

Step 5: Repeat the preceding four steps as often as needed until you feel free of that particular feeling.

NOTE: You will probably find yourself letting go a little more at each step of the process. The results at first may be quite subtle, but if you are persistent, very quickly the results will get more and more noticeable. You may find that you have layers of feelings about a particular topic, so be patient. However, what you let go of is gone for good and you will feel lighter and more peaceful.

Portions of the preceding exercise were excerpted from *The Sedona Method: Your Key to Lasting Happiness, Success, Peace and Emotional Well-being* by Hale Dwoskin. *Used by permission of The Sedona Method®, www.sedona.com.*

Happiness Habit for the Mind #3

Incline Your Mind Toward Joy

What a wonderful life I've had! I only wish I'd realized it sooner.

—Colette, twentieth-century French novelist

One evening a Cherokee elder told his grandson about the battle that goes on inside people. He said, "My son, the battle is between the two 'wolves' that live inside us all. One is Unhappiness. It is fear, worry, anger, jealousy, sorrow, self-pity, resentment, and inferiority. The other is Happiness. It is joy, love, hope, serenity, kindness, generosity, truth, and compassion."

The grandson thought about it for a minute and then asked his grandfather, "Which wolf wins?"

The old Cherokee simply replied, "The one you feed."

Because of our inborn tendency to register our negative thoughts, feelings, and experiences more deeply than our positive ones, we often feed the wrong wolf. When your brain is Teflon for positivity, happiness goes "slip-sliding away." To be happier, you need to even up the score a bit. You can do this by Inclining Your Mind toward Joy.

I first heard this expression from James Baraz, when I took his fabulous course, "Awakening Joy," a ten-month experiential program for developing one's natural capacity for well-being and happiness. In the first class, James began by telling us that the course was about inclining our minds toward joy. He suggested we gently shift our focus toward giving more attention and energy to thoughts that serve us.

Inclining your mind toward joy works by roughening up the Teflon, so your positive experiences will stick more than the negative ones. When I started consciously inclining my mind toward joy, I began to feel happier right away by simply registering the large and small hits of happiness that I hadn't stopped to notice before. As I continued doing this over time, my happiness increased exponentially, because as we know from the Law of Attraction, when you notice and appreciate the happiness you already have in your life, you draw more happiness to you.

I've noticed that the one place it's often hard to incline our mind toward joy is in the area of our self-worth. Surveys show that two out of three adults in America have low self-esteem. My friend Lenora Boyle is a transformational life coach and teacher of the Option Method, a powerful process that helps people eliminate their negative beliefs. Having worked with thousands of men and women, she says that the most commonly held limiting belief is "I'm not good enough." From my years of giving self-esteem seminars, I know that having such a tough inner critic limits our experience of happiness.

Lisa Nichols, a dynamic motivational speaker and fellow contributor to *The Secret,* struggled with feelings of not being good enough for many years. Although today she is one of the Happy 100, she had to work to overcome her barriers to being happy. Her story shows how inclining her mind toward joy helped her overcome the many ANTs that filled her mind.

Lisa's Story

The Woman in the Mirror

For many years I was unhappy because I felt that the cards I had been dealt by life just weren't a winning hand. My mocha complexion, full lips, and round hips were not the ideals of beauty I saw on television or in the movies. I qualified for the free lunch program, and on top of that, I lived in South Central Los Angeles, a low-income neighborhood with a high crime rate.

I woke up every day feeling sad. I wanted things that I didn't have—things that were absolutely impossible. I wanted to look like Farrah Fawcett. Impossible. I wanted to get a car at sixteen, as some of my school friends did. Impossible. I wanted to live in Beverly Hills. Again, impossible. To compensate, I became a superachiever: I was captain of the track team, head cheerleader, senior editor on my yearbook, and on the student council. But it wasn't enough. The things that were wrong with me far outweighed the good—at least in *my* mind.

For decades, because all my thoughts were focused on what I didn't like about myself, I made a lot of very poor decisions. I sometimes became intimate with the wrong partner, and after these encounters, I'd often feel emptier than ever.

It wasn't until I was in my early thirties that I stopped looking to others for love and acceptance. One day a friend of mine pointed out that intimacy can mean "into me I see." Wow, *that* really woke me up! Could I find love by looking into myself?

I started standing in front of the mirror, looking into my own eyes, and asking, "Who is Lisa?" The answers were simple and honest. A woman who has full lips, round hips, mocha skin, and an Afro. A woman who has battled her weight for years. A woman who's left an abusive relationship. A woman who's in search of her spirituality and now has a relationship with God.

There were so many things to love about that woman. I looked in my eyes and said things like, "I'm proud that you . . ." and talked about the great things that I did. I listed things that I put on my résumé and things that I wouldn't dare put on my résumé: I'm proud that you moved away from your family to start your own business. I'm proud that you got out of an abusive relationship. I'm proud that you recognized that you have to work with your weight. I'm proud that you have never said a negative word—ever—about your son's father. I'm proud of the work you do to help so many teens. Focusing on these things felt wonderful!

I stood in front of the mirror and began to validate, love, and celebrate *myself.* I began to celebrate the big things and the little, itty-bitty things. "I'm proud that you did ten sit-ups this morning." Whatever the hugeness, whatever the smallness, I celebrated. My face would be wet with tears, but I kept saying "I'm proud that you . . ." until I ran out of things to say.

Before I did this exercise, I'd looked in the mirror, of course. I'd study my face, sighing at the little bumps on my forehead and hating how big my lips were and how frizzy my hair was. I looked at the external things that I felt people were judging—and that I had been judging too.

It was the same reflection, but now I saw different eyes staring back at mine. Eyes that looked for the beauty and goodness in myself—and found them. Over the years, taking the time to savor the good things I recognize about myself has made me stronger and able to love others more.

I still do the mirror exercise every night and I am amazed at how much love and compassion I feel for the woman in the mirror. Sometimes when I'm traveling, I'll even slip open my compact mirror in the back of a cab or wherever I am, and I'll do the exercise in my compact. There are probably rumors around the country that I'm a little strange, but that's okay. It's worth it to be a happy woman.

I had an experience recently that showed me how important this skill really is. A few months ago, I bought a new car. The next day, excited with my new toy, I was driving down the freeway. But as I drove onto the exit ramp, my car began to lose power and the engine started making a *puddah-puddah, puddah-puddah* sound.

"Oh no," I thought, "what's the matter with my brand new car?" *Puddah-puddah, puddah-puddah,* the car coughed and then died.

I was livid! I got out, and in my funky high-heeled sandals and diva shades, walked down the long exit ramp to the gas station at the bottom. I marched inside and told the attendant, "My car is broken. Would you please come see what's wrong with it?"

The attendant walked up the ramp with me, put the key in the ignition, and turned it. Then, giving me a disgusted look, he said, "Ma'am, your car's not broken. You're out of gas."

I was shocked. I immediately pulled out my cell phone and called the dealer. I said, "I just bought a car from you yesterday. I put a ton of money down on it. Now I just ran out of gas."

Without a second's hesitation the salesman said to me, "Ma'am, it is not my job to fill your tank." His answer changed my life. He was right. It was one of those epiphany moments: I saw that it wasn't anyone else's responsibility to fill my tank—in my car or in my life!

Today, keeping my attention on what I appreciate about myself helps me to fill up my own "love tank." The years of sending love to myself in the mirror have paid off handsomely. Not only do I love Lisa, I really, really like her too. I know my job is not to beat Lisa up. It's not to be unhappy about the way things are, but to love myself through the journey.

The Mirror Exercise

Does the idea of standing in front of a mirror and appreciating your positive qualities feel uncomfortable and stupid? It did to me—which was a sign that I really needed to try it.

My cowriter Carol and I first learned the mirror exercise in 1990, when we took a week-long course from Jack Canfield on self-esteem. Jack assigned the exercise as homework every night, saying, "Make sure you do this behind a closed door so nobody walks by and thinks you're crazy." Carol and I were roommates at the course, so each night we took turns going into the bathroom, shutting the door, and whispering sweet nothings to our reflections: "I love you"; "You're beautiful"; "You have a loving heart."

The first night, I felt like a California New Age woo-woo nutcase, but soon I experienced a rush of sadness. I was such an expert at judging myself—why was it so hard to say nice things?

With practice, it gradually became easier to list reasons to love myself: "You're smart"; "You go out of your way to help others"; and so on. But the real power of this exercise came when I learned to express appreciation for myself for no reason—to look myself in the eye and simply love who I was, unconditionally.

If you're like most people, consciously recognizing the positive about yourself may feel conceited. After all, we're raised not to toot our own horns. So we end up not giving ourselves credit or acknowledgment, or, even worse, we beat ourselves up, which shuts down our hearts, contracts our energy, and—you guessed it—lowers our happiness set-points. Not surprisingly, people who are Happy for No Reason have a compassionate, encouraging, and validating attitude toward themselves. This isn't arrogance or self-centeredness; it's an appreciation and acceptance of who they are. Feeling this way about yourself is an important step in raising your happiness set-point.

Register the Positive

To incline your mind toward joy, start registering your happy experiences more deeply. The first step is to make a conscious decision to look for them. You can make it a game you play with yourself. Have the intention to notice everything good that happens to you: any positive thought you have, anything you see, feel, taste, hear, or smell that brings you pleasure, a win you experience, a breakthrough in your understanding about something, an expression of your creativity—the list goes on and on. This intention activates the reticular activating system (RAS), a group of cells at the base of your brain stem responsible for sorting through the massive amounts of incoming information and bringing anything important to your attention. Have you ever bought a car and then suddenly starting noticing the same make of car everywhere? It's the RAS at work. Now you can use it to be happier. When you decide to look for the positive, your RAS makes sure that's what you see.

Adelle, one of the Happy 100, told me about a unique method she has for registering the positive. As she goes about her day, she gives away awards in her mind: the best-behaved dog award, the most colorful landscape design at a fast-food drive-through award, the most courteous driver award. This keeps her alert to the beauty and positivity that is all around her. Charmed by this idea, I tried it myself. I liked it so much, I was inspired to include it as the exercise at the end of this section.

Once you notice something positive, take a moment to savor it consciously. Take the good experience in deeply and *feel* it; make it more than just a mental observation. If possible, spend around thirty seconds soaking up the happiness you feel. If you want to accelerate your progress, take time every day to write down a few of your wins, breakthroughs, and things you appreciate about others—and about yourself. This will shift the balance of power in your mind, tilting the Velcro/Teflon ratio in your brain toward happiness.

In my interview with Happy 100 member Paul Scheele, a human development expert and the author of *Natural Brilliance,* he explained that registering the positive more deeply is easier when you engage the unconscious mind, which is responsible for 90 percent of our thoughts. Every day, we're subject to an onslaught of negative images and messages from the world that go into our minds on an unconscious level. An effective way to counteract these insidious negative thoughts is through the use of Paraliminal audio programs, which work on the level of our unconscious awareness. Paraliminal recordings use multiple voices, in combination with music and scientifically proven brain technology. These programs, which you listen to through stereo headphones, are carefully designed to work simultaneously with both sides of your brain and shift your conscious beliefs while you simply relax and listen. I've found using Paraliminals to be a remarkably easy way to incline my mind toward joy.

Lean into the Thought That Makes You Feel Happier

The concept of inclining our mind toward joy is very similar to what Dr. Martin Seligman, who's considered the father of positive psychology, calls "learned optimism." In his book of the same name, Dr. Seligman, the director of the University of Pennsylvania Positive Psychology Center, draws on a vast body of research to support his thesis that it's possible to learn through practice to become more optimistic.

One of the most effective ways I've found to practice inclining your mind toward joy is *leaning into the thought that makes you feel happier.* The next time you're faced with a challenging situation that gives rise to negative thoughts and bad feelings, find an equally true thought about the situation that makes you feel better—and lean into it. The classic measure of optimism, seeing the glass as half full rather than half empty, is the perfect example of leaning into the equally true but happier thought.

Here's another example using a situation from my own life that I'm sure you've experienced as well. One day, as I bent over my computer, struggling to corral all my ideas into coherence, I had this negative, self-defeating thought: *I can't get this project done in time.*

I noticed how this thought made me feel: stressed out, panicked, and crummy, which didn't help matters.

Then I searched my mind for thoughts that were *equally true* and made me feel better, like *I always manage to get things done. I can ask for help. The more I relax, the more the ideas flow through me.* I inclined my mind toward joy by leaning into these thoughts. Rather than feeling contracted in my body, they made me feel relaxed and expanded.

Please notice that I'm not talking about forcing a positive thought or repeating an affirmation by rote in the mind—*I can get this done in time. I can get this done in time. I can get this done in time*—while you're still feeling that you can't. These still involve some degree of fighting with your negative thought. It's like having a shouting match in your mind: Who's going to win, the *can't* or the *can*? Obviously the winner will be the one that screams louder.

In contrast, when you lean into a happier thought, you're not trying to convince yourself of anything. You're simply shifting your focus from a part of your situation that makes you feel bad to a truthful part of your situation that creates a better feeling.

As the Cherokee grandfather pointed out, the wolf that wins is the one you feed.

Make a habit of feeding happiness.

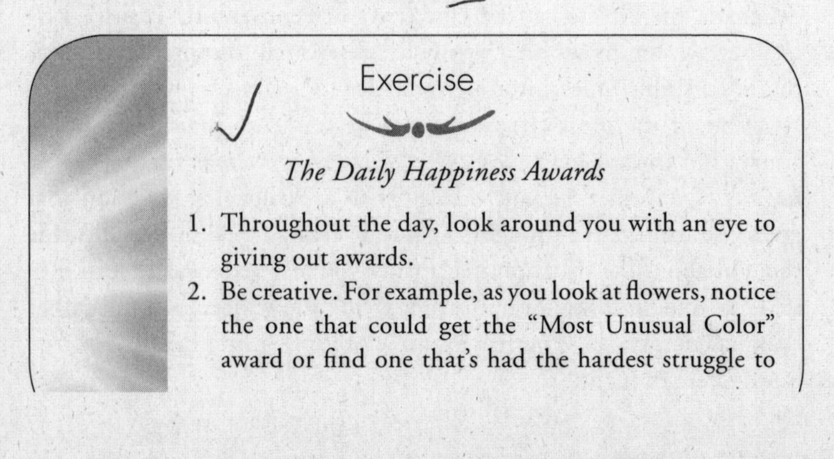

Exercise

The Daily Happiness Awards

1. Throughout the day, look around you with an eye to giving out awards.
2. Be creative. For example, as you look at flowers, notice the one that could get the "Most Unusual Color" award or find one that's had the hardest struggle to

survive, but made it, and give it the "Best Blossom of the Day" award. Look for extraordinary smiles, efficient service, or ingenious solutions to everyday challenges. There's no limit to the type or number of awards you can give in a day.

3. Invite other family members or friends to play this award game, and at the end of the day, tell each other the awards you've given out.

Summary and Happiness Action Steps

Thank God we don't have to believe everything we think! You strengthen the pillar of the mind by thinking in ways that support happiness: questioning your thoughts, going beyond the mind and letting go, and inclining your mind toward joy. Use the following action steps to practice the Happiness Habits for the Mind:

1. When you catch yourself thinking a negative thought, check to see whether it's telling you the truth by doing The Work.
2. To release sticky negative thoughts, practice the Letting Go Exercise.
3. To register the positive about yourself, try the Mirror Exercise once a day for at least a week, preferably twenty-one days.
4. Give Happiness Awards as you move through your day to keep your mind inclined toward joy.
5. Practice leaning into the thought that makes you feel happier.

The Pillar of the Heart—Let Love Lead

I would rather have eyes that cannot see, ears that cannot hear, lips that cannot speak, than a heart that cannot love.

—Robert Tizon, author

Try a little experiment with me. Point to yourself. Now, notice where you're pointing. If you are like the thousands of people I've asked to do this, you're pointing to your heart. Nobody ever points to their head or belly button or kneecap. Why? Because we instinctively feel the heart is the essence of who we are.

Imagine looking deeply into the eyes of someone special and uttering the words, "I love you with all my head." It just doesn't have the same ring to it, does it?

Throughout history, people of all cultures have considered the heart, the seat of our emotions, to be central to human happiness and wisdom. In many traditions, the heart is referred to as the diamond, the jewel, or the lotus—all symbolizing the deepest and most valuable essence of our being.

In the center of our own body, there is a small shrine in the form of a lotus flower,

And within it can be found a small space.

The heavens and the earth are there; the sun, the moon, and the stars, fire and lightning and winds—the whole universe dwells within our heart.

—adapted from the Upanishads

Our hearts are where the "juice" in our life comes from, and when that juice is flowing, we feel great. When it's not, we feel unhappy.

I know this all too well from my own experience. For many years, I lived on and off with a severe, stabbing, and often debilitating pain in my heart. It began over twenty years ago, right after I ended a relationship with a man I loved. Although I didn't plan to marry him, I fell apart when he started dating a good friend of mine. I figured my heartache would mend with time, or at least when I met someone new. But it persisted. At times, I felt I couldn't take another breath because the pain was so intense; at other times, I was afraid I was having a heart attack. I visited many doctors, but no one could find a physical reason for the pain. My heart was heavy, both physically and emotionally. It was only when I began to practice the Happiness Habits for the Heart you'll learn in this chapter that my pain finally diminished.

My interviews with the Happy 100 revealed an important truth: *Happy people let love lead in their lives.* Although they have the same kind of fears, pains, and disappointments as the rest of us, they simply have different habits that allow them to keep their hearts open in their daily lives. When you practice these habits, you'll experience a more loving and open heart—one of the pillars of your Home for Happiness.

The Heart Has an Energy Field

Think back to a happy time from your childhood: a special family outing, having fun with your best friend, or maybe getting your very first cat or dog. How do you feel recalling these memories? Chances are you feel a warmth and a sweet flow in your heart. This is your heart's energy.

When I was a child, my grandfather Poppa, whom I dearly loved, used to stay at our house every weekend. He'd arrive each Friday, bag of Hostess cupcakes in hand, and as soon as I saw him start walking up the steps to the front door, I'd practically vibrate with excitement and joy. I could feel the energy in his heart jumping out and meeting the energy in my heart. I couldn't wait to snuggle into his lap and hear more of his marvelous stories about the 1906 earthquake, his career in semi-pro baseball, and his many other adventures. Even as an eight-year-old, it was obvious to me that the heart has an energy that extends beyond the body.

Now science confirms my childhood experience: the heart *does* have a powerful energy field. The Institute of HeartMath, a highly esteemed research group whose work has been verified in studies conducted by Stanford University and Miami Heart Research Institute, among others, has found that our hearts generate an electromagnetic field around us that is several feet in diameter and five thousand times greater than the field generated by the brain.

One measure of your heart's activity that reflects your emotional state is called heart rate variability (HRV), which shows variations in the intervals between heart beats. In studies using EKG machines to measure HRV, Dr. Rollin McCraty and other HeartMath researchers have found that people's heart patterns look different when they're happy than when they're angry, frustrated, or sad. Look at the difference in the heart's patterns in these graphs.

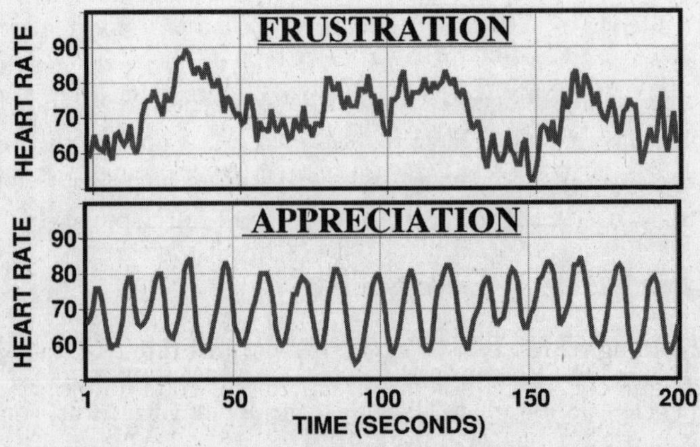

Negative emotions cause erratic patterns called heart rhythm *incoherence,* which has a damaging effect on your body. When you feel angry, frustrated, or sad, stress hormones and cholesterol are released into your body, your heart pumps faster, and your blood pressure rises. In contrast, when you're feeling appreciative, loving, and emotionally balanced, you create heart rhythm *coherence*—smooth, even patterns in the heart rhythms.

"It has a good beat and it's easy to dance to."

According to research published by the Institute of HeartMath, heart rhythm coherence increases production of good hormones, such as the anti-aging hormone DHEA, normalizes blood pressure, improves cognitive function, and strengthens the immune system. In a famous study, researchers at the University of Kentucky analyzed journals that 180 nuns had kept from the time they were in their twenties and found that the sisters who expressed more positive emotions lived, on average, seven years longer than the sisters who expressed more negative emotions. Positive emotions not only feel good, but are good for you!

Love and Fear

All of our emotions can be divided into two basic categories: Love and Fear. All the variations of love, such as gratitude, forgiveness, compassion, and appreciation, expand the heart and create heart wave coherence, while all the variations of fear, like anger, sadness, hurt, and guilt, contract the heart and create heart wave incoherence. At any given moment, either love or fear is running your life—and happiness or unhappiness will follow.

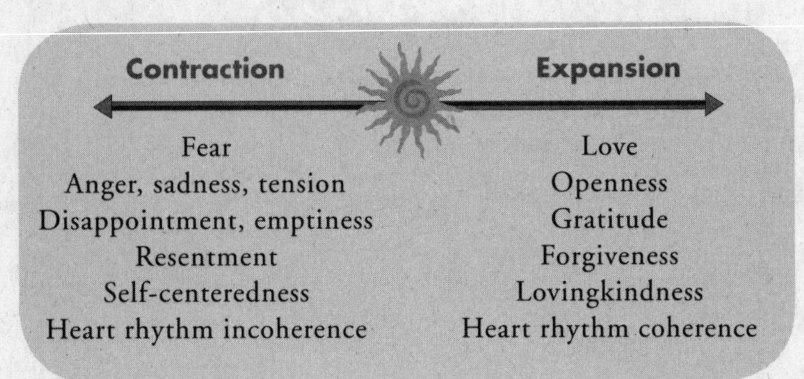

The HeartMath researchers discovered that when people focus on emotions such as appreciation, love, and gratitude, they're able to create more coherence in their heart rhythms *at will*. That means you can jumpstart the expansion of your heart any time you want. I'll show you how to do this later in the chapter using one of the techniques I learned at the Institute of HeartMath.

When I interviewed the Happy 100, I found that their ability to let love lead no matter what's going on in their lives is based on three powerful habits for opening the heart.

Happiness Habits for the Heart

1. Focus on Gratitude
2. Practice Forgiveness
3. Spread Lovingkindness

Happiness Habit for the Heart #1

Focus on Gratitude

If the only prayer you said in your whole life was "Thank you," that would suffice.

—Meister Eckhart, thirteenth-century German theologian

Have you ever felt your heart swell in gratitude? Have you ever wanted to spread your arms wide and shout, "Thank you, thank you, thank you!" Then you know what I mean when I say gratitude is a natural heart expander.

Yet it's easy to take things for granted. How much time during the day do you actually *focus* on gratitude, compared to the time you spend thinking about the problems in your life? We act as if gratitude and appreciation are our good china and our fancy tablecloth and bring them out only on really special occasions.

People who are Happy for No Reason don't necessarily have more in their lives to be grateful for; they simply focus more often on gratitude throughout their day. The difference is where they choose to put their attention.

The following story by Happy 100 member Rico Provasoli, a writer and chiropractor who has the energy and enthusiasm of ten people, illustrates the power of focusing on gratitude.

Rico's Story

Thank You for Everything

Imagine sitting in a dark room lit only by a candle that is almost burned down. As you watch, the candle flame flickers, splutters, seems to fade and then leaps up again—a drop of fragile light in the inky blackness around you. You see that it is only a matter of minutes before it is completely gone.

A number of years ago, my life was like that flame. A little longer, or the slightest puff of breath, and it would have been over. It was *that* close.

As a young man, I simply didn't know what I wanted to do with my life. At college, although my classmates were future elite corporate tycoons, high-profile politicians, and even a Supreme Court judge, I had no such ambitions. During my junior year abroad in France, I found my way to a Trappist monastery, where I spent nearly a year living as a monk. Although I loved my experience there, I soon realized I wasn't cut out for the monastic life. I left and began traveling around the world, sailing the high seas and visiting over fifty countries.

After a few years of adventuring, I ended up back in the States, where I eventually got married, had children, became a chiropractor, and built a clinic on the coast of Maine. I had a very good life, yet I wasn't happy. An inner restlessness dominated my mind and heart. For as long as I could remember, I had felt that way: aware most often of what I was missing in life, rather than grateful for what was working. After a period of deep soul-searching, my wife and I decided to divorce. I made sure that my ex-wife and children were taken care of, sold my practice, and began to travel abroad once more.

Then, in the course of a few months in 1991, my health began to unravel. I started to feel terrible all the time. I'd been sick before, but nothing like this. The list of symptoms kept lengthening, and no one could discover the cause. A friend of mine even hired an exorcist to try to cure me—candles, praying, the whole bit—to no avail. I was really in rough shape. This went on for almost ten years. Finally, in 2001, I hit rock bottom.

On Christmas Eve, I got a call from an eminent endocrinologist I'd recently seen: they had discovered a brain tumor in my anterior pituitary gland, and I would need immediate surgery. "Oh, and have a nice Christmas," he said as he hung up.

I was devastated. Hearing that you need to be opened up to have a tumor removed is never good news—on Christmas Eve or any eve. After spending a miserable Christmas Day, I went to the doctor's office to discuss the surgery. Right away, he told me that the pituitary tumor had been a misdiagnosis. Then he looked me in the eye and said, "You know, there's actually nothing wrong with you. It's all in your head. You're a hypochondriac."

It was the last straw. On top of all of my suffering, he was telling me that I was creating it for myself? The doctor prescribed antidepressants, but I resisted taking them. Finally, six months later, I was so desperate to feel like myself again that I agreed to give the antidepressants a try. After three days on the medication, I felt worse. In this state of total despair and hopelessness, I began to plan my death.

My sister-in-law, who is a psychotherapist, later explained that the particular antidepressant I took can sometimes prompt suicidal tendencies in the first fourteen days of use. At the time, all I knew was that I didn't want to live this way—couldn't live this way—any more. I didn't want to burden my family with the shame and the stigma of a suicide, so I figured I would take the ferry into the city and then simply walk in front of a bus. It would be a clean way out, just one of those terrible things that happens sometimes.

I sat at my kitchen table, contemplating my plan. I'd come to terms with the whole idea, accepting that it was the most sensible solution. It wasn't a passionate, charged decision; it felt very well reasoned. I thought, *You know, this is it. I've had a full life. I don't need any more of this. I'm done.* I felt a certain peace inside.

Then the mail arrived.

It was the day before Father's Day and there in the stack of mail was an envelope from my ex-wife, the mother of my children. I opened the envelope to find a card with beautiful artwork on the front that she had created herself. Inside the card, she had written a message that turned my world upside-down. She told me that she still felt deep love for me and was sincerely happy that I was the father of her children. She said that despite the challenges we'd been through, she had grown profoundly in my company and that she wished me nothing but wonderful health, good fortune, and happiness.

I was shocked. I thought, *Wow! Wait a second. I'm going to kill myself?* It was like a cosmic time-out. I saw that I'd been stuck again focusing on what was wrong in my life, rather than being grateful for what was working. But now my ex-wife's tremendous outpouring of love and gratitude had stopped me in my tracks. Her warm and genuine appreciation brought me back to my heart and helped open my eyes to all the good I had in my life. I abandoned my suicide plans and experienced the first taste of happiness I'd had in years.

These new feelings of gratitude carried me along like a wave. My life started turning around. Within twenty-four hours I met someone who recommended a tropical disease specialist. The specialist took one look at me and knew instantly what was wrong. Tests showed that I was infected with seven types of parasites, amoebas, and liver flukes—unwelcome guests I'd picked up on my travels abroad. I went through a course of powerful antiparasite medication, and to my great relief, I was cured. Finally, I felt like myself again. Actually, I felt *better* than my old self! The difference was my newfound appreciation and gratitude for my life. I was determined to keep this alive and, soon after, found two powerful tools that have helped me do this.

The first is a daily laughing practice: I simply spend ten minutes a day laughing. Although taking time out of my day to just sit and laugh sounds a little odd, my laughing sessions have been transformational. Along with the health benefits from the added endorphins, I find it cleanses me emotionally and keeps my happiness at a high level. I never miss a day.

Then, not long after I began the laughing practice, I received an anonymous fax that contained a mantra from a Zen master: "Thank you for everything. I have no complaints whatsoever." I decided to incorporate this expression of universal gratitude into my everyday routine as a daily renewal of gratitude and joy.

This phrase has become my anchor. Now, no matter what happens, I feel that I have no argument with life.

A few years ago, my sense of gratitude was put to the test when I got a phone call telling me that the bulk of my entire life savings had been embezzled. I had lost everything and would have to radically change my lifestyle. I set down the phone after hearing the news and stood for a moment, digesting the meaning of these events. My first response was "Oh, well." My years of ill health and my brush with suicide put it in perspective: in the larger scheme of things, it just wasn't that important.

I had learned from my days of open-water sailing that when trouble strikes, you keep moving—emergencies require action—so I immediately began to make calls: dissolving the lease on my home, arranging a move to a friend's house, and borrowing money to live on until I could figure out a Plan B.

An hour later, after I had set these things in motion, I was finally free to reflect on my situation. I smiled inwardly as the familiar words bubbled up inside of me: "Thank you for everything. I have no complaints whatsoever." Amazingly, it was true. Of course, I would have preferred things to be different, but I was at peace with what was. Then I sat down and began my laughing session.

Now, years later, through many ups and downs, I'm still laughing! A grateful heart has made all the difference.

Why Gratitude Works

How can something as simple as gratitude be such a powerful tool for creating more happiness in our lives? The answer lies in the Law of

Attraction. Remember the third principle of the Guiding Three: What you appreciate, appreciates. If you want more good in your life, rather than focusing your energy on the problems and obstacles, focus your attention on what's *already* good, what's working. This automatically draws more good to you.

I'm not suggesting you use gratitude as a way to deny, ignore, suppress, or sugar-coat painful feelings. Rather, gratitude is a way to incline your *heart* toward joy. Everyone has both challenges and blessings, but focusing your heart's energy on your blessings will make you far happier.

The Good Vibes of Gratitude

Gratitude is not only fundamental to being Happy for No Reason, it's good for your health too. A recent study conducted by Dr. Michael McCullough at the University of Miami showed that people who describe themselves as feeling grateful tend to have more vitality and optimism, suffer less stress, and experience fewer episodes of clinical depression than the population as a whole.

In an experiment by Dr. Robert Emmons at the University of California–Davis, people who kept a "gratitude journal," a weekly record of things they felt grateful for, enjoyed better physical health, were more optimistic, exercised more regularly, and described themselves as happier than a control group who didn't keep journals.

These studies confirm that gratitude creates a specific energy that affects our bodies in a positive way. A clue to why this happens can be found in the thought-provoking work of Dr. Masuru Emoto.

I first heard of Dr. Emoto and his amazing photographs in the movie *What the Bleep Do We Know?* Using high-speed photography, Dr. Emoto showed that crystals in frozen water had dramatically different forms, depending on the kind of energy that was directed toward the water. In some of his experiments, Dr. Emoto had people gather in a circle around a container of water and send different feelings toward it. "Love and Thanks" is the beautiful crystalline structure that formed when feelings of love and gratitude were directed at the water.

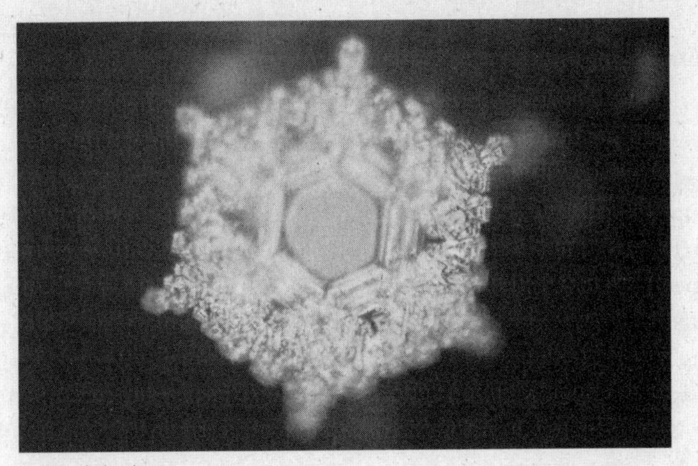

Love and Thanks

In contrast, "You make me sick, I hate you" is the pattern that emerged after feelings of hate and negativity were directed at the water.

You make me sick, I hate you

Our bodies are composed of 70 to 80 percent water. Which pattern would you rather create in your body?

Grateful for No Reason

If there's a VIP section in the Happy 100, Brother David Steindl-Rast would be in the front row! Brother David, a remarkably youthful Benedictine monk in his eighties, has written several books about the importance of gratefulness and is the founder of the Network for Grateful Living, a nonprofit organization that's committed to helping people awaken to gratefulness as the "core inspiration for personal change." I'd heard about Brother David for a number of years and had recently joined a monthly gratefulness group based on his work. When he'd agreed to come to our meeting, our host asked if I wanted to interview Brother David for my book. I jumped at the opportunity.

As I sat on the couch sipping tea with this delightful and wise man, I marveled at the love and joy he radiated. I started by asking him my standard questions, and within moments, I had tears in my eyes as he told me about the hardships he'd experienced during World War II and how they'd turned his heart toward gratefulness.

As a teenager in Austria during the Nazi occupation, he'd never expected to reach the age of twenty. Food was scarce—his family often lived on little more than soup made from weeds—and he was sure he'd be drafted and killed in combat. But he told me he'd been happy despite all the dangers and difficulties, because against the backdrop of impending death, he had seen life as the gift it was. That deep sense of appreciation has never left him.

Brother David offers a unique perspective on gratitude. I was particularly impressed when he said that gratefulness is not just about being grateful for the laundry list of things we have in our lives. "No matter how much or how little you have in life," he told me, "you can still be grateful." To Brother David, gratefulness means experiencing "great fullness," feeling full in every moment, appreciating exactly what is. What I call being Grateful for No Reason. He says, "Happiness is not what makes us grateful; it is gratefulness that makes us happy."

Brother David shared with me a wonderful exercise for increasing feelings of gratefulness in life. Each day, he picks a "theme for the day" to focus on. If he picks water, for example, every time he washes his hands, does the dishes, waters the plants, or brushes his teeth, he notices and appreciates the water and uses it as a reminder to be present in the moment in pure gratefulness. The next day, he might choose to focus on the sounds of traffic, and the next day something else. When I tried this powerful exercise myself, I loved it, and added it to the repertoire of gratitude techniques I practice regularly to keep my happiness level high.

Gratitude in Action

Marc Bekoff is another one of the Happy 100 who wakes up each morning happy. He jumps out of bed, goes to the window, and says good morning to the mountains, the sunshine, and the birds and trees outside his window. Once, when a houseguest heard him do this, he asked, "Who are you talking to?"

"The day, of course!" Marc told him.

It may seem corny, but Marc, like all people who have high happiness set-points, truly delights in the good things in his life. Like all of us, he has challenges, yet he still greets every morning like this, setting the tone for the rest of his day.

Marc's happiness is always there. As I explained in Chapter 1, the state of Happy for No Reason is like a backdrop, remaining even in the midst of difficult emotional situations. For example, when Marc's mother was dying, he flew to her Florida home to spend time with her. She'd had a series of strokes and was paralyzed from the neck down. She couldn't speak, and it was hard to know how much she understood.

To stay centered, Marc often took long walks or runs. One day, he came back from his run with a beautiful bunch of fragrant pink flowers for his mother. Her middle name was Rose and she'd always had a deep fondness for flowers. When he walked into his parents' condominium, smiling broadly, a neighbor who was visiting gave him a surprised look and said to him, "How can you be happy when your mother is in the next room dying?"

Marc answered, "Because it's such a beautiful day and I know if she were more aware, my mother would love this day."

He went to his mother's bedside and put the flowers on her lap. She looked at them, and though she couldn't respond, Marc likes to think that she enjoyed their beautiful scent. Even when his mother was dying, Marc was still able to be grateful for the gift of her presence and to see the goodness in the world.

During our interview, I asked Marc how he remained happy while he was going through deep sadness. He told me, "Happiness is just a part of who I am. At my core, I'm always happy—and there are times when I'm also profoundly sad. They aren't mutually exclusive. The sadness doesn't take away the happiness."

Saying Your Thank-Yous!

A year ago, at a get-together of a dozen girlfriends from college, I saw my old friend Therese Gibson. Therese had been one of the fun girls at school; she'd had an easy laugh and had always been up for an adventure. When she heard I was writing this book, she told me about the daily gratitude ritual she and her ninety-five-year-old father, Charlie, practice—they call it "saying their thank-yous"—that keeps them smiling and feeling good. Therese moved in with Charlie, who's still sharp as a tack, at a bad time in both their lives. Charlie's wife, Therese's mother, had just died, and Therese was at the tail end of a painful divorce. Money was tight and Therese says they were as glum as any two people could be. But both of them had heard that gratitude was a great way to feel better, so they decided to sit together for a few minutes each morning before Therese headed off to work and tell each other the three things they were grateful for in their lives.

"It was slow going in the beginning," Therese told me. "The first time we did it, I was feeling so low I had a hard time thinking of even one thing I was grateful for." Finally, she looked around the room and saw a vase she liked. She told Charlie, "I'm grateful for how pretty that vase is." It sounded silly, but it was the best she could do. Charlie wasn't any better at it, often waiting for Therese to give him a clue about what to say. But she and Charlie both noticed that even a thank-you for something superficial had a good effect.

Soon, their decision to focus on what was right in their lives began to pay off. Both Therese and Charlie started to feel happier and notice that more and more things were going their way. Even their money situation improved. Three thank-yous became five, became ten, and soon they had to stop listing the good things in their lives long before they ran out of things to say, or Therese would be late for work.

One day, they were feeling so light and happy after finishing their lists that Charlie, who'd always liked the musical *Oklahoma!,* started singing "Oh, What a Beautiful Morning." Therese joined in. It was the perfect expression of how being grateful made them feel. They added this song to their ritual and now, saying their thank-yous and singing together has become one of the highlights of their day.

What you're grateful for, you get more of. When you appreciate the happiness and love you already experience, more happiness and love come to you.

I've experienced myself how powerful gratitude is. After the heartbreak I described at the beginning of this chapter, a friend told me to write down five things I was grateful for each night before I went to bed for three weeks straight. I knew that psychologists say it takes twenty-one days to change a habit, so I agreed. At first I struggled, but my results kept me going. In fact, this simple little exercise worked so well that I continued doing it every night for the next three years, and over time, the pain in my heart eased.

I suggest you try the gratitude exercise yourself. Every night before you go to sleep, list five things that you're grateful for that day, and notice how you feel when you wake up the next morning.

Tools from the HeartMath Experts

Appreciation and gratitude are a must if you choose to become the architect of increased happiness and your own fulfillment.

—Doc Childre, founder of HeartMath

On several occasions, I've made trips to the Institute of HeartMath, two hours from my home, in the heart of the redwood forest. There I met with the brilliant visionary and founder Doc Childre and some of his top researchers. The Institute of HeartMath is on the leading edge of research and technology in the area of the heart's influence on health and happiness. They've even developed a computer program and a hand-held device called the emWave that give you real-time feedback of your heart's rhythms to help you habituate heart rhythm coherence. I use these technologies regularly and find that they help my heart feel more open, radiant, and bathed in warmth.

You can use the following Quick Coherence Technique they developed any time you want to focus on the love and gratitude in your heart.

Exercise

The Quick Coherence Technique

Quick Coherence is a powerful emotion-refocusing technique that connects you with your heart power to help you release stress, balance your emotions, and feel better fast. Once you've learned the technique, it takes only a minute to do.

Step 1: Heart Focus
Gently focus your attention in the area of your heart. If you like, you can put your hand over your heart to help. If your mind wanders out of habit, just keep shifting your attention back to the area of your heart.

Step 2: Heart Breathing
As you focus on the area of your heart, pretend your breath is flowing in and out through that area. This helps your mind and energy to stay focused and your respiration and heart rhythms to synchronize. Breathe slowly and gently, until your breathing feels smooth and balanced, not forced. Continue to breathe with ease until you find a natural inner rhythm that feels good to you.

Step 3: Heart Feeling
As you continue to breathe, recall a positive feeling, a time when you *felt* good inside. Now try to reexperience the feeling. This could be a feeling of appreciation or care toward a special person, a pet, a place you enjoy, or an activity that was fun. Allow yourself to *feel* this good feeling of appreciation

or care. If you can't feel anything, it's okay, just try to find a sincere attitude of appreciation or care. Once you've found a positive feeling or attitude, you can sustain it by continuing your heart focus, heart breathing, and heart feeling.

Used with permission courtesy of the Institute of HeartMath.

Happiness Habit for the Heart #2

Practice Forgiveness

To forgive is the highest, most beautiful form of love. In return, you will receive untold peace and happiness.

—Robert Muller, former Assistant Secretary-General to the United Nations

Sometimes it's hard to let love lead, especially when we've been hurt by someone. But whether the wound is big or small, you can't be truly happy until you forgive. No one can deny that sometimes people do terrible things or act in ways that appear cruel and wrong. Yet, even in instances like these, forgiveness is possible.

Many people think that feeling hatred, anger, and resentment toward the person who wronged them is a way to punish them—but IT'S EXACTLY THE OPPOSITE! Holding onto those emotions is like taking poison and expecting it to hurt the other person. It's *you* who's hurt. When you forgive, you heal your own anger and hurt and are able to let love lead again. It's like spring cleaning for your heart.

During my search for the Happy 100, one of my *Chicken Soup for the Soul* colleagues told me about Mary Lodge, whom she'd met through her work with prison inmates and their families. When I interviewed Mary, I was inspired by her strength and courage, and found that her story helped me reexamine the boundaries I place on my own forgiveness.

Mary's Story

Set Free

For years, my life was not what you'd call easy. Forced to stand up for myself on many occasions, including going through a divorce, I'd learned to be quite a scrapper. The truth is I found myself upset at people and situations—a lot. Unfortunately, this created a great deal of resentment and desire for revenge.

Then, one night in 1996, something happened that made all my previous upsets *put together* seem trivial in comparison. I woke up to the sound of the phone ringing at 3:00 in the morning. Filled with dread, I picked it up. It was my oldest son, Jay, telling me that my youngest son, eighteen-year-old Robbie, had been shot. "Mom, he's dead."

In that moment, I thought my life was over. The pain of losing Robbie was overwhelming. I wanted to crawl into a hole and never come out. But I knew I had to hold myself together for my other children, and to deal with the police, so I put my emotions on hold.

Shawn, the young man who had killed my son, was arrested and charged with murder. Shawn had known Robbie and shot him while the two had been arguing. He pleaded guilty, so there would be no trial, just a hearing at which the plea bargain would be arranged and his sentence handed down. I'd have to wait three long months for that hearing to arrive. I wasn't allowed to see or speak to Shawn throughout that time, which was probably wise—with my despair and fury at a boiling point, if I could've gotten my hands around his neck, I would have strangled him. This was my baby he'd shot!

The day of the hearing finally arrived, and I got my first glimpse of Shawn. As they led him into the dimly lit courtroom, he kept his eyes on the floor. Shadows masked his face, distorting his features and giving him a dark, sullen appearance. I felt a wave of white-hot anger shoot through me. *Why had he done it?* Shaking with emotion, I decided not to take the stand, but I made it clear to the judge that I wanted to speak to Shawn after the hearing was over.

Since Shawn had pleaded guilty, the verdict was no surprise and neither was the sentence: twenty to forty years in a state penitentiary. As the judge had promised, he summoned me to his chambers to meet with Shawn. I followed the bailiff down the hall, my heart beating faster with each step as I prepared to meet the young man who had taken my son's life. I'd waited a long time for the opportunity to let Shawn know how I felt about what he had done. Now, filled with rage and hatred, I had no idea what I was going to say, but I knew I wanted to let him have it.

I was frisked and led into a small, paneled office. Shawn stood trembling in the corner with his hands and feet shackled, wearing a baggy orange prison jumpsuit. His head was down, and although he was twenty years old, he was crying like a baby, sobbing his heart out. As I watched this boy, so forlorn—no parents, no friends, and no support—all I saw was another mother's son.

I asked the bailiff if I could approach Shawn. At this, Shawn looked up, revealing a childlike face stained with tears. Suddenly I found myself asking, "Can I give you a hug, Shawn?" He nodded his consent. The bailiff motioned me toward the prisoner, and I walked over to Shawn and put my arms around him. He just melted into my shoulder. It was the first compassion he'd had from anybody for a long, long time. As I stood there holding him, I felt my anger and hatred fall away.

Still, what came out of my mouth next surprised everyone, including me: "Shawn, I forgive you for this horrible thing you've done." Our eyes connected for a few moments. "I would rather my Robbie be where he is than be going to prison. I will pray for you every day." I asked Shawn to keep in touch with me, and then the bailiff escorted me from the room.

Soon after that, Shawn left for prison to begin serving his time. I felt little satisfaction at this. Robbie was gone and no sentence could bring him back, yet here was another boy whose life was destroyed.

Both his parents said they wanted nothing to do with him, so Shawn and I began corresponding. And for the first five years of his sentence, I was his only visitor. Five years ago, Shawn was transferred to a different prison, and the warden there does not allow victims' families to visit, but we still write often.

Some people don't understand how I can do it, but I've learned that forgiving doesn't mean condoning. I believe the compassion I felt in the judge's chambers that day was a gift from God. I know I could not have healed the deep, dark places of hatred and revenge, embedded within my heart and soul, had I not forgiven my son's murderer. Forgiveness set me free. It gave me the peace that I needed to get on with my life and eventually come to terms with Robbie's death.

Since then, I have become a Stephen minister, a type of lay minister, through my church. I help someone through a crisis or loss in his or her life simply by listening and just being there. It requires very little except commitment and compassion, two qualities I have found in great abundance in my heart since the day I forgave my son's killer.

I've learned that you only hurt yourself when you hold on to anger and resentment. Now, despite what happens, I feel truly peaceful and happy.

Hatred and revenge won't bring back my beloved son Robbie, but Shawn is someone's son too. The hatred has to stop somewhere. What better place to begin than with me?

Why Forgive?

Few of us are faced with experiences as heartbreaking as Mary's, yet I chose to include her story for precisely that reason. If Mary could forgive her son's killer, then maybe we can forgive the people who've wronged us.

Why is it so hard to forgive? Here are the five main reasons. Do any sound familiar to you?

1. We think forgiveness means condoning the wrong behavior.
2. We think forgiveness means we have to let that person back into our lives.
3. We think feeling hatred for that person somehow gives us control, power, or strength.
4. We feel that if we forgive, we might get hurt again.
5. We want to punish the offender.

As it turns out, they're all off the mark. Forgiveness isn't about the person or people being forgiven—**it's a gift you give yourself that allows your heart to stop being contracted**. When you forgive, you release the toxic resentment and anger you're holding in your heart, finally freeing yourself to get on with your life. There is a well-known Tibetan Buddhist story that illustrates this point perfectly:

> Two Tibetan monks meet each other a few years after being released from prison, where they had been tortured by their jailers.
>
> "Have you forgiven them?" asks the first.
>
> "I will never forgive them! Never!" replies the second.
>
> "Well," says the first monk, "I guess they still have you in prison, don't they?"

It also helps to remember that forgiveness is neither an erasing of what happened nor a free ride for the perpetrator. Eva Kor, an Auschwitz survivor, publicly forgave the Nazis who had killed her family and used Eva and her twin sister as human guinea pigs for medical experiments. Her act of forgiveness was not meant to absolve the Nazis for their acts; it simply lifted the burden of pain and hatred Eva had been carrying for so long. She says this about forgiveness:

> *I believe with every fiber of my being that every human being has the right to live without the pain of the past. For most people there is a big obstacle to forgiveness because society expects revenge. . . . We need to honor our victims, but I always won-*

der if my dead loved ones would want me to live with pain and anger until the end of my life.

. . . I do it for myself. Forgiveness is really nothing more than an act of self-healing and self-empowerment. I call it a miracle medicine. It's free, it works, and has no side effects.

Forgiveness as Medicine

Three years ago I sat in an auditorium, spellbound, as the director and cofounder of the Stanford University Forgiveness Project, Dr. Fred Luskin, spoke about his work in the field of forgiveness. Dr. Luskin, who travels all over the world to do his research, had recently brought together mothers in Northern Ireland who'd lost their sons on opposing sides of the conflict. Exuding love and compassion, he shared the miracles that forgiveness could bring.

His stories, which moved the entire audience to tears, demonstrated that people who forgive others are happier, have stronger, more loving relationships, and report fewer health problems and symptoms of stress. The medical community is starting to recognize the major role that anger and resentment play in creating disease and addictions. Dr. Luskin's research suggests that failure to forgive—holding hatred in your heart—is actually one of the risk factors in heart disease. Interestingly, he's found that people who just go through the *internal* process of forgiving their offender have immediate improvement in their cardiovascular, muscular, and nervous systems. So you don't even have to tell the other person that you've forgiven him or her to reap the benefits for yourself.

In his book *Forgive for Good,* Dr. Luskin describes Dana, who feels that the offense against her is unforgivable. Dr. Luskin tells Dana to imagine someone holding a gun to her head. Her only chance of survival lies in letting go of the anger and resentment she feels toward the person who wronged her. Now will she forgive? Put this way, Dana immediately says her pain isn't worth dying for—and finally realizes that she's been killing herself slowly by refusing to forgive.

Although no one's holding a gun to our head to get us to release pain and anger, our lives—and our happiness—truly depend on learning to let go of our pain and being able to forgive.

Compassion Is the Key

As Mary discovered, if you can set aside your pain long enough to really look at the situation, you'll see that the people who hurt you are inevitably hurt themselves.

I once had a neighbor who was always yelling about something. My garbage cans were too close to her driveway. People parked their cars in front of her house. The neighborhood dogs were digging in her garden. Understandably, she wasn't my favorite person. One afternoon, I heard an ambulance coming down the street. I looked out my window and saw it turn into her driveway. The paramedics loaded the woman into the vehicle and, lights flashing, took off for the hospital. That day I found out that my neighbor was a very sick woman; she had a serious liver disease and chronic back problems and lived every day of her life in constant and excruciating pain. My anger at her disappeared instantly. From the day she came back from the hospital until she died a year and a half later, I not only felt differently toward her, but I found myself doing anything I could to help her.

When you understand the suffering of others, like magic, it transforms your negative feelings into compassion, and sets the stage for forgiveness to occur.

If you thinks this sounds great but are wondering how to let go and forgive, you've already cleared a big hurdle. Just being willing to consider forgiveness is sometimes the hardest part.

Here is a powerful exercise that can guide you through the forgiveness process:

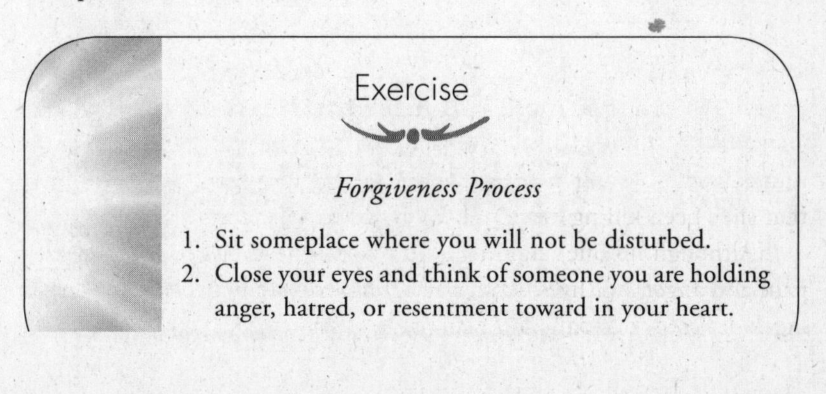

Exercise

Forgiveness Process

1. Sit someplace where you will not be disturbed.
2. Close your eyes and think of someone you are holding anger, hatred, or resentment toward in your heart.

3. Take a couple of deep breaths and let yourself feel your feelings without having to do anything about them. Just notice them.
4. Now, realize that the person's hurtful action can't be changed. It's in the past and there is absolutely nothing that can be done to affect it now. Feel the finality of that.
5. Also realize that this person may never change. They are the way they are. Take a few deep breaths as you accept the truth of that.
6. Now, see that the person is the way they are—and did whatever they did—because they have some pain, some lack, some woundedness. They may not even realize it themselves, but it's there. People hurt others only because they are hurt themselves. See them through the eyes of compassion for their own suffering. Imagine they are a child that is hurting, lashing out at others in their own pain. Can you feel compassion for them?
7. Sit quietly for a minute or two more, just feeling the expansion that compassion—in any amount—brings to the heart.

NOTE: It's okay if you still feel angry; the purpose of this exercise is to begin to release the pain in your heart, not to excuse others for their actions. Keep repeating this exercise until you feel a shift, however small, in your heart. Your forgiveness will grow as you feel more compassion.

Happiness Habit for the Heart #3

Spread Lovingkindness

Those who bring sunshine into the lives of others cannot keep it from themselves.

—J. M. Barrie, nineteenth-century Scottish novelist

When your heart flows in love, you naturally feel happier. But what about those times when you don't feel loving? It may not take much to feel your heart close. When your surly teenager, an annoying coworker, or a dense sales clerk upset you, how do you live in the flow of love then?

You can restart your heart's flow by sending lovingkindness to anyone and everyone you see. It doesn't have to be dramatic; sometimes simply wishing others well switches on the pump that generates love in the heart. This creates a strong current of love and happiness, because a heart overflowing in love is continually being filled with more love.

When I sent out the Happy for No Reason survey, I was profoundly moved by a response I received from CJ Scarlet. I interviewed her further and found her story shows the tremendous effect that sharing love, either silently or in words and actions, can have on others and on yourself.

CJ's Story

The Flow of Love

I was forty-one years old, but felt like an old woman. For twelve years, I'd been living with lupus and scleroderma, both incapacitating autoimmune diseases. The steroids I took caused my weight to balloon. I needed my walker or cane to make it to the mailbox, and some days I had to crawl on my hands and knees to climb the stairs. Frequently, I couldn't drive and had to depend on my family for everything.

My doctors said that heart failure could happen at any time. I was terrorized by every chest pain, but at times wished death would come quickly to end my suffering. Almost every night I had nightmares of being sucked into black tornados or going down in flaming airplanes.

Reading self-help books and going to therapy had helped a little, but I was still in very bad shape. Buddhist writer Thich Nhat Hanh's books had touched me deeply, so when I had the opportunity to meet a Buddhist lama (teacher) who lived in my city, I jumped at the chance.

Using a cane, I hobbled up the walk to the house where the lama lived. I told him my tale of woe, fully expecting him to turn his compassionate gaze on me and offer his sympathy. Instead, he told me, brusquely, though not unkindly, "Stop feeling sorry for yourself, and start focusing on the happiness of others."

But," I objected, "I'm too sick. I can hardly help myself." Disappointed, I thought, *He just doesn't understand.*

I was convinced that I was too exhausted and too ill to help anyone; nevertheless, I began to pray for the happiness of others. I brought to mind people I knew, family members and friends, and imagined them happy, healthy, and at peace. Then I began to focus on the happiness of strangers. When passing people on the highway, I would look at them and wish for their well-being and prosperity. Finally, I was even able to extend my good wishes and help to people I actively disliked.

One day I was in my scooter, waiting in the grocery checkout line, when a woman came up behind me who was clearly having a bad day. Harassed and harried, she seemed irritated at everybody. Her cart was full to the brim and it was clear she wanted to get through the line as quickly as possible.

Normally, I would have tried to stay away from her bad vibes and negative energy. In fact, my first thought was, *Look at how nasty she's being. I don't want to have anything to do with her.*

Then I remembered the lama's advice. *Okay,* I thought, *she's really having a tough day today. I know how that feels. Let me think about her happiness. What would help make her happier?*

I turned to her and said, "It looks like you're in a hurry."

Startled by my overture, she said tersely, "Yes, I am. I'm running late."

I said, "Why don't you go in front of me?"

Looking at the few items in my scooter's cart, she quickly shook her head."No, no, that's okay."

But I said, "Really, I'm not in a hurry. Go ahead."

The transformation was amazing. She went from being this angry person who radiated negativity and was probably going to chew out the clerk at the cash register to someone who felt validated, cared for, and appreciated. She steered her cart in front of mine, thanking me profusely, thanking the clerk, and when her groceries were all bagged up and ready to go, she left the store smiling.

I felt fabulous. Looking around, I noticed that everyone around me was smiling and friendly and talking to each other. "That was a nice thing to do." "Hope you have a great day today." We had all been affected by the interaction.

I started looking for more ways to think of the happiness of others. I smiled and rushed to help anyone in need, from giving money to homeless people to helping a woman arrange to buy a car so she could get a job. I bought a tank of gas for a woman who had no money and volunteered at the Red Cross during Hurricane Katrina. Every moment seemed to present an opportunity to improve the life of someone else, and I rejoiced in my physical, mental, and financial ability to do so.

I had done volunteer work before this—I had been very active in nonprofits for victim and child advocacy—but there had always been a trace of ego involved as I perceived those I helped as victims and myself as their rescuer. It had made me feel good about myself for helping. But this was different.

Now it was 100 percent about *them*. My focus was on their happiness directly. And when I wished them happiness, I felt a wave of love for them, which sometimes led to action and at other times was just a prayer, a heartfelt desire for their happiness. Very often they weren't aware of my intention at all. But it created a flow of love inside of me that grew stronger and stronger.

When I stopped focusing on whether other people were making me happy or meeting my needs and thought about what would make *them* happy, I started to see everyone as beautiful. I could understand that they were fighting their own heroic battles and trying to make their own way through life, and my heart went out to them. The more I focused on contributing to the happiness of others, the better I felt. And the better I felt, the happier I became. My dreams transformed into joyous celebrations.

Within a year my health was transformed. The pain that had wracked my body disappeared. I could once again take a deep breath, and I had more than enough energy to resume my life. Today, two years later, I feel better than I did at twenty-nine before I became ill. To my doctors' amazement, my once debilitating medical conditions are reversing themselves. I continue to live pain-free. I even work out at the local gym three times a week and am losing the steroid weight.

I met with the lama again, about a year after our first meeting. When I told him how my life was transformed from focusing on the happiness of others, he clapped his hands and smiled broadly at me. "Very good! Very good!" he kept saying.

His wise words had stopped my descent down a terrible slope and put me in touch with the most powerful force for good that there is: the loving compassion that resides in our hearts. It was the flow of that love that healed my body and today has become a bubbling, clear spring of happiness in my life.

Wishing You Well

What a simple idea, and yet so life-changing. I've started practicing CJ's technique with great results. I used to hate waiting in line or getting stuck in traffic, but now I spend the time looking around and silently wishing everyone around me happiness, ease, comfort, and peace. Instead of fuming, I find myself smiling and feeling good.

Sometimes I go beyond just wishing people well in my heart. Recently I was at an airport, buying a burrito from a server who was crabby and grumpy. I was tempted to get a little crabby back, but instead, I thought about this guy on his feet all day long, cranking out burrito after burrito for impatient flyers off to exotic destinations while he was stuck in one place, baking under the warming lights. A pretty thankless job. I caught his eye. "Boy, you must get really tired of doing this all day long."

My server was completely taken aback. Someone had reached out to connect with him. He just melted. He gave me the biggest, warmest smile—and extra chips!

I think we all underestimate the power we have to make someone else's day just a little better simply by beaming them a little light and love. I suggest that you try CJ's technique yourself. You can also set some time aside each day to do the following short lovingkindness exercise. It's adapted from a Buddhist practice for culturing *metta,* which is defined as the strong wish for the welfare and happiness of others. This isn't exclusively a Buddhist concept; in Christianity, the term for this kind of unconditional love is *agape*. In Judaism, *rachamim* is the love that motivates us to give to others and includes empathy and care. This same ideal of love is expressed in Islam with the word *mahabba,* which means spiritual love for others and the divine.

Choosing to feel love and wish the best for everyone—a natural habit of happy people—can help you cultivate more happiness in your life.

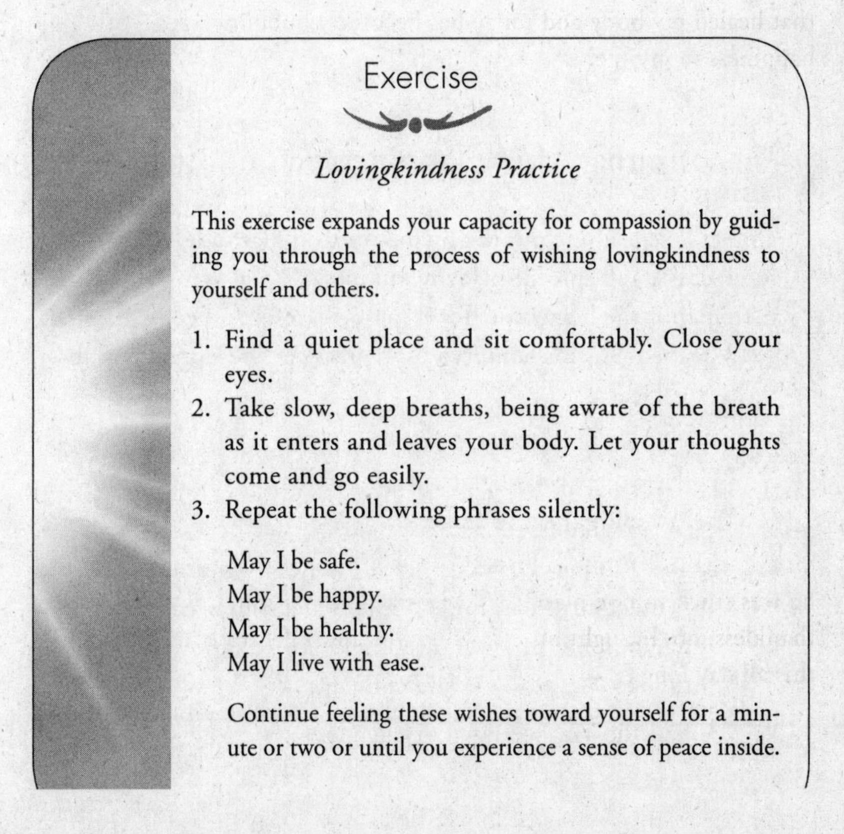

Exercise

Lovingkindness Practice

This exercise expands your capacity for compassion by guiding you through the process of wishing lovingkindness to yourself and others.

1. Find a quiet place and sit comfortably. Close your eyes.
2. Take slow, deep breaths, being aware of the breath as it enters and leaves your body. Let your thoughts come and go easily.
3. Repeat the following phrases silently:

   May I be safe.
   May I be happy.
   May I be healthy.
   May I live with ease.

   Continue feeling these wishes toward yourself for a minute or two or until you experience a sense of peace inside.

4. Now, move on to your friends and family. Picture one of them as you send the following wishes silently:

   May you be safe.
   May you be happy.
   May you be healthy.
   May you live with ease.

   Continue sending these wishes until you feel a flow of love in your heart.
5. Now send these wishes to all the living beings around the world. Continue until you feel a sense of expansion in your heart.

Summary and Happiness Action Steps

You let love lead in your life by focusing on gratitude, practicing forgiveness, and spreading lovingkindness. When you strengthen the pillar of the heart, you'll feel more peaceful and compassionate. Use the following action steps to practice the Happiness Habits for the Heart:

1. Play the Gratitude Game. Before you go to sleep, think of five things you're grateful for that day. Write them down in a journal if you'd like.
2. Try Brother David's "Great-Fullness" Exercise. Pick a theme for the day, for example, water, and when anything reminds you of water, use it as a cue to experience gratitude for no reason in the moment.
3. Like Rico, make a point to laugh for a few minutes each day.

4. Do the HeartMath Quick Coherence exercise to habituate heart wave coherence.
5. Try the Forgiveness Process. Find the compassion in your heart that will make it easier to forgive.
6. Do the Lovingkindness Practice every day, and spread lovingkindness through your thoughts or actions wherever you are.

The Pillar of the Body—Make Your Cells Happy

A sound mind in a sound body is a short but full description of a happy state in this world.

—John Locke, seventeenth-century English philosopher

Being happy is not just a state of mind—it's also a state of the body. In fact, our bodies are actually designed to support our happiness. The renowned neurophysiologist Dr. Candace Pert documented this mind-body-happiness link in her best-selling book, *Molecules of Emotion,* explaining that when we're happy, we're alive and buzzing with "happiness juices," the chemicals of body and brain that underlie our positive experiences.

There are no drugs more powerful than those you already have in your own head! More than 100,000 chemical reactions go on in your brain every second. Your brain contains a veritable pharmacopoeia of natural happiness-enhancing drugs: endorphins (the brain's painkiller, three times stronger than morphine), serotonin (which naturally calms anxiety and relieves depression), oxytocin (the bonding hormone), and dopamine (which promotes alertness and a feeling of enjoyment), among others. They're just waiting to be released to every organ and cell in your body. Because your brain's pharmacy is open twenty-four hours a day, you can create your own supply of these happiness chemicals any time you want. And when your cells are happy, you're happy.

In the previous two chapters we've looked at how your thoughts and feelings influence your happiness set-point. In this chapter, we'll look at how the way you eat, move, breathe, and rest, and even your facial expression can shift the balance of the brain's feel-good chemicals in your favor to overcome unhappiness.

Remember, when I refer to unhappiness in this book, I mean the garden-variety type of unhappiness and not clinical depression, which is a medical condition requiring professional intervention. If you're clinically depressed, it's important to work with a health care professional to address the chemical imbalances that may be a contributing factor. Nonetheless, strengthening the pillar of the body by practicing the habits in this chapter can be extremely helpful as an adjunct to standard treatment for depression.

The Body's Happiness Robbers: Stress and Toxins

If our bodies are designed to support happiness, then why aren't we all happier? Just take a look at our lives. Most of us zip around like overcaffeinated bees, multitasking madly and grabbing meals on the run. Our stressful lifestyles, which include unhealthy eating and a lack of exercise and proper rest, hinder our ability to create happy cells.

Stress is a huge robber of happiness and health. Scientific evidence indicates that over 90 percent of all diseases are stress-related. So many of us are stressed out and exhausted, yet we ignore our symptoms and power through the day, taking medication to dull the pain without dealing with the deeper cause.

Then there are the environmental toxins we're exposed to every day: chemicals in our processed food, pesticides in our produce, hormones in our meat and milk, and polluted air and water. Yikes! When our cells don't get the support they need, rather than singing a joyful chorus of vitality and well-being, they starve and die, resulting in low energy and unhappiness. Fortunately, there are ways to inspire the choir to warble songs of well-being once more.

Inspiring the Choir

There are many ways we can make our cells happy: we can stop bulldozing over our fatigue and discomfort, cleanse our bodies of accumulated toxins, reduce the new ones we take in, and use our brain's pharmacy to experience more happiness in our lives.

Studies abound showing how everyday activities—singing, listening to relaxing music, stroking a pet, getting a massage, enjoying a long hug, gardening—increase our happiness chemicals. Even smiling raises happiness levels.

Mona Lisa had the right idea. When we use our facial muscles to express emotion, we trigger specific brain neurotransmitters. Scientists studying the effects of Botox discovered that when depressed patients

"Good news — they found you a donor for a smile transplant!"

were treated for frown lines, they were no longer as depressed. Research by French physiologist Dr. Israel Waynbaum shows that frowning triggers the secretion of the stress hormones cortisol, adrenalin, and noradrenalin, chemicals that increase your blood pressure, weaken your immune system, and increase your susceptibility to depression and anxiety. Smiling decreases these substances and produces happiness chemicals such as endorphins and immune-boosting killer T-cells, relaxing muscles, reducing pain, and accelerating healing.

If you want to multiply the benefits of smiling, enjoy a good laugh. Dozens of studies confirm that laughter really is the best medicine. It too quells stress hormones and sends happiness hormones into high gear.

Happiness: Just What the Doctor Ordered

Being happy is good for your health. Over the past two decades extensive research has shown that contentment strengthens the immune system and prevents disease:

- Happy people are 35 percent less likely to get a cold and produce 50 percent more antibodies in response to flu vaccines than the average person.
- Individuals who score high on happiness and optimism scales have a reduced risk of cardiovascular disease, hypertension, and infections.
- People who maintain a sense of humor, an indication of inner happiness, outlive those who don't, and the survival edge is particularly large for people with cancer. One study showed that a sense of humor cut a cancer patient's chance of premature death by about 70 percent.

Happiness and health create a positive feedback loop: improving one will automatically improve the other.

Our physical habits either cause our energy to contract, making us feel tired and sick, or bring about a state of expansion, supporting our happiness and well-being:

Contraction	**Expansion**
Feeling stressed	Experiencing well-being
Eating processed foods	Eating fresh, whole foods
Having chemical and hormonal imbalances	Having a balanced system
Breathing shallowly from the chest	Breathing deeply from the abdomen
Being dehydrated	Drinking plenty of water
Being a couch potato	Having an active lifestyle
Frowning	Smiling
Ignoring the body's signals	Listening to what the body needs and wants

Though you may be doing everything you can to support your health, your body may still have its challenges. It's possible to be Happy for No Reason anyway. A number of people in the Happy 100 that I interviewed had health problems—even terminal disease—and remarkably, their pain and joy seemed to coexist. Their happiness showed up automatically, a state of peace and well-being underlying all of their experiences. Practicing the following Happiness Habits to make your cells happy will help reinforce that same unshakable state in you.

Happiness Habits for the Body

1. Nourish Your Body
2. Energize Your Body
3. Tune In to Your Body's Wisdom

Happiness Habit for the Body #1

Nourish Your Body

Tell me what you eat, and I will tell you what you are.

—Anthelme Brillat-Savarin, eighteenth-century French writer and epicure

For years, my cells were unhappy because I nourished them poorly. When I was very young, my diet consisted mainly of crisp bacon, juicy hamburgers, Hostess cupcakes (Poppa's weekly gift), crackers filled with a mysterious substance called "processed American cheese food product," and snowy-white Wonder Bread ("builds strong bodies twelve ways!"). Fruits and veggies came in only three flavors: carrots, celery, and apples, of which I ate the barest minimum so I'd have lots of room for McDonald's fries and shakes. I was always exhausted, so I'd rev myself back up with sugar, raiding the freezer for ice cream at all times of the day and night for an energy boost. Naturally, I'd enjoy my sundaes with a can of Tab—who wanted the extra calories from a regular Coke?

I fed my growing body so well that grow it did—an extra twenty pounds, which is a lot when you're five feet tall and sixteen years old. It wasn't just being chubby that bothered me; it was that I was tired, listless, and unhappy all the time. My temporary sugar highs were always followed by crashes that left me feeling more exhausted than ever.

When I got to college, I decided to clean up my food act. I drank my last can of Tab when I was seventeen, phased out the sugar, and became a vegetarian. When I switched from refined carbohydrates to whole foods, I was amazed to find that there are actually dozens of delicious fruits and vegetables.

At first this burst of virtuousness was prompted by my fear of wearing shorts in public. But I quickly discovered that any weight-loss triumphs paled in comparison to the sky-high levels of energy I felt once I'd gone off the bad stuff. I felt so much lighter, happier, and clearer—I felt more *me.* Now that I understand the relationship between my energy, mood, and food, I don't ever want to go back to the "Wonder Bread Years" and nonstop exhaustion.

It isn't always just a bad diet that causes unhappy cells. Sometimes a lack of balanced brain chemicals or hormones can also be a contributing factor. That was the case for my dear friend, actress Catherine Oxenberg, who at first glance seems to have it all: beauty, brains, a great husband, wonderful kids, and a fulfilling career. That's why it's so surprising for people to learn how she's struggled to overcome fatigue, illness, and recurring episodes of feeling blue, which she describes in the following story.

Catherine's Story

No More Sick and Tired

Most little girls dream of being a princess, but I can tell you from experience, it hasn't always been that wonderful. Though I was born a princess, descended from a long line of European royalty, I wasn't a happy little girl. When I was six, my mother, HRH Princess Elizabeth of Yugoslavia, divorced my father, a New York City businessman, and took my sister and me to live with her in London. At one point, I remember her saying to me, "Catherine, could you please stop moping around?"

I wanted to, but I just couldn't help the way I felt. Now, I believe that my "moping around" may have been the result of low levels of serotonin—a hormone that affects happiness. Later, as a teenager, I learned to make myself feel better by eating. On the outside, everything looked wonderful: I excelled in school, was admitted to Harvard, became a successful model and then an actress, making films and starring in the hit television series *Dynasty*. But I spent those same years self-medicating my inner pain by binge-eating and then throwing up.

The horrible cycle of my bulimia made me feel even worse, and at one point, a doctor prescribed antidepressants in an effort to help me.

The antidepressants were not the miracle cure I'd hoped for, though I did feel a little bit better. Then I discovered I was pregnant, and my doctor and I agreed that I should stop taking the medication. After my daughter was born, I didn't go back on antidepressants. I continued to struggle with bulimia, on and off, for the next few years. With a lot of work on myself, I eventually managed to free myself from bulimia's terrible grip, though I still had a tendency to slide into unhappiness easily and often.

Not long after that, I met actor Casper Van Dien, fell in love, and got married. But within a year, my body started hurting everywhere; it was like having a mild case of the flu all the time. I was diagnosed with fibromyalgia, a chronic condition characterized by widespread pain in the muscles, ligaments, and tendons. This made sense to me: instead of feeling miserable mentally, I'd transferred the unhappiness to a physical level. I believe that in my case, the fibromyalgia was my body's way of experiencing depression. And as it turned out, when I was given a low dose of antidepressants, my pain was reduced considerably.

Although Casper and I already had three children between us, we knew we wanted to have a family together. When we decided to get pregnant, I stopped taking the medication. Within a month I was pregnant, and the fibromyalgia went away.

But, two babies later, the physical reality of being a forty-three-year-old mother of five children, two of whom were under three, began to take its toll on my already fragile health and happiness. I was exhausted and sick all the time. I couldn't focus or concentrate. And my memory! I was sure I had early-onset Alzheimer's disease.

Mornings were particularly awful. Even after a full night's sleep, I still felt tired, so Casper was the one who got up and made breakfast for the kids and got them off to school. I remember one morning, India, my eldest daughter, came into my bedroom to wake me. She wanted me to come eat breakfast with everyone. "Darling," I told her, "I'm exhausted. I feel really sick." She looked at me with a sad expression and said, "Mom, you're always sick," before she turned and left the room. Devastated, I curled into a ball and cried. She was right.

I knew there was something very wrong with me, yet no doctor could find the problem. My blood work appeared completely normal, and the only thing they'd recommend was that I go on antidepressants again, but I didn't like the troubling side effects. There *had* to be a way to feel better naturally, but I had no idea how. I was at my wits' end—when help came to me in a way I could never have imagined.

It was 3 a.m. and I was sitting on an airplane en route to Florida to visit my in-laws for Christmas. The red-eye flight had been a nightmare. The two little ones had refused to go to sleep, fighting, whining, and generally being impossible. Finally, everyone had settled down. I took a deep breath and closed my eyes too. Exhaustion and despair descended on me like a three-hundred-pound weight.

I couldn't sleep so I reached for the in-flight magazine in the seat pocket in front of me. As I flipped through it, my eye was caught by a heading in large type across the top of a page: *ARE YOU SICK AND TIRED OF BEING SICK AND TIRED?* I instantly got chills and felt my hair stand on end. I continued scanning down the page. *Are you tired of being told by doctors that there's nothing wrong with you? That your blood work is "perfect" despite your symptoms of fatigue, lethargy, and mental cloudiness? Are you too tired to enjoy your life?*

I felt tears come to my eyes. I'd been so ashamed, convinced that my problems were all in my head. It was such a relief to realize I wasn't the only one who felt this way! I kept reading.

It was the description of a clinic that specialized in a natural approach to balancing the body and mind that used supplements, natural hormones, and proper nutrition. When I began reading the story of a forty-five-year-old woman who'd tried this approach, I was floored. The woman could have been me. I had every single one of the symptoms she listed, but by following the clinic's recommendations, she'd gone from being miserable to feeling better than she'd ever felt before. I ripped the page out and put it in my purse. Then I leaned back in my seat, sending up a silent prayer of thanks for what I considered divine intervention, before finally falling asleep myself.

When we got home from Florida, I made an appointment for a consultation with the doctor featured in the magazine. I discovered that what I was experiencing was extremely common for women of all ages, and for men as well. The bottom line was that my hormones were out of balance, which had started a disastrous domino effect, affecting my thyroid and adrenal glands and seriously compromising my health. I began taking nutritional supplements and bioidentical (nonsynthetic) hormones.

My diet was also contributing to the problem, so on Dr. Hotze's recommendation, I eliminated all sugar, dairy, alcohol, and grains for a month. I ate moderate amounts of healthy fats in the form of nut butters, avocado, olive oil, and coconut oil, lots of vegetables, and a variety of proteins, such as organic meats, eggs, and fish.

At first, I didn't see much change, but after just two weeks, I stopped having that 3:00 afternoon slump. (I've since discovered that that's the time that your body stops making serotonin in preparation for the night's rest.) When the thirty days were up, I was so encouraged by how I felt that I decided to keep on going with my new nutrition, supplement, and hormone program. After another month, I had to admit the results were pretty miraculous. I felt transformed in body, mind, *and* spirit.

Today, though I've added more things back into my diet, I continue to have only small amounts of sugar and processed carbs, because I can definitely feel the difference when I eat them. In general, I just feel so healthy. I don't have fatigue anymore. I feel energized and have much more mental clarity; my strength has returned, and even my excess weight has just melted away. Best of all, I'm able to be there for my kids. I remember one day about a month after I started the program, my youngest came into the bedroom first thing in the morning and asked me to get up and make breakfast. I immediately threw back the covers and raced her to the kitchen. I was reaching for the cup of chai, caffeinated spiced tea that I'd always needed to wake myself up, when I suddenly realized I was already awake! I felt clear and full of energy. Since then, I've become a regular at the morning breakfast party at our house, and I don't know who's more excited about it—me or the kids.

How ironic that the "airplane trip from hell" turned out to be the beginning of my journey out of purgatory. Now, with my brain chemistry and hormones in balance, I'm able to experience the natural happiness that I see in the faces of my children. It was finding the key to a healthy, balanced body that unlocked the door to a happy life.

The Power of the Plate

As Catherine discovered, a fundamental way to feel better is to get the natural chemicals in your body to function in a balanced way. What you eat can play a crucial role. *Happy for No Reason* isn't intended to be a diet book. (For some excellent books on nutrition and natural supplements to support your happiness, please refer to the resource section.) Still, I'd like to offer a few general guidelines to get you eating in a way that not only will improve your health, but will make your cells happy. Knowing the dramatic and cumulative impact that diet has on happiness has been one of my greatest motivators for sticking with this Happiness Habit.

The Make-Your-Cells-Happy Nourishment Guide

1. **Go for Happiness-Building Foods—Fresh and Whole:** A balanced diet of fresh, whole foods gives our brains the necessary raw materials to ensure that we produce abundant happiness juices every day. Without those building blocks, our biochemistry gets out of whack, causing elevated blood sugar levels, adrenal exhaustion, and a shortage of vital hormones that buffer stress in everyday life.

   Eating whole foods means giving your body food that's as close as possible to the way nature made it. Avoid what I call "fake food" that comes out of a box or a can, which is many times removed from its original source by processing, preservation, and synthetic packaging. Shop the outer aisles at your supermarket, where you'll find the fruits and vegetables, fresh meats, fish, and poultry, not the inner ones where the boxed, canned, and packaged foods live. Buy whole grains, organic produce, and hormone-free meat, dairy, and poultry products. Yes, the food generally costs more, but you'll more than make up for it in fewer doctor visits and a healthier life.

ZIGGY ©2005 ZIGGY AND FRIENDS, INC.
Reprinted with permission of UNIVERSAL PRESS SYNDICATE.

2. **Keep the Water Flowing:** Being dehydrated is a no-no for happy cells. We *need* water because our bodies *are* mostly water! To fully take in the nourishment in our food, our bodies require the chemical elements of hydrogen and oxygen found in H_2O (a fact I learned in high school biology and promptly forgot). People often feel hungry when what their bodies actually need is *water.* The next time you feel like reaching for a snack, take a sip or two of water first. Even better, do as the experts recommend: make it a habit to drink half your body weight in ounces each day. (A 120-pound person would drink 60 ounces.)
3. **Lose the Happiness-Robbing Foods:**
   - **Shake the Sugar:** Do you know how hard it is to get health experts to agree on anything? Yet every one I interviewed agreed that the biggest happiness destroyer in our diets is white sugar. It's powerfully addictive and wreaks havoc with your brain,

causing depression, anxiety, and that sluggish, low-energy state you recognize when your forehead hits the desk at 3 p.m. The synthetic sugar substitutes are unfortunately no better; numerous reports point to potentially negative side effects. When you take your sugar in its natural form, as in fresh fruit, the body can handle it better.

- **Curb the Carbs:** In the carb department, "whole" is the operative word. When you eat processed grains, such as white bread, white rice, or pasta and pastries made with white flour, you set off a high-glycemic alarm that causes your blood sugar levels to spike and crash, constantly altering your mood and energy levels. The Standard American Diet (SAD—what an appropriate acronym!) relies on too many starchy, refined carbs. Switching to whole grains like brown rice, quinoa, and millet is a simple but effective trick for feeling healthier and happier fast.
- **Kick the Caffeine:** When we need a lift, a lot of us reach for the caffeine jolt of coffee or soft drinks. Caffeine blocks the transmission of the brain chemical adenosine, which results in more adrenaline pouring into the bloodstream. After drinking a cup of coffee or a soda, you feel alert, motivated, and stimulated, but that high reaches its peak in 30 to 60 minutes, and then down you go. Instead, try decaffeinated green tea (regular green tea has caffeine), which not only offers powerful antioxidant protection to help make cells happy, but gives you a more sustainable level of energy.

Super-Nourishment to Promote Happiness in the Brain and Body

To make our cells happy, it's sometimes helpful to boost our body's nourishment in specific ways. Nutritional psychology expert Julia Ross, the author of *The Mood Cure,* believes that much of our unhappiness is the result of "critically unmet nutritional needs." She's developed a program based on research that links our moods to the balance of our body's four key neurotransmitters that produce happiness. These neurotransmitters are fueled by nutrients called amino acids, and if your amino acid levels are sufficient and these four key neurotransmitter levels are high, you'll generally feel positive in life. If you are low in any of them, you may develop symptoms specific to that neurotransmitter deficiency.

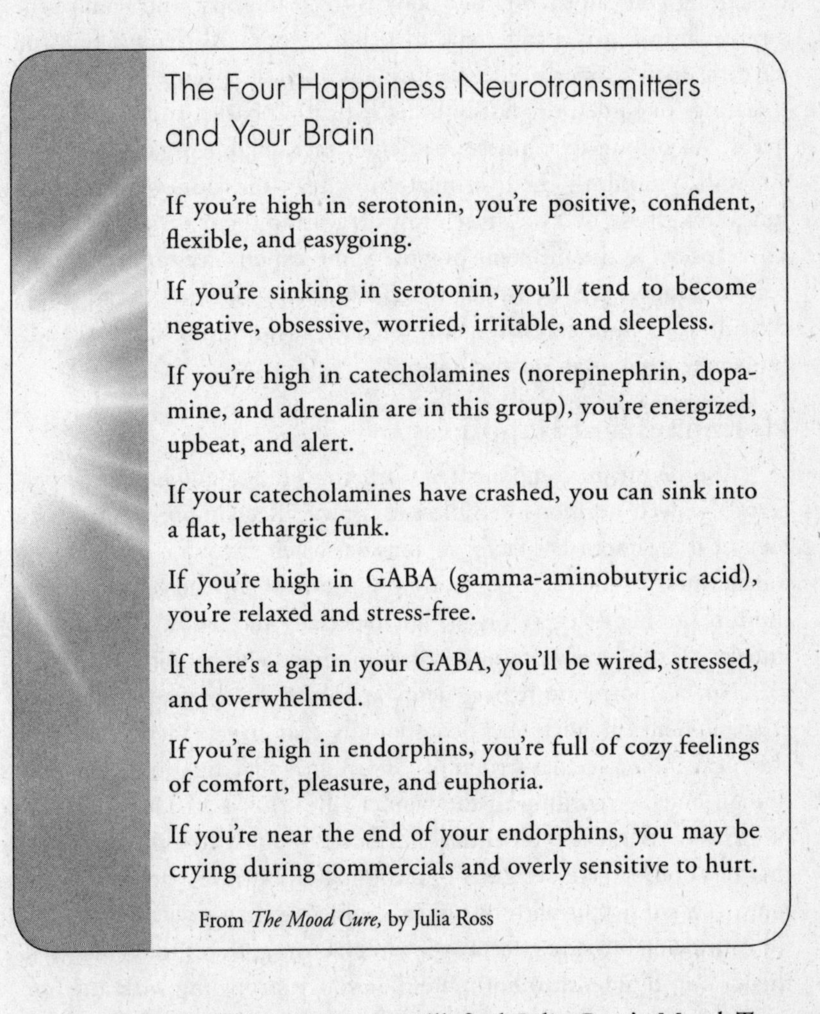

The Four Happiness Neurotransmitters and Your Brain

If you're high in serotonin, you're positive, confident, flexible, and easygoing.

If you're sinking in serotonin, you'll tend to become negative, obsessive, worried, irritable, and sleepless.

If you're high in catecholamines (norepinephrin, dopamine, and adrenalin are in this group), you're energized, upbeat, and alert.

If your catecholamines have crashed, you can sink into a flat, lethargic funk.

If you're high in GABA (gamma-aminobutyric acid), you're relaxed and stress-free.

If there's a gap in your GABA, you'll be wired, stressed, and overwhelmed.

If you're high in endorphins, you're full of cozy feelings of comfort, pleasure, and euphoria.

If you're near the end of your endorphins, you may be crying during commercials and overly sensitive to hurt.

From *The Mood Cure,* by Julia Ross

At the end of this section, you'll find Julia Ross's Mood Type Questionnaire that can help you determine more accurately if you have adequate amino acid levels.

Cleaning House

Many people's bodies are overloaded with "toxic gunk" that blocks the happiness juices from flowing. There are times when the best thing you can do for your body is to clean house and remove the gunk. Cleansing is a fast track to making your cells happy, but you have to do it properly. Cleanses usually include a temporary change in eating (or sometimes fasting), detoxification baths, and elimination herbs. According to Chinese medicine, each of our organs relates to a specific emotion—the liver relates to anger, the kidneys to fear, the lungs to sadness, and the spleen to worry—and there are specific types of cleanses for the different organs. Some experts recommend doing regular cleanses at the change of each season. IMPORTANT NOTE: Always consult your doctor before going on a cleanse; certain health conditions may make it an unwise option.

Hormones and Happiness

Another major component of Catherine's health and happiness program involved hormones. While this aspect affects more women than men, it is an important factor to consider when anyone is experiencing unhappiness in life. Hormones are nourishment for the cells, affecting the functioning of every organ, but especially the brain, so hormonal imbalances can have a profound effect on mood and happiness.

Not all hormone replacements are alike. Many people prefer to take bioidentical hormones, compounds that have exactly the same chemical and molecular structure as hormones that are produced in the human body. According to the women's health expert Dr. Christiane Northrup, "Because bioidentical hormones are just like the hormones that our bodies were designed to recognize and utilize, their effects are more . . . consistent with our normal biochemistry—with less chance for unpredictable side effects at low replacement doses than with synthetic, non-bioidentical hormones." If you're struggling with any hormone issues, make sure to find a health care practitioner who doesn't believe in the one-size-fits-all approach.

Exploring the many ways you can nourish your body is a worthwhile investment of time that will pay rich dividends in your happiness.

Exercise

The Four-Part Mood Type Questionnaire

Write down the number next to each symptom listed below that you identify with. Total your score in each section and compare it to the cutoff score. If your score is over the cutoff, or if you have only a few of the symptoms but they bother you on a regular basis, learn more about the amino acid indicated in Julia Ross's book *The Mood Cure* or at her website: www.moodcure.com. The exciting news is that you can easily get the amino acids your brain needs from nutritional supplements, and you can experience your moods improve in a short period of time as your neurotransmitters get the fuel they need.

Part 1. Are You Under a Dark Cloud? If So, Your Serotonin Levels May Be Low

3) Do you have a tendency to be negative, to see the glass as half empty rather than half full? Do you have dark, pessimistic thoughts?

3) Are you often worried and anxious?

3) Do you have feelings of low self-esteem and lack confidence? Do you easily get to feeling self-critical and guilty?

3) Does your behavior often get a bit, or a lot, obsessive? Is it hard for you to make transitions, to be flexible? Are you a perfectionist, a neatnik, or a control freak? A computer, TV, or work addict?

3) Do you really dislike the dark weather or have a clear-cut fall/winter depression?

2) Are you apt to be irritable, impatient, edgy, or angry?

3) Do you tend to be shy or fearful? Do you get nervous or panicky about heights, flying, enclosed spaces,

public performance, spiders, snakes, bridges, crowds, leaving the house, or anything else?

2) Have you had anxiety attacks or panic attacks (your heart races, it's hard to breathe)?

2) Do you get PMS or menopausal moodiness (tears, anger, depression)?

3) Do you hate hot weather?

2) Are you a night owl, or do you often find it hard to get to sleep, even though you want to?

2) Do you wake up in the night, have restless or light sleep, or wake up too early in the morning?

3) Do you routinely like to have sweet or starchy snacks, or wine in the afternoons, evenings, or in the middle of the night (but not earlier in the day)?

2) Do you find relief from any of the above symptoms through exercise?

3) Have you had fibromyalgia (unexplained muscle pain) or TMJ (pain, tension, and grinding associated with your jaw)?

2) Have you had suicidal thoughts or plans?

Total Score ____________ If your score is more than 12 in Part 1, you may have a serotonin deficiency.

Part 2. Are You Suffering from the Blahs? If So, Your Catecholamine Levels May Be Low

3) Do you often feel depressed—the flat, bored, apathetic kind?

2) Are you low on physical or mental energy? Do you feel tired a lot, have to push yourself to exercise?

2) Is your drive, enthusiasm, and motivation quota on the low side?

2) Do you have difficulty focusing or concentrating?

3) Are you easily chilled? Do you have cold hands or feet?

2) Do you tend to put on weight too easily?

3) Do you feel the need to get more alert and motivated by consuming a lot of coffee or other "uppers" like sugar, diet soda, or ephedra?

Total Score ____________ If your score is more than 6 in Part 2, your level of catecholamines may be low.

Part 3. Is Stress Your Problem? If So, Your GABA Levels May Be Low

3) Do you often feel overworked, pressured, or deadlined?

1) Do you have trouble relaxing or loosening up?

1) Does your body tend to be stiff, uptight, tense?

2) Are you easily upset, frustrated, or snappy under stress?

3) Are you easily chilled? Do you have cold hands or feet?

2) Do you tend to put on weight too easily?

3) Do you often feel overwhelmed, or as though you just can't get it all done?

2) Do you feel weak or shaky at times?

3) Are you sensitive to bright light, noise, or chemical fumes? Do you need to wear dark glasses a lot?

3) Do you feel significantly worse if you skip meals or go too long without eating?

2) Do you use tobacco, alcohol, food, or drugs to relax and calm down?

Total Score ____________ If your score is more than 8 in Part 3, you could be low in GABA.

Part 4. Are You Too Sensitive to Life's Pain? If So, Your Endorphin Levels May Be Low

3) Do you consider yourself or do others consider you to be very sensitive? Does emotional pain, or perhaps physical pain, really get to you?

2) Do you tear up or cry easily, for instance, even during TV commercials?

2) Do you tend to avoid dealing with painful issues?

3) Do you find it hard to get over losses or get through grieving?

2) Have you been through a great deal of physical or emotional pain?

3) Do you crave pleasure, comfort, reward, enjoyment, or numbing from treats like chocolate, bread, wine, romance novels, tobacco, or lattes?

Total Score ____________ If your score is more than 6, you may be low in endorphins.

Used by permission of Julia Ross.

Happiness Habit for the Body #2

Energize Your Body

There is a vitality, a life-force, an energy, a quickening that is translated through you into action. . . . Keep the channel open.

—Martha Graham, twentieth-century dancer and choreographer

You wouldn't expect your car to run well if you never shut it off or if you didn't fuel it. Yet we often neglect our bodies in similar ways and expect them to keep going like the Energizer Bunny. To access our natural joy and maintain balance in our lives, we need to energize our bodies through proper rest, breathing, and exercise.

Eastern systems of health and well-being have long recognized the presence of a vital life force or energy in the body. In China, this life force is called *chi* or *qi,* and in India, it's called *prana.* When this vital life force is increased in the body, it energizes the entire system, mobilizing healing forces and eliminating emotional blocks that dampen happiness.

I'd heard of Qigong, the ancient Chinese practice of cultivating the life energy in the body, but had never tried it. So I decided to take a class with Qigong master Chunyi Lin. I was impressed right away with Master Lin's energy, joy, and vitality. Although he is close to fifty, he looks like a man in his thirties. I interviewed Master Lin and immediately added him to the list of my Happy 100. His story shows how moving your body releases your vital energy and makes you happier.

Master Lin's Story

Moving Energy, Feeling Joy

I was born in the mountains of China. Both my parents had good jobs, and although we weren't rich, my parents were kind and loving people and we were happy.

When I was eight years old, the Cultural Revolution started. Chairman Mao, the Communist Party leader, wanted to get rid of everyone who had a different political opinion. Good people went to jail, teachers and professors were forced to work in the countryside farming, and hundreds and thousands of honest and learned people were killed. The whole country was in a terrible mess.

One night, as our family sat eating dinner, armed men came into our home. They grabbed my father, tied his hands behind him, and pushed him out of the house. They arrested him for what they eventually found were false charges. We couldn't see him for over six months; he was sent to jail and later, to a work compound.

Then one night, my mother disappeared. We didn't learn until later that she had been forced to flee for her life. Our nanny, an elderly widow my parents had taken in to live with us, was left alone to care for my two brothers, my sister, and me. We were still reeling from our mother's disappearance when, a few days later, a group of our neighbors, people my parents had liked and helped, stormed into our house holding weapons and ordered us out into the street. They did this to show their loyalty to the local people in power and to avoid sharing my parents' fate.

The wind was blowing with cold evening rain as we watched the neighbors seal off our house. We huddled together, four little children and an old woman, walking in the rain down our narrow street, trying to find shelter.

We were on the street for three days with no food. Nobody dared to take us in or give us anything to eat. On the third night, as we crowded together on the side of the street trying to keep warm, a gun battle broke out between two rival factions. Bullets were flying all around us and there were explosions everywhere.

Terrified, we ran from one house to the other, desperately trying to find a safe place to hide, but no one would let us in. As we pressed together in a doorway, shivering from fear, a very elderly lady opened the door. We recognized her as a landlord, who we'd been told by the government were all devils. Frightened, I jumped behind our nanny to hide.

The elderly lady looked at us and said, "Oh, you poor little children. With all this fighting, it's too dangerous for you to be outside. Please, come inside. You'll be safe."

At great personal risk to herself, this wonderful old lady fed us and then hid us, along with many others, in a storage shed at the back of her house. For weeks, we never ventured out of the shed for fear of discovery. Then finally, our parents managed to locate us.

They sent a family friend to escort us, and after a long and dangerous trip we made it to my grandmother's house in the country. We lived with my grandmother for over a year, before my parents determined that it was safe for us to come and live with them again.

My experiences during the Cultural Revolution colored my life for many years. Everything had been turned upside down. So-called good friends turned out to be the ones who wanted to take your life. So-called evil people turned out to be your angels. I didn't even trust my parents. In my child's mind, they had simply abandoned us. Feeling betrayed by everyone and everything, I withdrew from my family and friends.

In high school, I began studying Qigong, an ancient healing system of balancing energy in the body through movement, which is widely taught throughout China. When I was little, I'd heard many stories of Qigong masters and miraculous healings. I'd always loved those stories and wished that one day I could become a healer like that. During the Cultural Revolution, teaching or studying Qigong was forbidden. Anyone caught even practicing Qigong was arrested. It wasn't sanctioned by the communist government, so my teacher, a revered Qigong master, taught me in secret. I learned some very basic Qigong movements and found that when I did them, I felt so peaceful.

After high school, many students like me were taken by soldiers and forced to live on farms in the country. For five years, we worked like slaves, often without enough to eat. The work was very hard and I suffered many injuries and diseases in the country. I would often sneak off at night by myself to practice my Qigong. It was the only time of the day that I felt okay, and it helped keep me going.

Finally, Chairman Mao died and the Gang of Four was purged from power. Things began to return to normal in China. I was able to attend college and my life started to improve, but I was still a very depressed and angry young man. I didn't want to talk to anybody. I had no friends. Although I didn't act like it outwardly, I actually hated people. In fact, I hated everything. Sometimes I just wanted to kill myself and leave this world. I began searching hard, trying to find out how to be happy in life.

Then one day as I was playing basketball, I had an accident that severely damaged the cartilage in both my knees. I was in constant agony and could hardly walk, and nothing, including painkillers, could stop the pain.

I heard that a very powerful, nationally renowned Qigong master was coming to town to give a workshop and that many people, just by attending his workshop, had their serious problems go away. I didn't believe this was true, but I thought it couldn't hurt to try. Besides, I needed a miracle.

Fifteen thousand people attended the workshop, which was held in a soccer field. It started at noon. This master taught a very potent form of Qigong and led us through many different movements and meditations. I had amazing experiences during those hours. The energy I felt was like a volcano. My body rocked and shook as the Qi began to flow through the energy channels inside of me. First I cried just like a baby, and then I began to laugh uncontrollably. I laughed and laughed until my stomach muscles ached. I knew this was a Qi reaction, and after half an hour, it gradually stopped, leaving me comfortably tired.

Then I felt a tingly sensation, starting with my toes and working its way up the length of my body. This feeling was not only in the skin; it was in the muscle and in the bone. It felt as though my body was winter ice melting in the spring sunshine—it was so peaceful, so beautiful, so nurturing. The feeling of my own life force flowing unimpeded through my body was like a breeze sweeping through my bones. I felt so relaxed and happy. It wasn't the kind of happiness that comes from getting a birthday gift or earning a promotion at work. This happiness was from the bottom of my heart. At 7:30 that night, the master finally guided us through the ending exercise. I stood up—and found a miracle *had* happened! The swelling in my knees had disappeared and the pain was 80 percent gone. I began running and jumping on the soccer field like a little kid.

I continued to practice the very simple movements that I'd learned during the workshop, and after two months, all the pain in my knees was gone. What's more, by getting the energy or Qi moving in my body, I began to be flooded by feelings of peace and beauty, and everything in my life started working.

This flow of vital energy allowed me to feel the blockage in my heart that had caused the depression, anger, and emotional pain I had felt for so many years. Whenever I felt that block in my heart, I focused on feeling forgiveness. Over the months and years that followed, the impressions I'd held in my body from my many difficult experiences were released, and I felt happiness in every cell in my body. I became such an easygoing person. I was able to forgive all the people in my life who had hurt me and my family. The daily practice of increasing and balancing my energy through movement healed me completely—both physically and spiritually.

Naturally, I wanted to share Qigong with other people, so that they could have the same joy in their lives that I was experiencing. I developed my own system of Qigong and eventually began to teach this beautiful practice in China and then in America. I've seen how, when people move their bodies with conscious awareness, they get happier.

It's been nearly twenty years since that day on the soccer field when I first fully experienced the power of the Qi, and today I am flourishing. I have a wonderful family and I do exciting and meaningful work in the world, helping thousands of people to heal themselves. Every day is a good day—whatever happens.

Motion with Meaning

Phys. Ed. class should have been called Happiness 101! Research overwhelmingly shows that people who exercise are happier. Like Master Lin, you can transform your life by making some form of exercise or movement, such as walking, running, swimming, dancing, Qigong, or yoga, a regular habit. When you exercise, your brain gets more oxygen, but even more important, it causes your body to produce valuable chemicals and hormones that impact energy, mood, and health. In a recent study done on athletes, the Harvard psychiatrist John Ratey found that dopamine, serotonin, and norepinephrine—those wonderful happiness chemicals—were all elevated after exercise. In fact, dozens of studies indicate that exercise is often as effective for reducing depression as the typical medications prescribed.

Exercise can also help relieve and prevent anxiety, creating a calming effect that lasts for about four hours after exercising. Try getting in a fight right after a rigorous workout. It's not likely to happen! Exercise also increases endorphins, the "bliss" neurochemicals responsible for that wonderful exercise high, by about 500 percent.

Dr. Henry S. Lodge, assistant clinical professor of medicine at Columbia University and coauthor of *Younger Next Year,* explains how exercise works at the cellular level to keep you vital and healthy. He says that every day you replace about 1 percent of your cells, getting a whole new body every three months. When you exercise, your muscles release specific substances that tell your cells to grow. When you sit around like a couch potato, your muscles let out a steady trickle of chemicals that tell your cells to die. What powerful motivation! If you started exercising in January, you could have a whole new body of strong, happy cells by April.

To turbocharge the effects of exercise, bring awareness to your movement. Moving with conscious intention is one of the reasons Qigong is so effective. You can take this same approach to any exercise. For example, as you set out on your next walk, Master Lin recommends telling yourself, "On my walk, all my channels are going to become clearer, I will open my heart to nature, and by the time I'm finished, my energy will be much stronger." He says this intention will dramatically boost the impact of movement on your happiness.

You can even energize your body without leaving your chair. Brian Siddhartha Ingle, an osteopath specializing in a neuromuscular education program called Hanna Somatics, told me that he sees daily how people's posture affects their energy and level of happiness. Next time you're feeling stressed, anxious, or blue, notice if your shoulders are coming up toward your ears. Instead of trying to pull your shoulders down, Dr. Ingle suggests exaggerating this movement by bringing your shoulders even closer toward your ears—then, SLOWLY, letting them come down. Do this three to four times and see if your stress and anxiety levels go down.

Breath of Life

You can live for weeks without eating and a few days without water, but you can last for only a few minutes without breathing. Our breath is the most important fuel we have for energizing our bodies. For millennia, many traditions have understood the importance of skilled, mindful breathing to maintain optimal health and well-being. In the past thirty years, hundreds of clinical studies involving thousands of participants have been conducted showing how breathing techniques can relieve anxiety, depression, and chronic fatigue and increase mental clarity. Today, even our own FDA approves breath training as a recognized treatment for hypertension.

Stop and notice how you're breathing at this moment by putting your hand on your stomach. See if your hand goes out on your inhale and back in on your exhale. If you're like most people, you breathe from your chest cavity alone and your hand doesn't move at all. In my interview with Dr. John Douillard, an Ayurvedic practitioner and the author of *Body, Mind, and Sport,* he told me, "While shallow breathing will keep you alive, the oxygen isn't getting to the deeper cellular levels where it's needed to cleanse cellular pathways and open the way for happiness-enhancing chemicals to flow. Breathing deeply from the stomach is one of the most powerful waste-removal techniques we have; it increases the *prana* or Qi in the body and helps to create a happy, feel-good physical state. We have 26,000 opportunities a day, each time we breathe, to support our happiness."

The way we breathe is intimately connected with our emotions. Each emotional state has its own pattern of breathing: when we're anxious, we breathe quickly and shallowly; when we're sad, we sigh deeply; and when we're angry, we breathe in short, forceful bursts. But this connection works the other way too: if you start breathing as though you're anxious, sad, or angry, you stimulate the area of the brain associated with that emotion and quickly begin to experience it. The next time you're feeling agitated or anxious, try taking five to ten deep "belly breaths" in a row and notice the immediate calming effect it has on your body.

Sleep Your Way to Happiness

Sleep is nature's way of recharging our batteries. Though we all know we're happier when we get enough sleep, ask most people whether they're getting eight hours a night, and they'll usually respond with a hollow laugh. Who has the time, they say, when there's the Letterman or Leno monologue to watch, bills to pay, children to tend to, problems to worry about?

When I was working as a consultant to Fortune 500 companies, I was always amazed to hear people talking about sleep as though it were a contest. One executive would say, "I get by on only five hours of sleep a night." Her colleague would say, "Yeah? I never get more than four hours." They'd brag that if their to-do lists got too long, they'd just lop off a couple more hours of sack time so they could accomplish more to get ahead. The person who slept the fewest hours a night won.

Getting too little sleep is definitely nothing to brag about. According to the Centers for Disease Control and Prevention, there's a strong correlation between the amount of restful sleep a person gets and his or her level of happiness. I was blown away when I read a December 2004 study in the journal *Science* reporting that the quality of our sleep has a greater influence on our ability to enjoy our day than household income or marital status. Who knew that snoozing trumps salaries and spouses?

I subscribe to the Ayurvedic wisdom (Ayurveda is the ancient medical tradition of India) that "an hour of sleep before midnight is worth two hours of sleep after midnight." I once went to see an Ayurvedic doctor, a little old man no taller than I was, who must have been at least a hundred years old. He was as wrinkled as a raisin but still had all his hair, a wide smile, and the twinkliest eyes I'd ever seen. He told me that if I was ever feeling unhappy or out of sorts, I should try going to bed before 10 (ideally by 9) three nights in a row, and then see how I feel. Every time I do that, I find a whole new world out there by the third day. I once again become an energetic, joyful, and rested person! I call this "catching the 10 o'clock angel train," and it's definitely one of my favorite happiness habits. Over the years, I've recommended this to lots of people, and everyone who's done it has thanked me profusely.

As an experiment for the next week, make getting a good night's sleep your priority. Letterman and Leno will soldier on without you, and you'll be so much happier.

To energize your body, return to these basics: keep your body moving, breathe deeply, and get enough rest. Here's a simple Qigong exercise you can use to raise your happiness level through conscious movement, regardless of whether you're sitting on a mountaintop or taking a break at work.

Exercise

Spring Forest Qigong—Breathing of the Universe

Don't be fooled by the seeming simplicity of this exercise. As Master Lin (pictured in the accompanying photos) says, "The most powerful is also the simplest." This exercise is subtle, yet extremely effective for opening blockages in the whole body, especially the lungs.

1. **Relax in the proper position:** Stand with your feet a bit more than shoulder-width apart, knees slightly bent, and look forward. Smile and relax. Draw your chin back slightly to straighten the spine. Drop your shoulders and move your elbows out a little. Open your hands and spread your fingers.

2. **Breathe deeply:** Slowly take three deep, gentle breaths through your nose. Imagine using your whole body to breathe. Visualize energy coming in and collecting in your belly. When you exhale, visualize any pain or sickness changing into smoke and shooting out from every cell into the universe.

3. **Silently say the phrases:** Close your eyes and silently say the phrases, "I am in the universe. The universe is in my body. The universe and I combine together." Take a moment to feel the quietness, the stillness of the universe.
4. **Move your hands:** As you inhale, slowly move your hands wide apart and to the sides. (Use the pictures as a guide.) As you exhale, slowly bring your hands back together (don't let your hands touch each other). When you open your arms, feel the energy expanding in the space between your hands. When you bring your hands toward each other, feel the energy compressing in the space between them.

Do the exercise for five to six minutes. When finished, take three slow, gentle, deep breaths, and allow yourself to relax for another minute or two.

Used by permission of Spring Forest Qigong.

Happiness Habit for the Body #3

Tune In to Your Body's Wisdom

We will be in tune with our bodies only if we truly love and honor them. We can't be in good communication with the enemy.

—Harriet Lerner, PhD, clinical psychologist and author

My interviews with the Happy 100 revealed that they consistently tune in to their body's wisdom when making choices that affect their health. Knowing when it's time to rest, time to drink more water, to take a bath or exercise—the self-nourishing activities that keep us in balance—is a habit all of us can develop.

Though our body knows exactly what is best for us at any given moment, we often don't listen. When we start loving and trusting the wisdom of our body, it's "the beginning of a beautiful friendship," one that makes our cells infinitely happier.

During my interview with Happy 100 member, author, and consciousness pioneer Gay Hendricks, he told me the following story that illustrates the powerful effect of living in tune with what your body really wants.

Gay's Story

The Magic Key

I was fat practically from the moment I was born. During my entire boyhood and well into adulthood, I thought being fat was a curse. I blamed it on fate, on God, on my parents. Sometimes I blamed it on all the enticing food I gorged myself with. But most of the time I blamed it on myself: my insatiable appetite, my lack of willpower, my craving for rich food. On really bad days I believed there was a pit inside of me—a fundamental fault so deep it felt bottomless. I'm not sure if being fat was making me unhappy, or being unhappy was making me fat. It didn't really matter—the fact was: I was very fat *and* very unhappy.

Things went this way until I was in my mid-twenties. Then one day during a graduate school psychology class exercise, a fellow student named George looked me in the eye and asked, "What is your weight all about?"

I was so taken aback that all I could do was stutter, "W-what do you mean?"

He simplified it for me: "Why are you so fat? Why are you trying so hard to kill yourself at such a young age?"

I was horrified. He was asking me about the one thing that must never be mentioned. Although my family had taken me to see a dozen different medical specialists in futile attempts to handle my weight problem, they never talked about it in front of me. My classmate did the one thing no one had ever done: he looked me in the eye and asked me why I was fat.

I froze up, breaking eye contact with him, and mumbled something about having glandular problems and a family history of obesity. He looked at me with pity tinged with disgust. "That's it?" he asked. "That's all you're going to say?"

When I didn't respond, he sighed, and then, to my relief, we continued our class work. The problem was that I couldn't sleep that night. I must have replayed his question in my mind a hundred times, but could find no answer.

Over the next week, I couldn't get his question out of my mind. I became more and more frazzled, my work became sloppy, and I argued incessantly with my wife. Then, one wintry day, I went out for a walk down a deserted stretch of country road.

Picture a pear-shaped, three-hundred-pound man trudging down the road, his body stuffed into an orange parka. The day shimmered, and all was peaceful and quiet around me. The only sound was the crunch of my boots on the dry snow as I tramped along the road, lost in thought.

Suddenly, both my feet shot straight out from under me and I fell. I'd stepped on a patch of ice that was covered with a fine dusting of snow. As the back of my head smacked on the icy road, I saw an explosion of stars and a blast of pain wracked my body.

In the very next moment, the pain disappeared, and I found myself having the strangest experience. Suddenly I was in two places at once! I was up in the air, looking down at my body, and at the same time looking up through my body toward the sky.

From this unique two-way vantage point, I could see deeply into myself for the first time. I saw that my mind, body, heart, and soul weren't as separate as I'd always believed. In a slow-motion, altered state of consciousness, I saw all the emotional defenses I had mounted on a daily basis to protect myself. Suddenly I had the answer to George's question: eating was my body's way to avoid pain! I had created an armor of fat that insulated me from my feelings of fear, sorrow, loss, and shame. The problem with this strategy is that it left me with a painful emptiness inside that further fueled my craving for food. It was the perfect vicious cycle.

Now as I lay there, I could feel my misery draining away as I simply relaxed into the spacious fullness that I realized was my soul. It permeated every part of me—my mind, body, emotions—and filled me to the brim with a vibrant contentment. I felt a strange sensation: I was completely satiated, maybe for the first time in my life!

This was the feeling of completeness I had sought with snacks, sandwiches, and sodas. I felt more than full; I felt nourished. I saw that by walling myself up inside to avoid painful feelings, I had lost touch with my body's wisdom and starved myself of spirit. No wonder I had a hunger no food could satisfy!

At that point, my eyes flickered open and the everyday world returned. I got up off the icy road, dusted myself off, and stood looking around. I felt a singing-humming exhilaration of clarity in me as I made a choice in every cell of my being. "From now on," I said, "I'm choosing to listen to my body's wisdom and truly nourish myself from the inside." Then, smiling with a newfound joy, I headed home.

Over the course of the next twelve months, I lost over a hundred pounds. I won't kid you and say it was easy. However, I can tell you sincerely that it was simple. My fall on the ice had shown me a magic key, which was just one action: Before I did anything, I tapped into my body's inner knowing and asked myself, "Would this truly feed me?"

For years, I'd known everything there was to know about protein and carbohydrates, calories and dieting—but nothing about nourishing myself from within. The magic key changed everything, including my relationship with food. The morning after my fall, I considered my standard breakfast: cereal with milk and a few spoonfuls of sugar. My favorite part was when I finished the cereal and got to the layer of undissolved sugar in the milk at the bottom of the bowl. I loved that sweet milky taste, even though I knew it made me feel bloated and irritable an hour later.

Force of habit pulled me toward the cabinet that held the cereal. But this time I paused and reminded myself of my commitment to listen to what my body really wanted. I looked at the cereal box and asked, "Would this truly feed me?" My body immediately said "No," with a slight contraction in my throat and stomach. It was like stepping on the brakes of a car and hearing the metallic squeal.

I went to the refrigerator and looked in. My eyes were instantly drawn to a box of fresh blueberries. They were the kind of thing I would never have eaten in a million years. Yet that day, the box of berries stood out like a beacon. They were actually quite beautiful. I took out the box and looked more closely. I picked up a blueberry and asked the same question, "Would this truly feed me?" My body said "Yes" with a sensation of expanding space and lightness inside me. I popped the blueberry in my mouth and chewed it slowly. It was absolutely delicious. To this day I can remember the burst of fresh aliveness in my mouth. I thought, "Could everything taste this good if it truly fed me?"

I took another blueberry and started to eat it, but stopped abruptly when I realized I was about to eat it simply because the first one had tasted so good. I asked myself again, "Would this particular blueberry also truly feed me?" When my body said "Yes," I popped the berry into my mouth. In response to my fourth inquiry, my body said "No." So, on the first morning of my new life, I had three blueberries for breakfast—and I felt great! When I got hungry an hour later, I just repeated the process. It was like magic; my stomach *and* every other part of my being felt full.

The magic key made life incredibly straightforward. It showed me what food to eat, told me when I needed to take a walk and when to turn off the light and go to sleep. It showed me which friends had to go and which ones I could continue to spend time with. It showed me the changes I needed to make in order to have a successful career. I've used it for everything, and it's always worked.

In retrospect, I think being fat was the best thing that ever happened to me. Struggling with my weight led me to an awakening that showed me what I had always wanted to know: how to be alive and in harmony with all things, including the one thing I'd never been in harmony with—myself. Today, being in touch with my body's wisdom in every moment has become an automatic choice, one that keeps me feeling vital and full of joy.

The magic key completely transformed my body and my life, showing me how to be nourished from the inside. My marriage, my career, my books and courses are all based on that nourishment. It took a sledgehammer-like blow to the head to knock the sense back into me, but it has led me to the life of my dreams.

Body Talk

You can tune in to your body in any situation by asking yourself: Is this what my body *really* wants or needs? Or by posing specific questions: *What am I hungry for? Am I listening to my body's cries for relaxation and relief from stress? What do I need to recharge my batteries?* If you listen closely, your body will tell you what's best for your health and happiness every time. Sometimes, as Gay experienced, just mentally asking the question will bring an instant answer in the form of a physical sensation.

This is the perfect time to use your inner GPS to see whether something you're planning to do will expand or contract you. When you consistently choose the things that bring about a state of expansion in you, it dramatically increases your experience of happiness and well-being.

Learning a New Language

Want to reverse the aging process? According to the life coach and author Martha Beck, PhD, when people connect with their bodies, they start to "age backwards." This connection comes, she says, when you accept all that's going on in your body, even the things you don't like. A lot of people don't listen to their bodies because they have strong negative feelings about them. In our interview, Dr. Beck told me that when you experience deep compassion for everything you're presently feeling instead of rejecting it, you come into harmony with your body and you can hear what it wants. Imagine feeling the same tenderness and concern for your body that you'd feel for a baby or a beloved pet in your care. Having this kind of acceptance for your body activates the areas of the brain associated with happiness, falling in love, and feeling a sense of oneness with everything around you.

When we learn our body's language and begin to treat ourselves gently, we feel more and more comfortable living in our own skin, which supports our experience of being Happy for No Reason.

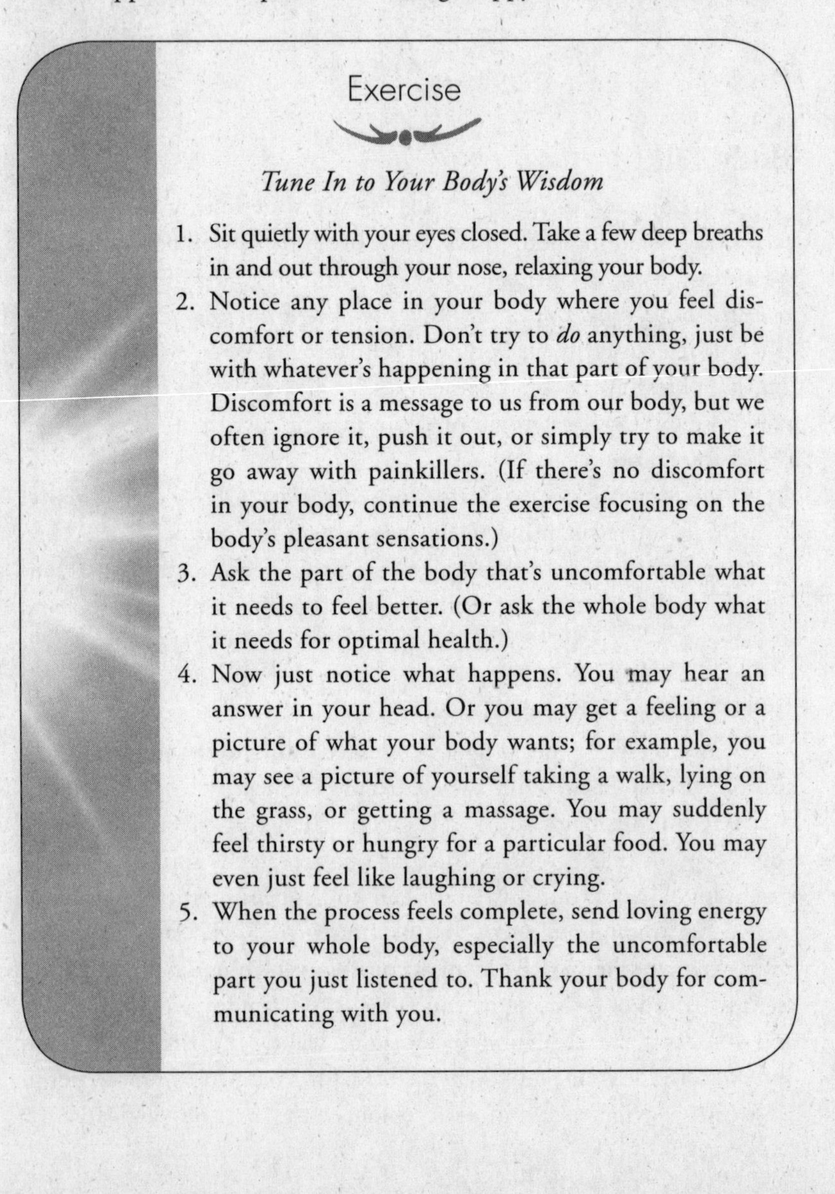

Exercise

Tune In to Your Body's Wisdom

1. Sit quietly with your eyes closed. Take a few deep breaths in and out through your nose, relaxing your body.
2. Notice any place in your body where you feel discomfort or tension. Don't try to *do* anything, just be with whatever's happening in that part of your body. Discomfort is a message to us from our body, but we often ignore it, push it out, or simply try to make it go away with painkillers. (If there's no discomfort in your body, continue the exercise focusing on the body's pleasant sensations.)
3. Ask the part of the body that's uncomfortable what it needs to feel better. (Or ask the whole body what it needs for optimal health.)
4. Now just notice what happens. You may hear an answer in your head. Or you may get a feeling or a picture of what your body wants; for example, you may see a picture of yourself taking a walk, lying on the grass, or getting a massage. You may suddenly feel thirsty or hungry for a particular food. You may even just feel like laughing or crying.
5. When the process feels complete, send loving energy to your whole body, especially the uncomfortable part you just listened to. Thank your body for communicating with you.

Summary and Happiness Action Steps

When you practice nourishing your body properly, energizing it, and tuning in to its own wisdom, you make your cells happy, which strengthens the pillar of the body and supports greater happiness in life. Use the following action steps to practice the Happiness Habits for the Body:

1. Reexamine your eating habits to see whether they're supporting happy cells. Favor the happiness-building foods.
2. For one week, kick the caffeine, shake the sugar, and curb the carbs, and notice the effect on your body.
3. Drink enough water—half your body's weight in ounces—every day to see if you feel more energized.
4. Consult your health care professional to determine whether your hormones are in balance and to see whether your body would benefit from a change in amino acids or a fast.
5. Experiment with different forms of exercise to find ones that energize you, and use Master Lin's suggestion to bring conscious awareness to your movement.
6. Practice deep belly breathing, particularly when you're feeling stressed.
7. Catch the "10 o'clock angel train" for three days in a row and see how you feel.
8. Listen to your body's wisdom by checking in regularly to see whether you're giving it what it needs.

The Pillar of the Soul—Plug Yourself In to Spirit

There are only two ways to live your life. One is as though nothing is a miracle. The other is as though everything is a miracle.

—Albert Einstein

Think of a time when you felt that life was miraculous: watching early-morning light fill a mountain valley, holding your newborn baby in your arms for the first time, or maybe looking up into the vast night sky ablaze with stars. Every one of us has had at least one moment when our appreciation for life was so intense, it became awe. It's at those times, when you feel both humbled and exalted, that you know you're plugged in to Spirit.

It doesn't matter what you call it—Spirit, Higher Power, Universal Source, Creative Intelligence, the Unified Field, Nature, or God—we're talking about the same thing. Plugging in to Spirit is the experience of feeling connected to an energy bigger than yourself. The more deeply you experience that connection, the richer and more joyful your life feels.

Our souls are the individual expression of this larger Spirit. When you experience that the beauty and mystery surrounding you is inside you as well, your life takes on another dimension. You realize you aren't just getting by in life, just going through the motions. Everything—your drive to work, your evening meal, your conversation with a friend, even your reaction to a piece of bad news—becomes permeated with a sense of grace. Living from that place of wonder and joy strengthens your connection to your soul, raising the fourth and final pillar of your Home for Happiness.

Although each of the Happy 100 have inspired me, the ones who stand out are the ones who have the greatest sense of oneness and unity with Spirit. They come from all different traditions: Christian, Jewish, Buddhist, Hindu, and Muslim. Others don't have a formal religion, yet experience a feeling of oneness with all life. The common thread that runs through all their experiences is a feeling of reverence, wonder, and gratitude for the remarkable gift of being alive. Happy 100 member Brian Hilliard, whose happiness set-point is off the charts, wakes up every morning with a big smile on his face. (His wife, Arielle, says he even smiles in his sleep!) Like so many of the people I interviewed, Brian attributes his state of perpetual well-being to his habit of tapping into the Source and feeling grateful for his life.

People who are Happy for No Reason don't always need to figure everything out or be in control; they live in the flow of life, trusting the underlying benevolence and wisdom of that larger wholeness.

Feeling separate from the Divine is what many consider the number one cause of human suffering and unhappiness. Looking back, it's clear to me that one of the main reasons I was unhappy when I was young was that I felt disconnected from Spirit. I knew there had to be more to life than my body, thoughts, and feelings. I truly had a hunger for the soul, but didn't know how to satisfy it. My first breakthrough in the spiritual arena came when I was sixteen and learned to meditate. It immediately started to relieve some of the existential angst and low-grade depression I'd felt since I was a little girl. Every morning, I'd get up twenty minutes early, settle into an oversized chair perfect for sitting cross-legged, and meditate before going to school. In the beginning, I often wondered if I was meditating correctly, but I felt so much expansion, peace, and well-being, I knew I was doing something right. Many times I felt a sense of coming home.

I was hooked. Meditation became as important a part of my daily routine as brushing my teeth. I'm convinced that meditating is what kept me from escaping my unhappiness through addictions and the other unhealthy behaviors I saw a lot of the other kids doing. Though I still had a way to go to be Happy for No Reason, it set me in the right direction. My parents noticed such a change in me that they learned to meditate too. Today, meditation still helps me stay connected to Spirit. Of all the things I've done to become happier, this is the step that's helped me the most.

Studies show that people who have a spiritual dimension in their lives—defined not as an affiliation with an organized religion, but an internal sense of the spiritual meaning in life—are happier than those who don't: they have happier marriages, are more effective parents, and in general feel better able to cope with whatever happens to them in life. Young people who consider themselves spiritual have higher grades and are less inclined to drink or do drugs.

Spirituality is good for your body as well. It's been found to improve blood pressure, strengthen the immune system, and reduce the rates of stroke, cancer, and heart disease. This has become so well accepted that 25 percent of medical schools in America now offer courses on spirituality and health!

The bottom line? When you feel connected to a Higher Power, you're happier and healthier and can handle the problems that come up in your life more easily.

The World Is Too Much with Us

What keeps us from being plugged in to Spirit? If our souls are always accessible, why do so many people feel empty and dissatisfied?

Part of the problem lies in the hectic pace of life today and the emphasis on material achievement and accomplishment. The poet William Wordsworth wrote, "The world is too much with us; late and soon / Getting and spending, we lay waste our powers." (He wrote those lines in 1888. Can you imagine what he'd think of the world today?)

From the moment you were first able to walk and talk, the notion has been drummed into your head: "Don't just stand there! *Do* something!" You might even feel, like so many others, that unless you're being constructive, rushing around and accomplishing things, you aren't a worthy person.

On top of that, we seem to have a strong aversion to being bored. If we're not working or checking off the items on our to-do lists, we're amusing ourselves: reading magazines, books, or newspapers, playing computer games, doing crossword or sudoku puzzles, listening to radios and iPods, surfing the Net, watching television or movies. The list, like our TV screens, keeps getting bigger and bigger. Heaven forbid we have an unfilled moment in our day! We're settling for what entertains us, rather than going for what will deeply fulfill us.

Add our new global obsession with being available 24/7 wherever we are—did you know that one in six people *on the planet* owns a cell phone?—and you can see how easy it is to get lost in the material world and not give time to your soul. Life has become a multimedia, multidimensional, multitasking extravaganza!

"I've tried letting my mind drift off to my happy place, but I can't get cell phone reception there."

This insane level of activity disconnects us from the inner silence that gives our lives meaning and depth. So how do you plug yourself in?

By making it a priority to experience your connection to Spirit. This requires routine time-outs from your busy life and a willingness to be quiet. In that silence, you can both listen and speak to your Higher Power, which cultivates a greater sense of acceptance, surrender, and trust.

When we make conscious connection to the soul, we're infusing the essence of being Happy for No Reason.

There are many ways to feel connected to your soul. It's a very personal thing, but from my research and interviews with the Happy 100, I've discovered some general guidelines. Practicing the following Happiness Habits can help anyone plug in to Spirit more easily.

Happiness Habits for the Soul

1. Invite Connection to Your Higher Power
2. Listen to Your Inner Voice
3. Trust Life's Unfolding

Happiness Habit for the Soul #1

Invite Connection to Your Higher Power

God is the friend of silence. See how nature—trees, flowers, grass—grows in silence; see the stars, the moon and the sun, how they move in silence. . . . We need silence to be able to touch souls.

—Mother Teresa

We're swimming in a sea of beauty and mystery—yet we often don't take the time to stop *doing* and notice. Turning inward is one of the most powerful ways you can nurture a conscious connection to your soul. Even just 15 minutes a day can make a huge difference. I know that for a lot of people that may seem like a tall order, but really, it's the best investment of your time you can make. When you feel stronger, happier, and more centered, it benefits everyone in your life—especially you.

There are many ways to cultivate a connection to a Higher Power. You can learn a formal meditation practice; you can take a walk and be in nature; you can sit in silence; listen to inspiring music; or you can use prayer to open the lines of communication with a power greater than yourself. It doesn't matter which you pick, as long as it works for you and you do it regularly. The Happy 100 have all found ways to keep their connection to Spirit flourishing in their everyday lives.

The actress Goldie Hawn is one of those "plugged-in" people. I've loved Goldie since the days when I first saw her in the comedy-variety show *Laugh-In.* The following story from her glowing memoir, *A Lotus Grows in the Mud,* describes her first experience of meditation. It's a beautiful account of connecting to your soul by closing your eyes and going inside.

Goldie's Story

The Space between Thoughts

I rejoice in the spaces between thoughts.

A beautiful woman leads me into a quiet room. The warm California breeze drifts through the open window, gently billowing the curtains and lifting my hair.

There is a lone chair in the room. She offers me the seat and whispers a secret mantra in my ear. Just before she leaves the room, she says, "Repeat this in your mind, over and over again." She closes the door behind her, leaving just me and my secret mantra.

I have always been drawn to unseen powers, to the mystical and the magical in life. With her help, I am about to discover the power of my own mind.

Closing my eyes, I feel the breeze lightly brushing my skin, while in my mind I dutifully repeat my mantra. I can smell incense burning in the room and the rose petals scattered all about me. This is my first experience of attempting to quiet my mind.

I chuckle to myself at first. What a cliché I am, sitting here in this room, in the seventies, with flower power at its peak, the latest celebrity to join the Transcendental Meditation bandwagon.

Whoops! That's a thought. Shhh. I have to go back to my mantra. She said thoughts would come in and out of my mind. "Just witness them," she whispered. "Don't judge them or give them any credence. Let them drift away, and then go back to your mantra."

It is not so easy to do.

The more I repeat the mantra, over and over, the more I feel my body relax. My breathing falls away to an almost imperceptible rate.

My heart beats more slowly, and the blood it pumps through my veins lessens its pressure.

Thoughts roll into my busy mind again—people I must call, places I must go—and I push them away, hoping for a longer period of calm before the next wave of thoughts.

Listening to my mind saying the words of my mantra, sensing their rhythm and primordial sounds in my head, an inexplicable feeling begins to wash over me.

Deep inside, I feel I am going down and reconnecting to something I know, like an old friend, that deep place that is ever constant, ever joyous, ever alive with creativity. It is the deeper part of me that knows something. It is such a great connection, and fills me with such joy, that I feel like giggling.

Pushing the temptation aside, I carry on, wanting to feel it again. The more I repeat my mantra over and over, the more I let go. As my thoughts flow in and out, I become quieter and quieter in my mind.

My consciousness feels like a teabag being dipped into a glass of hot water and lifted out again. I can feel it becoming slowly saturated with nothingness. When I say nothingness, it is sort of a space in time in which no thought takes place.

Each time I repeat the mantra, the phenomenon becomes stronger, and the teabag becomes heavier and heavier, sinking deeper and deeper, its rich essences seeping into the water.

After a while—I can't say how long—I lose my sense of place. I can visualize the clear glass full of the rich goodness that is my life. I feel like I am merging my spirit with something that is very familiar to me, very safe, and it tickles my joy center.

I am filled with a sense of purity, such clarity, like I have never experienced before. There is no ego, no self, no thought. I am just here. Nothing matters. I am coming back to the purest state of being. I feel unadulterated bliss.

Doing Nothing Can Bring You Everything

It isn't surprising to learn that the happiness Goldie radiates is rooted in her deeply spiritual nature. As a teacher of meditation, I've seen over and over how happiness grows in people's lives when they meditate regularly.

Meditation practices based in Eastern spiritual traditions became popular in the West in the '70s, but meditation has actually been a part of the Judeo-Christian and Native American traditions for thousands of years. The process of turning inward through meditation is universally recognized as a way to plug yourself in to Spirit.

Meditation takes many forms: focusing on a mantra or the breath, contemplation, visualization, or using sound. It's any process that quiets the mind and helps connect you to your source and innermost essence, that state of pure Truth and Love.

I love this beautiful story about how meditation works:

> A wise teacher, instructing his students to meditate, told them, "The process is like filling a sieve with water." All of the students were confused by this statement. How it was possible to fill a sieve with water? Some thought it meant meditation was very difficult, and others thought it meant they could only expect temporary gains from their practice. Discouraged, they stopped meditating. One student, however, approached the teacher and asked him to explain.
>
> The teacher took the student to the edge of the ocean, gave him a sieve, and told him to try to fill it with water. The student scooped the water into the sieve, but it immediately ran out. The teacher took the sieve from the student and said, "I will show you how." The teacher threw the sieve into the water, where it sank almost immediately. He told the student, "The sieve is full of water now and will stay that way forever. Meditation works the same way. It's not about scooping small amounts of Spirit into your individual life, but about dropping yourself into the ocean of Spirit and merging with that Spirit more and more each day."

Meditation and the Happy Brain

Whether you are aware of them or not, whether you recognize them as spiritual or not, you probably have had the experiences of silence, or transcendence, or the Divine—a few seconds, a few minutes that seem out of time; a moment when the ordinary looks beautiful, glowing; a deep sense of being at peace, feeling happy for no reason. When these experiences come . . . believe in them. They reflect your true nature.

—Sri Sri Ravi Shankar, spiritual teacher and humanitarian

Though meditating is relaxing and enjoyable, its greatest valuc comes from the influence it has on your life outside of meditation. Hundreds of studies have been done over the past forty years showing the powerful effects of meditation on our bodies, minds, and emotions. Some of the first research, done in the early 1970s by physiologist Dr. Robert Keith Wallace, studied the effects of meditation, specifically the Transcendental Meditation (TM) technique, and found that it offered many physical and psychological benefits, including normalization of blood pressure, decreased anxiety, and better immune functioning. Many more studies on all different types of meditation followed, and today meditating has become an accepted form of stress management the world over.

Meditation does much more than just help you cope with stress. Some of the most exciting research being done today shows that meditating puts you on the fast track to being happy by enhancing activity in areas of the brain associated with happiness and compassion.

Psychologist Dr. Paul Ekman at the University of California San Francisco Medical Center tested Buddhist monks—expert meditators—and found that their meditation practice seemed to calm the brain's amygdala (the adrenaline on-switch I talked about in Chapter 4). What's more, in and out of meditation, the monks were more serene. They were far less likely to panic or get upset, no matter what happened to them.

Dr. Richard Davidson, whose research on neuroplasticity I mentioned in Chapter 4, has also done groundbreaking work with Buddhist monks, whom the Dalai Lama persuaded to volunteer for experiments studying the relationship between meditation, neuroplasticity, and brain activity. Dr. Davidson asked novice meditators as well as the monks, who'd spent more than 10,000 hours over the past thirty years practicing meditation, to engage in five different kinds of meditation while they measured their brain activity. The one that had the greatest effect was a "lovingkindness" meditation designed to focus on compassion. Dr. Davidson discovered that during meditation, the more experienced monks had much higher levels of brain activity in their left prefrontal cortex, indicating happiness, empathy, and other positive emotions, than in their right prefrontal cortex, the area associated with anxiety and depression. This positive style of brain functioning was also found outside the period of meditation. In her book, *Train Your Mind, Change Your Brain,* the science journalist Sharon Begley explains that the enduring effects of meditation are due to the brain's neuroplasticity: "Brain wiring responsible for negative emotions withers and that [wiring] responsible for compassion and happiness becomes stronger."

If you're bummed thinking you can't be happy because you haven't been a Buddhist monk for the past thirty years, don't be. Dr. Davidson's research showed that people who'd been meditating for only three months, twenty to thirty minutes a day, experienced significant physiological changes, reflecting greater happiness and health. Happily, you don't have to meditate for decades to have results.

Different Strokes for Different Folks

Sitting down for a twenty- to thirty-minute meditation session each day is a great habit for plugging in to Spirit, but it isn't the only way to meditate. In our interview, Happy 100 member and Tibetan Buddhist lama Anam Thubten Rinpoche told me about a meditation practice that anyone can do, anytime. I call it the Pause Practice: Seven times throughout the day, simply pause and just "be." Become aware of your breath, and for a minute or two let yourself experience the present moment—the only time you can really experience happiness. When I do the Pause Practice regularly, I notice a greater sense of peace, perspective, and renewed energy.

You can also find great stillness and serenity simply by being in nature. Karen, one of the Happy 100, told me that whenever she takes a long walk alone in the woods or on the beach, she finds herself falling naturally into the rhythm of her breath as she walks along. Listening to the sound of the wind, the birds, and the water quiets her mind and heart. When she can't get away, just looking out the window for a few minutes at the trees or the clouds will often melt away tension and touch something deep inside her.

At the end of this section, you'll find a meditation exercise that anyone can use to experience more inner calm and relaxation.

The Power of Prayer

Every spiritual tradition in the world includes prayer. For thousands of years, people have opened their hearts to a Higher Power through praying, a kind of hotline to the Divine.

Like meditation, prayer can take many different forms. In times of trouble, we pray for comfort, guidance, and healing, either for ourselves or for people we love. At other times, when beauty, love, or gratitude overwhelm us, we're moved to offer up prayers of thanksgiving and praise. What inspires us to pray isn't important—it's the prayer itself that plugs us in to Spirit.

Many studies show that praying has a strong impact on happiness, with thousands upon thousands of people reporting that prayer increases their sense of well-being, life satisfaction, and general happiness. Prayers can also have an influence on others, even from a distance. According to research, remote intercessory prayer has a positive effect on hospital patients' rates of recovery and healing.

In his book, *Healing Words,* Larry Dossey, MD, one of the world's foremost experts on the link between spirituality and health, describes experiments conducted by the Spindrift Organization of Salem, Oregon, measuring the effect of praying on simple biological systems such as sprouting seeds and yeast cultures. Repeated studies showed that seeds that were sent prayers germinated more quickly than identical seeds that weren't prayed for, and that the amount of prayer was also an important factor in effectiveness. The most fascinating finding of the Spindrift research is that *nondirected* prayer, which simply asks for

God's will to be done or for the best thing to happen, was more powerful than *directed* prayer, which asks for a specific result.

You can see the power of prayer in these two photos by Masuru Emoto, whose work I introduced in Chapter 5. On the left is a picture of crystals formed in regular tap water. On the right, the same tap water after people had sent it prayers from a distance.

Tap water before prayer

Tap water after prayer

A remarkable demonstration of the beautiful energy prayer creates!

When you cultivate your connection to your Higher Power, you begin to recognize the presence of that Power underlying everything around you more and more. Making time each day to find what the poet T. S. Eliot called "the still point of the turning world" is a crucial piece of the Happy for No Reason puzzle.

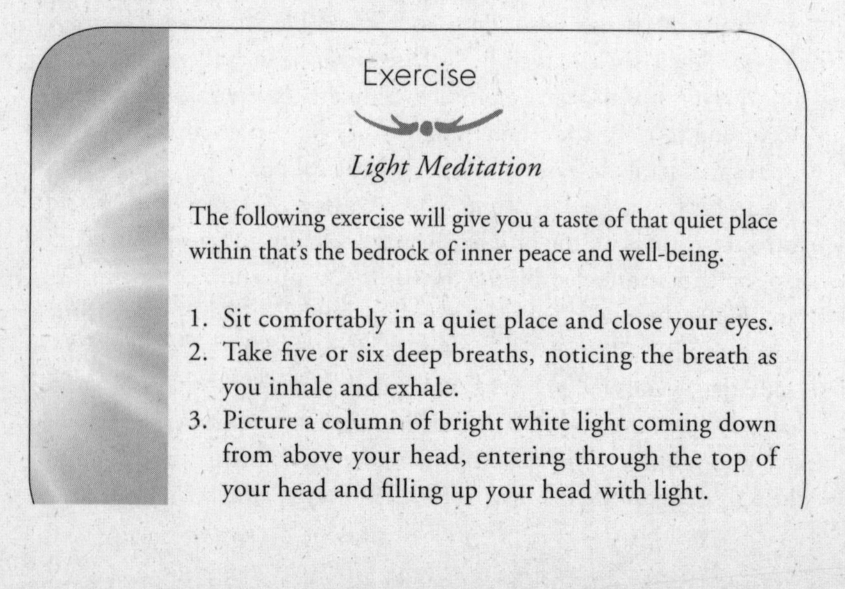

Exercise

Light Meditation

The following exercise will give you a taste of that quiet place within that's the bedrock of inner peace and well-being.

1. Sit comfortably in a quiet place and close your eyes.
2. Take five or six deep breaths, noticing the breath as you inhale and exhale.
3. Picture a column of bright white light coming down from above your head, entering through the top of your head and filling up your head with light.

4. Feel that white light flowing from your head down through your neck and into your chest, lighting up your heart. Feel the warmth and expansion in your heart area.
5. Continue to see the light flowing down your arms, your torso, your spine, and your hips, filling those areas with light. See the light flowing down through your legs and into your feet, lighting up the soles of your feet.
6. Feel your entire body flooded with warm, bright light. In this state, sit for ten minutes and just allow any thoughts and experiences to arise. Don't try to push away thoughts or control your mind—simply be with whatever comes. If you'd like a focus for your attention, notice your breath as you inhale and exhale.
7. When you feel ready to end your meditation, become aware of any peace and serenity you feel. Rest in this peaceful feeling for a moment. Take a few deep breaths and savor this feeling. This is the essence of being Happy for No Reason.
8. Slowly open your eyes. Have the intention to carry this experience with you as you return to your normal activities.

Happiness Habit for the Soul #2

Listen to Your Inner Voice

To make the right choices in life, you have to get in touch with your soul. To do this, you need to experience solitude . . .because in the silence you hear the truth and know the solutions.

—Deepak Chopra, MD, physician, author, and speaker

In the previous chapter, we discussed tuning in to your *body's* wisdom; here, we'll focus on listening to your *soul's* wisdom to guide you. Your inner voice is the part of you that knows what to do—at all times and in all situations. For some people, it's like finding the wise parent you always wished you'd had. For others, the experience of inner knowing is vaster and more cosmic. Whatever the flavor, the Happy 100 listen to this inner voice.

When I read Elizabeth Gilbert's book *Eat Pray Love,* I was immediately charmed and inspired by her description of her first "conversation" with God. After finishing the book, it was clear to me that Liz was one of the Happy 100, and I called her to set up an interview. I'm happy to report that Liz is as delightful in life as she is on the page; our interview added wonderful material to what she'd already shared in her book. The following story describes the transformation Liz experienced when she learned to hear "the still, small voice" inside her.

Liz's Story

Hello, God. I'm Liz.

I was in the upstairs bathroom of the big house in the suburbs of New York which I'd recently purchased with my husband. It was a cold November, around three o'clock in the morning. My husband was sleeping in our bed. I was hiding in the bathroom for something like the forty-seventh consecutive night, and—just as during all those nights before—I was sobbing. Sobbing so hard, in fact, that a great lake of tears was spreading before me on the bathroom tiles, a veritable Lake Inferior of all my shame and fear and confusion and grief.

I don't want to be married anymore.

I was trying so hard not to know this, but the truth kept insisting itself to me. In daylight hours, I refused that thought, but at night it would consume me. What a catastrophe. How could I be such a jerk so as to proceed eight years into a marriage, only to leave it? We'd only just bought this house a year ago. Hadn't I wanted this nice house? Hadn't I loved it? So why was I haunting its halls every night now, howling like Medea? Wasn't I proud of all we'd accumulated—the prestigious home in the Hudson Valley, the apartment in Manhattan, the eight phone lines, the friends and the picnics and the parties, the weekends spent roaming the aisles of some box-shaped superstore of our choice, buying ever more appliances on credit? I had actively participated in every moment of the creation of this life—so why did I feel like none of it resembled me?

I don't want to be married anymore.

My husband was sleeping in the other room, in our bed. I equal parts loved him and could not stand him. The many reasons I didn't want to be this man's wife anymore are too personal and sad to share here. Much of it had to do with my problems, but a good portion of our troubles were related to his issues, as well. And because I would not ask anyone to believe that I am capable of reporting an unbiased version of our story, the chronicle of our marriage's failure will remain untold here.

I will also not discuss here all the reasons why I did still want to be his wife, or all his wonderfulness, or why I loved him and why I had married him and why I was unable to imagine life without him. Let it be sufficient to say that, on this night, he was still my lighthouse and my albatross in equal measure. The only thing more unthinkable than leaving was staying; the only thing more impossible than staying was leaving. I didn't want to destroy anything or anybody. I just wanted to slip quietly out the back door, without causing any fuss or consequences, and then not stop running until I reached Greenland.

This part of my story is not a happy one, I know. But I share it here because something was about occur on that bathroom floor that would change forever the progression of my life—almost like one of those crazy astronomical super-events when a planet flips over in outer space for no reason whatsoever, and its molten core shifts, relocating its poles and altering its shape radically, such that the whole mass of the planet suddenly becomes oblong instead of spherical. Something like that.

What happened was that I started to pray.

You know—like, to God.

Now this was a first for me. Culturally, though not theologically, I'm a Christian. Traditionally, I have responded to the transcendent mystics of all religions. I have always responded with breathless excitement to anyone who has ever said that God does not live in any one scripture or in a distant throne in the sky, but instead abides very close to us indeed—much closer than we can imagine, breathing right through our own hearts. I respond with gratitude to anyone who has ever voyaged to the center of that heart, and then has returned to the world with a report to the rest of us that God is *an experience of supreme love.*

In the middle of that dark November crisis, though, I was not interested in formulating my views on theology. I was interested only in saving my life. I had finally noticed that I seemed to have reached a state of hopeless and life-threatening despair, and it occurred to me that sometimes people in this state will approach God for help.

What I said to God through my gasping sobs was something like this: "Hello, God. How are you? I'm Liz. It's nice to meet you."

That's right—I was speaking to the creator of the universe as though we'd just been introduced at a cocktail party. But we work with what we know in this life, and these are the words I always use at the beginning of a relationship. In fact, it was all I could do to stop myself from saying, "I've always been a big fan of your work . . ."

"I'm sorry to bother you so late at night," I continued. "But I'm in serious trouble. And I'm sorry I haven't ever spoken directly to you before, but I do hope that I have always expressed ample gratitude for all the blessings that you've given me in my life."

This thought caused me to sob even harder. God waited me out. I pulled myself together enough to go on: "I'm not an expert at praying, as you know. But can you please help me? I'm in desperate need of help. I don't know what to do. I need an answer. Please tell me what to do. Please tell me what to do. Please tell me what to do . . ."

And so the prayer narrowed itself down to that simple entreaty—*Please tell me what to do*—repeated again and again. I don't know how many times I begged. I only know that I begged like someone who was pleading for her life. And the crying went on forever.

Until—quite abruptly—it stopped.

Quite abruptly, I found that I was not crying anymore. I'd stopped crying, in fact, in mid-sob. My misery had been completely vacuumed out of me. I lifted my forehead off the floor and sat up in surprise, wondering if I would now see some Great Being who had taken my weeping away. But nobody was there. I was just alone. But not really alone, either. I was surrounded by something I can only describe as a little pocket of silence—a silence so rare that I didn't want to exhale, for fear of scaring it off. I was seamlessly still. I don't know when I'd ever felt such stillness.

Then I heard a voice. Please don't be alarmed—it was not an Old Testament Hollywood Charlton Heston voice, nor was it a voice telling me I must build a baseball field in my backyard. It was merely my own voice, speaking from within my own self. But this was my voice as I had never heard it before. This was my voice, but perfectly wise, calm and compassionate. This is what my voice would sound like if I'd only ever experienced love and certainty in my life. How can I describe the warmth of affection in that voice, as it gave me the answer that would forever seal my faith in the divine?

The voice said: *Go back to bed, Liz.*

I exhaled.

It was so immediately clear that this was the only thing to do. I would not have accepted any other answer. I would not have trusted a great booming voice that said either *You Must Divorce Your Husband!* or *You Must Not Divorce Your Husband!* Because that's not true wisdom. True wisdom gives the only possible answer at any given moment, and that night, going back to bed was the only possible answer. *Go back to bed,* said this omniscient interior voice, because you don't need to know the final answer right now, at three o'clock in the morning on a Thursday in November. *Go back to bed,* because I love you. *Go back to bed,* because the only thing you need to do for now is get some rest and take care of yourself until you do know the answer. *Go back to bed,* so that when the tempest comes, you'll be strong enough to deal with it. And the tempest is coming, dear one. Very soon. But not tonight. Therefore:

Go back to bed, Liz.

I call what happened that night, not a religious *conversion,* but the beginning of a religious *conversation.* The first words of an open and exploratory dialogue that would, ultimately, bring me very close to God, indeed.

In the years since then, I've found that voice again and again in times of code-orange distress. I've learned that the best way for me to reach it is through written conversation. I take out my most private notebook, which I keep next to my bed in case I'm ever in emergency trouble, and begin to write. And even during the worst of suffering, that calm, compassionate, affectionate and infinitely wise voice (who is maybe me, or maybe not exactly me) is always available for a conversation on paper at any time of the day or night.

At the beginning of my spiritual experiment, I didn't always have such faith in this internal voice of wisdom. I remember once reaching for my private notebook in a bitter fury of rage and sorrow, and scrawling a message to my inner voice—to my divine interior comfort—that took up an entire page of capital letters:

"I DO NOT BELIEVE IN YOU!!!!!!!!"

After a moment, still breathing heavily, I felt a clear pinpoint of light ignite within me, and then I found myself writing this amused and ever-calm reply:

"Who are you talking to, then?"

I have never doubted its existence again.

Today my connection to God, the voice inside my heart, is the foremost relationship in my life. And the way that I honor that relationship is to keep my life as calm as possible so that I can hear that voice. I consider this my primary devotional practice.

Still, it's not as if I'm laminated over with bliss. When crises come up, they shake me and shock me, just like everybody else. I definitely live in the real world, reacting to all the unexpected and unexplainable events that occur. The difference now is that I try not to react in a way that fights what is happening; instead I surrender to what's in front of me.

This doesn't mean that it's always easy or that when my life appears to be destroyed, I can run around being happy and excited about it. What it does mean, is that my job—and this is where prayer comes in—is to remain connected and conscious enough to ask the universe (or God or whatever I choose to call this power at that moment) the question, "What is it exactly that you're asking me to do here that I'm not getting yet? Open my eyes to see how I'm supposed to be using this."

Instead of praying as a lament, I pray as an information-gathering inquiry: "Can you please show me what I'm supposed to do right now?" I always assume there is something that I'm supposed to do or understand, even if I can't see it right at the moment.

What generally happens is that I get clearer about my reaction. It's like doing a CAT scan on myself that shows me my pockets of resistance—where I'm saying, "No, I don't accept that." Where I'm holding on and holding out. Where I'm saying, "I'm totally in accordance with the universe, and I really do trust the Divine force, but not this one thing—that's the deal breaker." And that's not surrender.

When I stop resisting what's happening and surrender, then I'm happy again. But that surrender only seems to come to me through that question and answer sesson, that prayerful inquiry.

Since that night in the bathroom, when I first I introduced myself to God, my life has turned around completely. Where there was neurosis and misery, there's now peace and fulfillment.

The loving wise voice is such a part of me now. When I find myself getting anxious or upset, that voice always asks me, "Are you really going to fall for this after all we've been through? Don't you know better? Haven't you learned?" I *do* know better and I *have* learned.

Which is why praying has become a moment-by-moment practice—a commitment I've made about how I'm going to live. It is this repeated experience of talking to God—asking and listening and then hearing the answer—that keeps me on the path toward greater and greater happiness. The other night I said, "How can I ever thank you, God?"

The calm, amused voice inside made me smile: *"Keep in touch."*

✵ ✵ ✵

Opening the Lines of Communication

Many of us have a tendency when making decisions to run around asking everybody and their mother what we should do, forgetting that whenever we check in and *ask ourselves,* we get a reliable answer. As Liz discovered, we each have an inner wisdom that's connected to Spirit, and it's available to us at all times.

Listening to your inner voice plugs you in to something bigger than yourself. You can ask questions of this inner voice about your life purpose, relationships, career—anything you want to know. You'll know you've made contact by the peace and utter fearlessness you experience in connection with the answers you receive.

There are many techniques for inner listening. Here are a few ways to pose a question and see what answers emerge:

Write it Down: Like Liz, some people find that inner listening works best on paper. When you have a question, sit quietly, inquire within, and then write whatever comes to you *without censoring.* No one is going to see this but you. Let the deepest part of your being flow through you.

Go to a Book: Another way to ask for guidance is to go to a book you are drawn to, open up randomly to a page, and see what message you discover there. You may pooh-pooh this technique, but I've found that it's often remarkably apt and helpful. Some people find that it allows them to break free of their own fixed ideas about a situation and see a new angle or perspective. I find it amazing how many times the exact answer I need is right there.

Look for Signs: Here's another one that may have your eyes rolling, but when I was writing my *Chicken Soup* books, I was astounded at how many people sent in stories about asking for signs. The most common sign people received came in the form of a bluebird or a cardinal. It got to the point where my coauthors and I had a separate file drawer for what we called the Bluebird/Cardinal Stories. The sheer number of these stories was impressive and made me look at asking for signs—and bluebirds and cardinals—in a whole new light.

Sergio and I were once stumped about whether or not we should rent a certain house. There were a lot of great things about this particular house, but we were genuinely torn. Thinking, *Why not?* I asked for a sign. As we walked toward the house to look at it one more time, I saw a dead bird, right in the middle of the path. It wasn't a bluebird or a cardinal, but it gave me enough pause to make me decide to wait until the next day before calling the landlord and taking the house.

First thing the next morning, I noticed a new listing in the paper for a house that sounded promising. Sergio and I ran right over to look. As we walked toward the front door, a beautiful deer crossed the path. Deer are my favorite animals, so I took it as a sign. The house was perfect. We immediately signed a lease and lived there happily for two years before buying our present house. Was it really a sign? Who can say? In this case, being open to a larger source of wisdom helped me get in touch with how I was really feeling about the house and guided me toward the better decision.

When you know that you can always go inside to find direction and wisdom, an unshakable peace and confidence dawns. The following exercise guides you through an inner listening process.

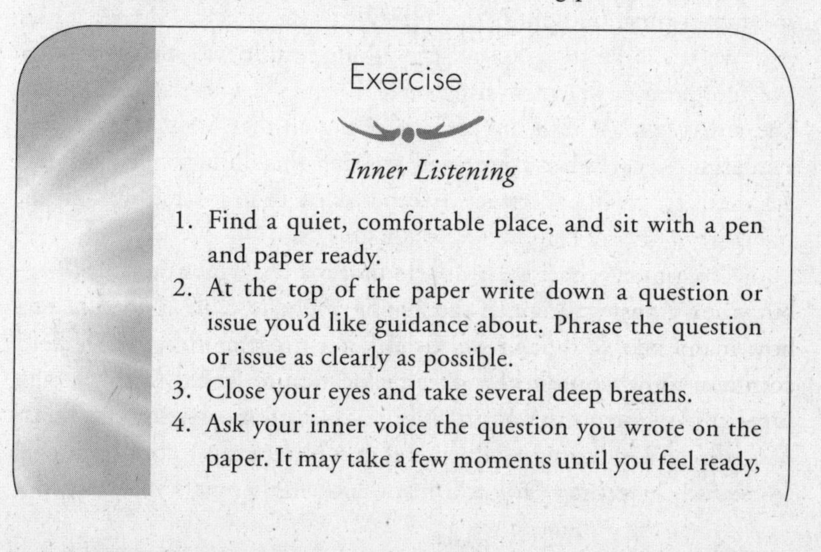

Exercise

Inner Listening

1. Find a quiet, comfortable place, and sit with a pen and paper ready.
2. At the top of the paper write down a question or issue you'd like guidance about. Phrase the question or issue as clearly as possible.
3. Close your eyes and take several deep breaths.
4. Ask your inner voice the question you wrote on the paper. It may take a few moments until you feel ready,

but when you do, open your eyes and start writing whatever comes to you. It doesn't matter whether it makes sense or not. Keep writing until your hand feels like it won't move any longer, not reading what you have written as you go.

5. Now read over what you've written. You may be quite surprised at what wisdom has come out. Even a single word or phrase may be the key to your answer.

Happiness Habit for the Soul #3
Trust Life's Unfolding

The winds of grace are always blowing, but you have to raise the sail.
—Sri Ramakrishna, nineteenth-century Indian saint

I discovered in my interviews that the vast majority of the Happy 100 experience a sense of surrender in their lives and feel profoundly taken care of by a universal power. They trust that the universe is out to support them (Guiding Principle #2).

We try so hard to control everything in our lives that we forget the profound power of putting our faith in the universe and letting go. When you get into the habit of doing all that *you* can, then surrendering to a Higher Power and trusting that things will work out for the best, you'll experience a deeper sense of peace and well-being, hallmarks of being Happy for No Reason.

Reverend Michael Beckwith, founder of the Agape Spiritual Center in Los Angeles, is one of the Happy 100 whose life is lived in surrender. Anyone who has met Michael, been to one of his services, or seen him on TV can feel his deep connection to Spirit. Michael, who appears with me in *The Secret,* is also a colleague of mine on the Transformational Leadership Council, a group of 100 top transformational leaders who meet regularly to enhance our effectiveness and contribution to the world. Every time I'm with Michael, I feel so uplifted, I just want to shout *Amen!* Interviewing Michael was a treat, and his story, which follows, has stayed with me, inspiring me to let go and trust in new ways.

Michael's Story

Love-Beauty

As a child, I can remember feeling naturally attuned to the divinity all around me. Children, so fresh from their Source, often feel this way. There were times when I just knew I was standing face-to-face with my Higher Self, my God-essence—though I didn't call it that at the time.

An example of that connection occurred on my eleventh birthday, when my mother and I were visiting my grandmother. I was sent to the corner store to buy some groceries. As I stood in the bread aisle pondering which loaf to choose, all at once time suspended. Space dissolved, and my sight was no longer limited to Roman Meal versus Wonder Bread. I "saw" that a jar of baby food was about to fall in the next aisle. I tore around the corner just in time to catch it, much to the amazement of the man who had knocked it off the shelf. "How . . . how did you do that?" he stuttered.

"I don't know," I innocently replied, "I just saw it."

Walking home I felt an expansive oneness with all that was before me: the trees were singing, the grass had its own language—everything was alive, shimmering with a high-frequency life force. As I approached the house, my mother, grandmother, and uncle were standing on the stoop, affectionately smiling down at me. A mystical pain entered my heart as I realized that the boy they saw was not the Michael I knew myself to be. At that moment, I consciously shut down my cosmic connection and began conforming myself to labels that boxed me into being someone that everyone would be comfortable around. The price was the loss of my contact with Divinity.

I lived inside that box for another ten years. Whenever an expansion in awareness popped up, I managed to shut it back down. One of these incidents took place in my first year of junior high, when I was nominated to be school treasurer. I was terrified of public speaking and had to face a campaign trail that took me from class to class, and ultimately before the entire student body to present my four-point plan for "Banking with Beckwith." When the big day arrived, I sat in my seat, dreading the moment I would have to speak. When my name was called I walked up to the podium, forced open my mouth, and was shocked to hear myself talking about excellence and the greatness within each of us waiting to emerge—none of which was even one of my four points! My audience was as astonished as I was, evidenced by the hundreds of wide-eyed stares that followed me to my seat. I had been flung out of my box. To cover my embarrassment, for the next week I uncharacteristically exuded a bad attitude and got into fights—anything to conform to the unwritten preadolescent rule to be a regular guy. I wasn't yet ready to break my agreement with mediocrity.

The religious affiliation of my youth shed no light on my mystical experiences. In high school, disillusioned by ministers who didn't practice what they preached and dogma being taught that just didn't add up, I announced my atheism. By my freshman year of college at Morehouse, my atheism had evolved into agnosticism. I hadn't yet come into contact with a spiritual path that matched my inner experience.

From Morehouse I transferred to the University of Southern California as a psychology major. I'd grown up in an era when smoking marijuana was somewhat the norm, so, like many students, I smoked some pot. To supplement my income for this extra expense, I began selling a little pot myself. What started off as a simple cottage industry became a network that stretched from Los Angeles to Atlanta, Nashville, and New York, bringing in thousands of dollars a week.

While I was attending classes, writing term papers, and running my business, I was also entering a spiritual awakening. During this period I had visions and heard voices. But when I did a psychology internship working with mentally ill prisoners who also heard voices and saw visions, I began to consider my experiences pathological. My first antidote was to cut back on smoking weed, but this only intensified my experiences! Then something happened that made it impossible to keep turning my back on God.

For about a year I'd been having a recurring dream of being chased by three men. I'd always wake up before they grabbed me, but with each recurring dream they got a little closer. Finally, one night, they caught me.

As I struggled with my dream captors, I saw a tent with hundreds of people I knew standing in line to enter. I shouted to them for help, but they all turned their backs on me. While two of the men held me down, the third plunged a knife into my heart. The pain was excruciating. I screamed out, and then I died.

When I awoke from this dream, reality as I knew it had profoundly shifted. I clearly sensed a luminous presence connecting everything and everyone. It penetrated my soul with total and unconditional love; its beauty, as it moved through the animate and inanimate objects all around me, was beyond my power to describe. Still agnostic, I didn't give this presence a name—I simply called it Love-Beauty. The person who had spent so many years burying his connection to God had died; I could never fit back into that box again.

I began a voracious study of both Eastern and Western spirituality and mysticism. I discovered that when the culture and history of the world's religions are stripped away, what remains are universally applicable spiritual principles. These explorations in consciousness were the final motivation I needed to stop selling dope. There was one last shipment—the only one ever stored at my house—that required handling. But before I could get rid of it, I got busted.

Because of the size of my operation, the charges were serious, and I was facing significant jail time. Well-meaning friends offered their advice, from "Plea bargain" to "Take your money and leave the country." But I could no longer relate to myself as a drug dealer. My spiritual transformation had made me a new person and I knew, even beyond faith, that the new me wasn't going to jail.

Throughout the days of the trial I sat in the courtroom calmly reading books on spiritual subjects. On a day that seemed no different from any other, my lawyer suddenly shot out of his chair and made a point about a technicality. The judge called for a three-day recess. The day court resumed, I don't think I will ever forget the sound of the judge's gavel striking his podium as he pronounced: "Case dismissed!" However, he wasn't quite finished with me and asked that I approach his bench. "That was a lucky break, young man. I hope I *never* see you in my court again," he admonished.

I looked him straight in the eye and said, "You never will."

I went home. The wind was blowing fiercely, which caused me to look up at my neighbor's weathervane as I walked up the path to my door. I couldn't resist an urge to demand one last validation of my transformation, so, concentrating on the weathervane, with inner authority I said: "I believe. Heal any remainder of my unbelief. If the Presence is as real as I know it is, make the weathervane go against the wind, point in my direction and . . ."

Before I could complete my sentence the weathervane was pointing right at me, even though the wind current had not changed. I started crying. In that moment I completely surrendered my life to the Presence, knowing that this Presence was going to somehow make use of my life in its service.

By the age of twenty-seven, my hair was on fire to know truth. Whenever I heard about a teacher who lived the Presence authentically, I was there. From silent retreats, to long hours of meditation, to spiritual discourses, nothing broke the blissful tempo of my days on this profoundly private path. Until the day when, in a gentle yet firm tone, the voice within said, "It's time to go public."

Perhaps the greatest proof of my transformation was my resounding "Yes!" I left the anonymity of my solitary spiritual journey and enrolled in a New Thought–Ancient Wisdom school of ministry, clear that my purpose was not to become a minister, but rather to find a context in which to honor my "Yes" to the Presence. Besides, I wanted my weekends free! Eventually, I became a licensed spiritual counselor and for many years had a practice doing one-on-one prayer sessions and spiritual therapy.

Still, my inner voice relentlessly urged me to go more public. Little by little my resistance dissipated. As I spoke about universal wisdom to increasingly larger audiences, I experienced that I could stand in a place that was inwardly comfortable—the presence of God—and that when I got out of the way that presence could flow through me.

In 1985 an inner vision revealed a transdenominational, transreligious spiritual community where God's only religion—Love—was taught and celebrated. It was a foretelling of the Agape International Spiritual Center, which I founded in 1986 and which has grown to include thousands of members.

Today, the "Yes" is always there. Though I don't always know what serving the Presence will look like, I always have faith and trust in it. When I surrender to the Presence, it always works out.

The Presence is not going to let me down, because I'm here representing it. Like each one of us, I've been hired by the Universe to be myself.

Having a Yes Mind

Sometimes, when I feel frazzled and tired of my self-appointed position as general manager of the Universe, I think of Michael and remind myself that I, too, am being taken care of by Love-Beauty. Though he's one of the lucky ones who was born feeling his oneness with Spirit, we all have the same connection. Our experience of Happy for No Reason grows exponentially when we trust that connection enough to let it direct our lives.

Throughout history, the wisest men and women have known that their highest good came from surrender—not as in losing a battle, but as in letting go of their personal limitations and aligning totally with an intelligence greater than themselves. Remember the Spindrift experiments? According to their research, the prayers that have the greatest effect are the ones that simply invite the presence and influence of a Higher Power rather than asking for a specific outcome. This demonstrates the power of that classic expression of surrender, "Thy will be done."

Trusting and letting go in this way brings enormous peace and freedom and creates what I call a "yes mind." Instead of saying no and resisting what's happening, you say yes. I had my first experience of the yes mind when I took improvisational acting classes many years ago.

One of the rules of improv is to respond instantly and enthusiastically—to say yes—to whatever another actor throws at you. During my first class, when my improv partner told me that I was an elderly rock star, I immediately began to play the part: strumming air guitar, clutching my lower back, and belting out lyrics as I gyrated like an eighty-year-old. In the next moment, the scene switched. Suddenly, I was supposed to be an alien coming to earth to rob a bank—and I had to go with it. I just said yes. The exercise broke my boundaries and freed my energy. I found it was a great practice for how to live.

When you say yes, it's like being a trapeze artist; you're able to let go of the trapeze you're holding on to and sail through the air toward the next one. Without letting go and then trusting that the next trapeze is there, that forward motion is impossible. Surrender and trust create a feeling of flow in every moment.

Amazing Grace

One of my greatest spiritual mentors is Bill Bauman, a former priest and the most centered and grounded person I've ever met. Though Bill has a deceptively unassuming demeanor—he'd fit right in as a greeter at Wal-Mart—I like to call him the enlightened Mister Rogers, for beneath that comforting cardigan beats the heart of a spiritual hero. He's been the guardian angel of this book, and both Carol and I deeply appreciate his help and counsel.

Bill was one of the first of the Happy 100 I interviewed, one of the handful of people obviously Happy for No Reason I knew personally when I began the book. When I think of Bill, I think of a life filled with grace.

Grace, Bill explains, "is just a fancy word for the infinite, unconditional, all-responsive love of God flowing in our lives." He uses the analogy of the unconditional love a mother feels for a newborn child. "The mother sees no flaws in the child, only utter perfection and utter deservingness; in her love, she wants nothing more than to give and give and give. Now move that example up to the infinite level. Our Higher Power sees the perfection, the worthiness, the absolute wonder of who we are—and in that love, wants nothing more than just to give gifts, to give blessings, to give solutions."

In our interview, Bill told me about an experience that illustrates how he allows grace to flow in his life:

> A number of years ago, my wife, Donna, and I decided to "start over" in a whole new area of the country. We left our old lives behind—including our old level of income. About a year after our relocation, we found ourselves low on funds; we were doing our best, but there just wasn't enough money coming in yet.
>
> We decided to take a day off and spend some time at a nearby Trappist monastery, hanging out in their church and opening ourselves to grace.
>
> As Donna and I sat together in the chapel, we didn't ask for anything specific; we didn't say "Please give us money"; we just invited grace. We sat quietly, with an attitude of openness and receptivity, and put ourselves in the presence of Divine Grace, in the presence of Abundance, in the presence of the maternal, all-loving expression of Universal Power. I remember thinking, "I don't have the ideal solution. Your response is always so much bigger than what I'd come up with anyway. I put myself in total connection to You. Whatever You send as the perfect response to this situation, I'm open to."
>
> That was Phase One. After an hour or so, we left the monastery and started Phase Two, which was to just let it all go. We went about our lives, trusting that the perfect response would happen.
>
> The very next day, we received a call from our accountant telling us that he'd just come across a mistake he'd made and was sending us a check for $6,000. That same afternoon, Donna got a call from the local college, offering her a summer teaching job and a full-time position for the next year.
>
> Then, two days later, we got a $3,500 check in the mail from an insurance company we'd never heard of, paying on a policy we never knew we had. An hour later, another phone call came in, offering me a consulting job.

I was surprised and I wasn't. Though I had no doubt that something would happen, the generosity and speed of the response was astounding. I guess that's why they call it amazing grace.

When I asked Bill how we can all learn to live in grace, he said, "By practicing surrender. Look for opportunities to be open to blessings, without defining too clearly what they should be, and then trust and let go."

For those of us locked in the "I'm in charge" and "I have to take control" approach to life, surrendering starts by simply inviting ourselves to believe that our Higher Power will respond to our needs and being open to the flow of grace when it comes. This gentle invitation is a great tool for letting go and trusting life to unfold—gracefully.

People living in that perpetual state of surrender and trust often report increased experiences of synchronicity in their lives: amazing coincidences, uncanny "luck," unexpected aid, and perfect timing—simply being in the right place at the right time. When you experience a lot of synchronicities, it's a sign that you are plugged in to Spirit.

Exercise

Inviting Grace

This simple exercise reinforces the *No Tension* step of the Secret Formula you learned in Chapter 2: Intention, Attention, No Tension.

1. Sit quietly and write a letter to your Higher Power about a situation in your life that you would like assistance with (for example, relationship, health, job). Write from your heart.
2. Ask that the perfect people, places, and circumstances be brought to you for the deepest fulfillment of that situation. You may want to ask for right understanding or forgiveness, if appropriate.

3. Put the letter somewhere meaningful to you where it won't be disturbed. Some people like to put their letter in a special book, in a sacred place in their home, or under a rock in their garden. You won't be looking at it again for a while.
4. Now, *let go*. Turn the situation over to a Higher Power. Relax, feel grateful, and invite yourself to believe that the universe is always supporting you.
5. Notice what happens over the next days or weeks. You may want to look at your letter in a month or two and see how the universe responded.

Summary and Happiness Action Steps

When you plug in to Spirit by taking time for silence, listening to your inner voice, and trusting life's unfolding, your experience of Happy for No Reason inevitably grows. Plugging in to Spirit strengthens the final pillar of your Home for Happiness. Use the following action steps to practice the Happiness Habits for the Soul:

1. Make silence, meditation, or prayer part of your daily routine.
2. Do the Pause Practice seven times a day for a week and see how you feel.
3. Look for guidance by posing questions in a journal, opening to a page in a book, or asking for a sign.
4. Practice surrender: invite yourself to believe that the universe is out to support you, send out an intention for your higher good, and then *let go*.

*T*he Roof—Live a Life Inspired by Purpose

There are two great days in a person's life—the day we are born and the day we discover why.

—William Barclay, twentieth-century Scottish theologian

I'm sure you've heard at some time in your life, "We're all here for a purpose." Yet if you polled the first 100 people you met on the street about their purpose, most of them would probably answer with a sigh, "I don't have a clue." Although there are people who sail through life graced with a sense of direction and clarity, many others feel they've missed the boat.

Happy people feel they are on the planet for some purpose. In my interviews with the Happy 100, I heard the same thing again and again: they live inspired, moment to moment, by a sense of purpose and meaning.

So, what is your purpose? Contrary to popular belief, your purpose isn't your job or profession—it's much bigger than that. It's an overarching intention to do what's meaningful to you in your life. For example, my purpose is sharing my love and energy by inspiring others to lead their highest life possible. Right now I happen to be a transformational speaker and writer, but I could fulfill that purpose in any number of other ways. I could be a teacher, a musician, a secretary, a doctor, a gardener. Living inspired by purpose can take many forms—the real key is to first discover the sense of meaning and purpose within you.

The research on happiness clearly shows that people who are deeply committed to whatever gives their life meaning are much happier than those who don't have this greater sense of purpose. According to the psychologist Edward Diener, who researches subjective well-being in the Department of Psychology at the University of Illinois at Urbana–Champaign, one of the vital ingredients for happiness is "having a meaning in life . . . and having goals embedded in your long-term values that you're working for, but also that you find enjoyable." Health and longevity studies show that when people live with a sense of purpose, no matter how big or small, they live longer and healthier lives.

Purpose, Meaning, and Work

Your purpose is the roof of your Home for Happiness. When you don't have that sense of purpose, it's like having a leaky roof; it can rain unhappiness over every other aspect of your life. Unfortunately there seem to be a lot of leaky roofs in the world today. According to a 2005 study released by the research company Harris Interactive, only 20 percent of working Americans are passionate about their work. That means that four out of five people aren't inspired by what they do. This statistic makes it clear why the largest number of heart attacks occur on Monday mornings. People would literally rather die than go to work.

Many people work at jobs just to pay the bills, feeling they don't have the freedom, skills, or opportunity to find employment they really like. They resign themselves to a life without a sense of deeper purpose, making the best of a bad situation and living for the weekends. Others spend years searching for the perfect job, like Goldilocks, trying to find something that's *just right*. Of those, a lucky few do find careers that are fulfilling, but unless they're inspired by a sense of inner purpose, that fulfillment is fragile. Their happiness depends on their job, so if they lose their job or retire, they feel adrift and quickly lose that sense of direction and satisfaction in life.

The statistics on retirement bear this out. It's been reported that the happiest retirees are those who still feel a sense of purpose even after their career is over. These people often transfer their skill set to another setting. A retired banker might volunteer at a job training center, or an employee who was always handy might become the neighborhood Mr. Fix-it. The important thing is to let your purpose lead the way.

Job, Career, or Calling

Do you consider your daily activity a job, a career, or a calling? The following story illustrates the difference:

> One day an old woman walked up to a dusty building site where three strong, young men were working hard laying bricks. She walked up to the first man and asked him what he was doing. He replied rather rudely, "Can't you see? I'm laying bricks. This is what I do all day—I just lay bricks." She then asked the second man what he was doing. He replied, "I'm a bricklayer and I'm doing my work. I take pride in my craft, and I'm happy that what I do here feeds my family." As she walked up to the third man, she could see that his eyes were full of joy and his face was as bright as the day. When she posed the same question to him, he replied with great enthusiasm, "Oh, I'm building the most beautiful cathedral in the whole world."

It isn't the activity in your life that defines your feeling of purpose, it's your perspective. Organizational psychologist Amy Wrzesniewski of New York University conducted research on people's work orientations based on these three categories: job, career, or calling. She found that, regardless of the job itself, those who feel they're following a calling experience greater satisfaction from their work and more happiness in their lives.

If You're Not in the Job You Love, Love the Job You're In

People who are Happy for No Reason, whether or not they're in their ideal career or calling, bring a sense of purpose with them wherever they go and to whatever they're doing—even the most mundane of tasks. Whether they're changing the oil in the car or preparing a family meal, they're still inspired by purpose. Their sense of purpose isn't "out there." In fact, if you took away whatever a happy person is currently inspired to do, he or she would simply find something else to be inspired by.

I once heard a story about the great conductor Arturo Toscanini. On his eightieth birthday, someone asked Toscanini's son, Walter, what his father ranked as his most important achievement. Walter answered, "For my father there can be no such thing. Whatever he happens to be doing at the moment is the biggest thing in his life—whether it's conducting a symphony or peeling an orange."

As we were writing this chapter, Carol told me how a sense of purpose once saved her from misery in a job:

> When I graduated from college with a degree in literature, there wasn't a huge demand for literature grads in the marketplace. Although I wasn't sure what I wanted to do with my life, I needed to pay my rent, so I took a position as a receptionist for a busy stock brokerage firm. While the job had a lot of perks, there was one big problem: I hated being a receptionist. Answering a phone all day was alternately stressful and boring. Within a month, I loathed getting up in the morning, and my unhappiness at work was coloring my whole life. I knew I had two choices: I could find another job or find a way to like the one I had. I decided to do both. While I looked for other employment, I searched for a way to be happier where I was.
>
> I challenged myself to become "the best receptionist in the world." Because I'd always had a very strong sense of wanting to serve others and make a difference, I wrote the word SERVICE in big letters across the blotter on my desk. I answered the phone with a smile in my voice, learned to recognize frequent callers' voices and address them by name. I'd heard the quote from cosmetic tycoon Mary Kay Ash, "Pretend that every single person you

meet has a sign around his or her neck that reads, Make Me Feel Important," and I put that concept into practice. I joked around with the brokers and other staff and generally made my work day a party. Not only did my happiness level skyrocket, but within a month, I was promoted to a more interesting job within the brokerage. Though I eventually found a way to make my living that suited me much better, I've never forgotten how I managed to turn that job—and my happiness level—around.

Being connected to purpose expands you and helps you feel inspired in each moment, which naturally leads to more success. As Albert Schweitzer said, "*Success is not the key to happiness. Happiness is the key to success. If you love what you are doing, you will be successful.*"

Look at the symptoms of contraction and expansion to see if you are "on course" in the purpose department.

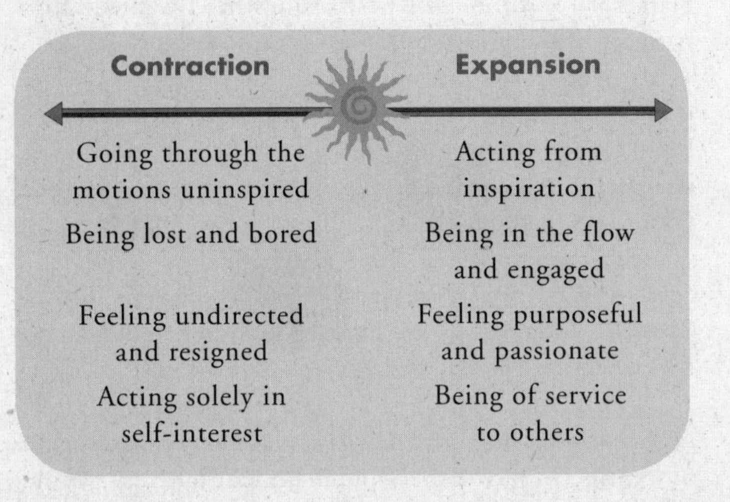

Living an inspired life supports your happiness and the happiness of all those who are touched by you.

Happiness Habits for a Life of Purpose

1. Find Your Passion
2. Follow the Inspiration of the Moment
3. Contribute to Something Greater Than Yourself

Happiness Habit for a Life of Purpose #1
Find Your Passion

When we learn to say a deep, passionate yes to the things that really matter, then peace begins to settle onto our lives like golden sunlight sifting to a forest floor.

—Thomas Kinkaide, artist

All right, you're saying, *I'm sold! I want to live inspired by purpose. But how do I start?* The clues that lead you to your unique and individual purpose are yours for the asking. All you need to do is stop.

That's right—just stop.

Take the time to step out of your busy life and investigate your inner landscape. Being totally honest and fearless, ask yourself: What am I passionate about? What do I love to do? What *truly matters* to me? The answers—your passions—are like a bread-crumb trail leading you to your purpose.

A great way to get in touch with your passions is to take The Passion Test, developed by Happy 100 member Janet Attwood. Janet has been one of my dearest friends for twenty-five years, and I've seen how using The Passion Test has transformed her life and the lives of so many others. She's a shining example of the joy that comes from this inner connection to purpose. Her story describes the path that led her to discover The Passion Test, now a #1 best-selling book, coauthored with her ex-husband, best friend, and business partner, Chris Attwood.

Janet's Story

Singing and Dancing under the Streetlight

There was once a little girl who loved everyone and everything—especially her mommy. The little girl and her mother used to read stories, watch movies, laugh and sing together for hours. For both of them, every moment they were with each other was filled with the most delicious joy.

In those happy days, the little girl would sometimes go outside in the evening and sing and dance under the streetlight on the sidewalk in front of her house. She imagined herself performing someday in front of thousands of people, touching their hearts.

When the little girl was about seven, her mother started drinking. Gone was the gentle sweet voice that had so lovingly sung her to sleep and tucked her into bed every single night of her life. Instead, the little girl heard her mother and father screaming at each other at the top of their lungs. No matter how many promises the little girl's mother gave, she continued to drink. Things just got worse and worse, until one day the little girl's mother was committed to a mental institution.

When she was finally released, she just started drinking again. After that, the little girl's mother moved away, going in and out of halfway houses. The little girl lost track of her mother and used to read the obituaries in the paper, terrified she'd find her mother's name there. Unable to understand the anger she felt, the little girl took it out on everyone around her—and on herself.

As the years passed, the little girl became more and more unhappy.

At seventeen she was physically abused.

At eighteen she was strung out on drugs.

At nineteen she was living with heroin addicts and riding with the Hell's Angels. Life became one long rhythm of drugs, sex, and depression. The little girl knew if she didn't change her life, she would end up just like her mother . . .

That little girl was me.

At twenty, determined to avoid my mother's fate, I cleaned up my act. With the help of my brother, I found a place to live, got a job, and learned to meditate. I began reading transformational books and listening to personal growth tapes. My life took a turn for the better, but I still felt something was missing. The jobs I took were all right, some better than others, but they barely paid the bills. At one point, I found myself working in Silicon Valley, recruiting disk drive engineers. This was *not* the job for me. I felt even more discouraged, and I wondered where I was going with my life.

One day I saw a poster for a seminar in San Francisco called "Yes to Success." *Maybe a little shot of positive attitude will turn my job around,* I thought.

The day of the seminar, I watched, intrigued, as Debra Poneman, an elegantly dressed woman in her early thirties, stepped to the front of the room and began to speak. Within a matter of minutes she had us all completely captivated and excited.

Debra told us about a survey that had been done of 100 of the most successful people in the United States, showing that all of these enduringly successful people had one thing in common.

"Can anyone guess what that one thing was?" she asked, looking around at the audience.

When no one raised their hand, she continued. "Each and every one of them had achieved the five most important elements in their lives *they felt* were necessary for their own success and fulfillment."

In that moment, the earth stood still.

"Would you please repeat that?" I asked, hardly able to contain myself.

"The one thing they all had in common was that each and every one of them had achieved the five most important elements in their

lives *they felt* were necessary for their own success and fulfillment."

Inside my head a voice screamed, "That's it! That's all I have to know. I just have to figure out what *I* feel are the five most important elements to living an ideal life, and then I can become just like those hundred successful people."

As I sat watching Debra speak, I thought about the elements I felt were necessary to create my ideal life—and realized that sharing transformational knowledge, in just the way Debra was doing, was what I wanted to do more than anything else in the whole world. The realization was so intense, it was almost painful. I felt as if I were birthing a whole new life! Then, in the very next moment, I became aware of an incredible inner calm, followed by the most peaceful feeling of happiness I had ever experienced. It came from the core of my being as I connected with what really mattered to me.

Driving home with the radio blaring, singing at the top of my lungs, I knew something miraculous was about to happen. I just didn't know what.

Within three weeks I'd quit my job as a recruiter and convinced Debra to hire me to give "Yes to Success" seminars. I never looked back. I spent the following years getting clearer and clearer about the five elements that would bring me my ideal life. I experimented, sometimes following what I thought I *should* do (not so good), and other times following my heart's desire (always good). When I was doing what I loved from the inside, the outside flowed in ever-widening streams of success and happiness.

This experience of clarifying the five things that mattered most to me was the beginning of The Passion Test, the simple process I developed for finding your purpose in life by identifying what you truly love and care about most. I firmly believe that what you love and God's will for you are one and the same.

A few years later, after taking hundreds of people through The Passion Test and seeing the dramatic results so many had, my best friend, business partner, and ex-husband, Chris Attwood, and I wrote a book called *The Passion Test* that became a #1 national best-seller. We also cofounded *Healthy Wealthy n Wise Magazine,* which has become the largest online transformational magazine in the world.

Today, I facilitate The Passion Test all over the world and work with thousands of people from all walks of life. I am living my passions, and life has truly become a magical adventure. The impact of it all really hit me some months ago when I was speaking to 200 homeless women in transition in Miami. These women had quit believing, quit dreaming, and given up. They mostly thought their life was over, except for the painful process of trying to eke out a mundane existence.

I shared with them some of the stories of my early life and then I took them through The Passion Test. I asked them to start making choices every day in favor of what they most cared about, what most lit their fire. I promised them that if they did this, little by little, they would find the energy to move toward a happier life. They would find the greatness that I knew was inside each of them.

As they gave me a standing ovation, excited about what they had discovered about themselves, tears welled up in my eyes. I thought of that little girl singing and dancing under the streetlight so many years ago, who had just wanted to touch people's hearts. I was living that little girl's dreams. The journey had brought me here to give the gift of love to these beautiful women, so much like my own mother.

Do What You Love, Love What You Do

The important thing is not to think much but to love much; and so do that which best stirs you to love.

—St. Teresa of Avila, sixteenth-century Spanish nun and mystic

What is it that makes your heart expand? What makes your soul sing? Most people are so busy going through the motions of their day that they don't pay attention. Sometimes it's subtle, but the clues to your passion always involve being interested, drawn, and intrigued.

The psychologist and author Mihaly Csikszentmihalyi, who is considered one of the world's leading researchers on positive psychology, calls that feeling of pure enjoyment you experience when you're fully involved doing something, "flow." Time may stop, or hours go by in what seem like minutes. You're naturally focused and not easily distracted. According to the University of Pennsylvania's Positive Psychology Center, one of the hubs of happiness research in this country, engaging in an activity that produces *flow* is so gratifying that people are willing to do it for its own sake, rather than for external incentives such as money. Looking for the places you experience flow in your life will help you steer toward your passions.

Janet says, "Once you've identified what you truly care about, choose in favor of your passions every day." Life is made up of choices; when you choose over and over to do the things that matter to you, it leads you to express your unique purpose in all areas and helps you draw more of what you want into your life—there's that Law of Attraction again!

I learned about doing what you love and loving what you do from my father. Dad absolutely loved being a dentist. He retired at age seventy-two, reluctantly. He wanted to find a new outlet for his talents, so he analyzed what he loved about dentistry. He realized it wasn't about putting fillings in people's mouths—it was that he loved working in intricate ways with his hands, in ways he felt were artistic.

So, at age seventy-two, Dad took up needlepoint—and loved it. He became a master needlepoint artist, winning awards throughout California. I remember going home one day for a visit when he was about eighty-five. He'd just begun the biggest and most intricate needlepoint project I've ever seen, a detailed depiction of the Tree of Life.

I asked him, "Dad, how long is this going to take you to finish?"

And he said, "Honey, I figure at the pace I'm going it's going to take me about four years."

Imagine, an eighty-five-year old man beginning a four-year project—but his passion for expressing his artistry gave him a strong sense of purpose. And did he complete that project? You bet he did! It was his greatest work of all. Today, it hangs proudly on the wall of my mother's living room in the same house that my parents shared for fifty-three years.

My dad taught me that feeling a sense of purpose allows you to bring joy to whatever it is you're doing.

Exercise

Identifying Your Passions

This exercise by Janet Attwood and Chris Attwood is the first step in getting clear about what really matters to you. When you go through the complete Passion Test, you will discover how to identify your top five passions and how to align your life with them. You can find the complete test in the book *The Passion Test,* or go to www.PassionTestOnline.com

1. On a piece of paper list at least ten things that will make your life and your work ideal. Complete the sentence, "When my life is ideal, I am____________." For example, "When my life is ideal, I am inspiring others with my love of writing" or "I am feeling healthy, fit, and energetic" or "I am enjoying healthy relationships with my friends and family."

   If you're stuck, think of things you absolutely don't want to have in your life, then turn them around. For example, if you feel, "When my life is ideal, I will never be around people who lie, cheat, or steal," turn it around to "When my life is ideal, I will always be surrounded by people who are honest, have the highest integrity, and love to give."
2. Now, think of four people you know who are not passionate about what they're doing in their lives. What do they talk about? Where is their attention focused? How do they treat the people they spend time with? List at least five behaviors you notice in these people.

   Do you see any of these behaviors in yourself? Can you see how any of these behaviors might sabotage your ability to live a purposeful life?
3. List five things you can do in the coming week to start changing these behaviors and begin aligning your life with the things you wrote down in Step 1 so you can live the passionate, purposeful life you deserve.

Happiness Habit for a Life of Purpose #2

Follow the Inspiration of the Moment

When you follow your bliss . . . doors will open where you would not have thought there would be doors; and where there wouldn't be a door for anyone else.

—Joseph Campbell, twentieth-century scholar and professor

When you're clear about your passions, you're lit by a fire inside that shows you what to do in each moment. You are led to inspired action. You know *what* you want to do in life, but you may not know *how* it will happen. Inspiration will lead you to the *how.*

Following your inspiration doesn't mean you do only the things that are easy. Inspiration gives you the courage and persistence to do *whatever* has to be done to fulfill your purpose—even if it's challenging or scary. When you're inspired, you act from a sense of inner purpose, not out of obligation or to get others' approval.

Rhonda Byrne is a shining example of someone who radiates happiness and is absolutely led by the inspiration of her soul. This guided her to create the film and book *The Secret,* which the *New York Times* calls the biggest phenomenon in the history of self-help. Rhonda was also named by *Time* magazine as one of the 100 most influential people in the world in 2006. Rhonda told us her story in an interview, and Carol and I then wrote the following account of the inspiration behind the remarkable unfolding of her film's release.

Rhonda's Story

Spreading *The Secret*

I'd always been a happy person. I had a wonderful family, dear friends, and a successful career as a television producer that I deeply enjoyed. But in 2004, after making six movie-length television specials in the course of twelve months, I was exhausted. Plus, my father had just died, and on top of dealing with my own grief, I was sick with worry about my mother, who was taking Dad's death especially hard. One night I got off the phone with her and was in such despair, I couldn't stop crying.

My twenty-three-year-old daughter, seeing how upset I was, handed me a book saying, "Mom, I think this will really help." It was *The Science of Getting Rich* by Wallace Wattles. I was mystified how a book about getting rich could help me deal with my sadness about my mother, but I opened it and began to read.

With every sentence my astonishment grew. The book was about getting rich all right, but money was only one part of it. *The Science of Getting Rich* tells you how to be overflowing with happiness and abundance on every level of your life. Though I'd never read anything like it, I knew right away it was absolutely true.

By the time I finished reading, I was a totally different person. It was like looking up and noticing the sun for the first time. I saw *everything* in a new light.

For the next few weeks, all I did was study—reading book after book as I traced back through history the ideas I'd been introduced to by Wattles. By the end of those weeks, I knew I'd stumbled onto the most valuable secret in the world: What you think, feel, say, and do, you attract to yourself. In truth, we all create our own reality!

When I put this principle to practice in my own life, my entire existence was transformed. Before long, I knew I wanted to share this secret with as many people as possible. With my television and film background, I thought the best way to do this would be to create a film.

I spent the better part of the next year working with my production company to make *The Secret,* which is what I decided to call the film. The whole experience was a fabulous adventure. We used the principles of the Law of Attraction that we were presenting in the film at every stage of its creation and development—for scripting, props, interviews, even the distribution.

From the very beginning, I had it in my mind that we would distribute the film through the conventional paths: either through cinemas or television networks. But before we'd even finished filming, the television avenue completely closed and wasn't a possibility. Then, once we'd completed the project, the cinema avenue closed as well. We'd talked to television networks and movie studios around the world, but we'd come to a dead end. There we were, sitting with this film we wanted to get out into the world with no idea how to do it.

I felt stuck until I realized I was getting caught up in the *how,* trying to figure out the way my intention should unfold. I knew from the Law of Attraction that my job was to stay focused on the *what* I wanted to create: to feel the gratitude and joy that would come from my successful outcome, and to trust and have faith that the way would be shown. So I let go of all my worries and plans about the distribution. This left me totally in the dark, unable to see the path ahead of me. Still, I kept holding to my purpose and feeling the joy in my heart.

The moment I let go of the *how,* an extraordinary sequence of events brought a company called Vividas into our lives. At the time, Vividas was the pioneer in the field of online streaming video, a breakthrough technology that allowed viewers to watch videos on their computer without downloading the material first. Up to that point, it had been used only for short videos like the movie trailers Vividas produced for motion picture studios. No one had ever done a whole film in this way before, but Vividas was game. Remarkably, we'd looked all over the world for distribution, but ended up working with a company located only two streets away from our offices in Australia! We collaborated with their experts, and *The Secret* became the first movie in history to be streamed online. What was even more amazing was that this new technology allowed us to release the film worldwide within a twenty-four-hour period, something I'd dreamed about and known would happen, but had been told was impossible.

The Secret carved a whole new path for movies to be released. Films usually go into cinemas or retail stores first, but *The Secret* became a phenomenon through online streaming video and Internet sales of the DVDs and *then* went into retail stores and other conventional outlets. After our success, movie studios and distribution companies everywhere came to us, asking for our template for releasing a movie in this way. People thought we'd known exactly the path we were taking, but we hadn't. It all came from trusting and feeling our way through the joy within us.

When I discovered the Law of Attraction, my purpose became clear to me: to be in joy and through every action and word to share that joy with billions. I've learned to pay special attention to my inner purpose—to be in that joy.

Sometimes I'll take a step in a particular direction and I'll get blocked very quickly. It's as if the Universe is saying to me, "Whoa, you just hold on here, Bessie. Where do you think you're going?" Then I just come back to the trust and joy and gratitude and say, "Okay, you lead me." I wait and from that place of joy, I soon see a whole different path open up.

That happened to me this year. I was so eager to move into the next film, excited about everything I wanted to include in it. I stepped forward in all of my passion and excitement and was instantly blocked. I knew straight away the Universe was saying, "Rhonda, you need to look after this baby—before you go off giving birth to another baby. Let *The Secret* grow and mature, and give everything that you can to this baby first. You are jumping the gun." I absolutely knew it with every fiber of my being. So I shifted my attention back.

The "new baby" is still there and it's burning away inside me, but I have a calm and a peace about it. I've let go of any schedule for it to happen. I'm certain that I'll feel the timing in my heart, and will know exactly—in the very second—when it's right to move on that.

When I was writing the book *The Secret,* I waited to feel the push inside me that would let me know the time was right. I didn't write a single word until I felt that the whole project had already been done. I kept feeling the outcome and feeling the outcome—which was more joy, more clarity, and more love. When I felt the real push to begin, I never sat down at the computer without first having tears of gratitude, love, and joy streaming down my face. Every day my heart was in a total meltdown and when that happened, my mind got out of the way and the creative power just flowed through me. Through joy, that joy spoke, so it could share itself with the world.

Your Job Is the *What*, Not the *How*

When you're inspired by purpose like Rhonda, you just need to keep following what you're led to do. You can absolutely trust that inspiration will carry you from one step to another. In the film *The Secret,* Jack Canfield talks about the experience of traveling in a car at night, the road lit only 200 feet in front of you by the car's headlights. He says that even though you can't see your destination, the lit portion ahead is all you need to stay on the road and get where you're headed. In life, the fire of your inspiration acts as those headlights, allowing you to see what's next. Your job is to follow that light.

Precession: Small Steps, Big Results

When you do what you're inspired to do in the moment, you're often unaware of the effects your actions will have or where they'll lead you. A honeybee buzzing from flower to flower isn't aware that it's cross-pollinating the plants and making life on earth possible. As far as it's concerned, it's just drawn to one flower after another to collect nectar, which will be converted to honey.

Rosa Parks, the African American woman who refused to take a back seat on a public bus, had no idea that her one courageous act would be the start of the civil rights movement in the South. She simply took the step that felt right to her at that moment, making what she thought was a small statement about freedom.

Buckminster Fuller, the famous architect and visionary, used the term "precession" to describe this phenomenon of a series of small steps leading to an astonishing, unforeseen conclusion.

I've experienced precession in my own life many times. If you had told me twenty years ago that I'd be a best-selling author, I would have thought you were crazy. I only wanted to be a speaker. I hated writing!

In fact, in my job at the Austrian crystal company, everyone in the company knew my well-established method for writing important business letters and memos. I would delay writing a letter for as long as I possibly could. (The office staff would know this by how clean my desk was: the cleaner my desk, the more I'd been procrastinating.) Finally, after putting the letter off as long as I could and struggling unsuccessfully to get a few sentences down, I'd go to my buddy Jay's office and cajole him into writing the letter for me. I was convinced that I was the worst writer in the world.

When I left that job to become a corporate trainer, the only position I could find was teaching business writing. On the surface, I thought, *No way! What kind of cosmic joke is this?* But on a deep level, it felt like the right thing to do. I took the job, learned all about writing and editing, and found I actually did have some skill and talent. Six years later, when I had the idea for *Chicken Soup for the Woman's Soul,* I was prepared: I had the exact skills I needed to co-create that book. I certainly didn't plan for it, but that's where life took me.

Some folks hear the fanfare of trumpets when they have their Big Idea. Many don't. You may feel you have a special and unique gift but haven't quite tumbled on how to express it. Rest assured: if you keep your sights on the lighted road, the opportunity is bound to sneak up on you when you least expect it.

Exercise

Acting from Inspiration

I like to think of inspiration as being *in spirit,* being led by my soul throughout the day. A wonderful way to act from inspiration is to start your day by asking yourself the following questions, which are adapted from the book A *Course in Miracles.* Here's what you do:

1. Close your eyes, and take a few deep, slow breaths.
2. Ask yourself these three questions:

   What would Spirit have me do?
   Where would Spirit have me go?
   What would Spirit have me say, and to whom?

3. As you move through your day, use the answers you receive to "light the 200 feet in front of you" on your way.

Happiness Habit for a Life of Purpose #3

Contribute to Something Greater Than Yourself

I don't know what your destiny will be, but one thing I do know: the only ones among you who will be really happy are those who have sought and found how to serve.

—Albert Schweitzer, physician and humanitarian

The happiest people contribute to something greater than themselves in life. When Stewart Emery interviewed people with enduring success and happiness for his book *Success Built to Last,* he found that their goals weren't fame, wealth, or power. People with those goals inevitably ended up feeling empty and unhappy. My interviews with the

Happy 100 showed me that people who are Happy for No Reason may be famous, wealthy, and powerful, but those are outcomes of living fully and passionately, engaged in meaningful service to a larger cause. Oprah Winfrey once said, "I never went for the money, I just said, *God use me. Show me how to take who I am, who I want to be, and what I can do, and use it for a purpose greater than myself.*"

Happy 100 member Lynne Twist is also someone who passionately devotes her life to a greater purpose. She's sometimes referred to as a modern-day Mother Teresa. I've been fortunate to spend time, personally and professionally, with Lynne, and whenever I'm around her, I'm so moved by the way her beauty and goodness shine from her in everything she does. She's often so full of gratitude that her eyes fill with tears. In our interview, Lynne shared the story of how she found her call to serve.

Lynne's Story

The Calling

As a teenager, I led a double life. To most people I appeared a typical 1950s high school girl. I earned straight A's, was a cheerleader and homecoming queen, and even dated the captain of the football team. But there was also another Lynne. This Lynne was deeply religious: she woke every morning before dawn to go to morning Mass, idolized Mother Teresa, and entertained dreams of becoming a nun. Which was the real me? They both were.

This double life began with the death of my father, whom I'd adored. A big-band leader like Glenn Miller, he'd turned our home into a joyful, fun place, filled with musicians, dancing, and singing. Then, two days before my fourteenth birthday, my father died of a heart attack, peacefully, while he slept. He was only fifty years old.

His death was incomprehensible to me. My shock and grief made me look for a deeper meaning to my life, and I turned to God and the church. It was then that my aspirations for a life of service—a life that made a difference—started.

I hid my spirituality from all the kids I knew because it wasn't cool to be religious, but I tried to bridge the gap between my inner and outer life by becoming involved in community service projects and roping in all my friends to help. We tackled all kinds of jobs, from collecting clothes for a local fund-raising sale to tutoring disadvantaged kids who had dropped out of school. It was so satisfying to help other people, and we all had fun doing it.

After high school, I went to Stanford, where studying the mystical poetry of Rilke and Rumi, among others, took the place of my daily churchgoing. I was still searching for the mission I was put on earth to accomplish when I fell in love with Bill Twist. We married during my senior year, and after graduation, in very short order, our daughter and two sons were born.

Although those were happy years, my search for greater meaning was always simmering below the surface. It spurred me to take a personal growth seminar called est, which I found profoundly transformational, and also to study with the renowned inventor, designer, and futurist Buckminster Fuller, whose books I'd read in college and admired greatly. As a young man of thirty-two, Bucky had contemplated suicide. Deciding against it at the last moment, he'd said to himself, "I may be a throw-away person, but perhaps I can take this throw-away life and devote it to making a difference." (It was actually Bucky who coined the phrase, "Make a difference with your life.") He'd launched an experiment to see if one ordinary individual could change the world and benefit all humanity.

In 1977, I helped to introduce Bucky to the founder of the est program, Werner Erhard, and from that relationship, the Hunger Project—the commitment to end world hunger by the year 2000—was born.

When I heard about the project a few days later, it created an inner earthquake in me. I knew without any doubt that this was what I was meant to do. I stepped out of "the movie of my life starring me" and became a supporting player in a much larger film. Suddenly, my personality and my agenda took a back seat to this greater calling. This commitment woke me up in the morning, showed me what to wear and where to go. It gave me an eloquent voice and the words to speak.

I took on a leadership role at the Hunger Project and soon found myself stretched to the max. Once again I was leading a double life—now a suburban mom and a crusader—although this time it wasn't a secret. I had a wonderful husband and three kids, six, eight, and ten, and was committed to being there for them; I was also committed to doing whatever it took to end world hunger by the year 2000. My two commitments lived side-by-side—sometimes literally. People from places like Bangladesh, Sweden, Japan, and Ethiopia often stayed in our home with us during their Hunger Project training in the States, and because I traveled constantly, I brought the kids and Bill with me whenever possible. Other families went to Disneyland and Aspen for vacations; we went to Zimbabwe and Indonesia.

We had enough money so that I could hire a terrific housekeeper, which helped enormously, but I still made a concerted effort to always be home on weekends. This sometimes meant flying to India on a Monday and flying back home on Friday! I felt the strain of always being pulled in two directions.

One Saturday, distraught that I had missed my daughter's choral concert and my son's championship soccer game, I called a family meeting. We sat on the floor in a circle and I told Bill and the kids, "I'm feeling so guilty that I didn't make the Halloween costumes this year, and that I missed the concert and the game. I need your permission to go on. I'm so dedicated to my work with the Hunger Project, but I feel torn that I can't do everything." By the time I finished, I was sobbing.

Summer, my eight-year-old daughter, came over and put her arms around me and said, "Mom, if you can help end world hunger, we don't want you driving us to the orthodontist. Someone else can do that." She went on, "We have the coolest life and the most amazing people living with us. We're so *lucky* and so proud of you."

My two sons and my husband joined in, putting their arms around Summer and me, as my husband said, "Go for it. We're just thrilled with your commitment; it lights up our lives." We hugged and cried and laughed, and in that moment, the schism between the two things I held so dear closed up and any lingering traces of a double life vanished.

Ending world hunger became a family commitment after that. The kids volunteered at the office, often lying on the floor beneath my desk to do their homework, and we all became world citizens. I realize now that my kids didn't have to have two separate lives, one "normal" and the other "spiritual." We melded the two—and have been all the better for it.

People often think that living a life of meaning means sacrifice, but for me, it's been exactly the opposite. I've had opportunities to do things and meet people I could never have imagined. When I finally met my childhood hero, Mother Teresa, our connection was immediate and natural. She called herself "God's pencil" and felt that God wrote his story to the world through her and people like her. I could relate to that—I also felt I was being used by God to write the end of hunger and the end of the suffering that goes along with it.

Living a committed life gave me the opportunity not only to work alongside Mother Teresa, but also to sit with the Dalai Lama and to have an ongoing relationship with Archbishop Desmond Tutu and Nelson Mandela. These were people that I never in a million years thought I'd know, let alone have an opportunity to work with. It's also provided me the equally valuable privilege of being in the presence of wise and courageous people all over the world. Following the famine of 1984–1985, I sat around a dry well for five days and nights with a group of Ethiopian mothers whose children had died of starvation. These women and others like them inspired me to keep going for the goal we'd set.

When we started the Hunger Project in 1977, 44,000 people a day were dying of hunger and starvation, most of them children under five years old—and those numbers were rising every year. Today, though the world's population has grown by over 50 percent, the number of deaths from hunger and starvation is 19,000 people a day, less than half of what it was in 1977. It's still too many, but it's a staggering accomplishment.

I always thought that I'd be working for the Hunger Project for the rest of my life: I'd either end hunger or die trying. But in 1994, to my great surprise, I heard something new calling me. At first, I ignored it, thinking it was just a distraction from the work in front of me, but its voice was so persistent and so persuasive, in the end it made me look inside and take a new direction in my life. In 1996, Bill and I founded the Pachamama Alliance to work with the indigenous peoples of South America to preserve the rain forests and to create a new global vision of sustainability for all life. Scientists predict that without the rain forests, South America will become barren, creating a hunger crisis that will affect millions of people and endanger the health of the planet as a whole. This goal is not as far from my original mission as it may seem: rather than working to end world hunger, I'm working to ensure that it doesn't happen in the first place.

Over the past thirty years, giving myself to the larger purpose that calls me, in whatever form it appears, has led me to a life happier than any I could ever have imagined.

Making a Difference with Your Life

It's not necessary to be a Mother Teresa or a Lynne Twist to contribute to something greater than yourself. When you discover what matters to you, your everyday actions can serve others and the world in ways large and small.

It really doesn't matter what you choose to serve. All of us are drawn to different causes. For some people, it's wildlife; for others it's social justice, ending poverty, or making sure all children have access to the arts. The details aren't important. When you serve a purpose larger than yourself it brings more meaning and joy to your life. I've experienced this myself being a part of the local Big Brothers/Big Sisters program. Spending time with my fantastic little sister, Leah, brings me great delight.

Your desire to make a difference can influence even routine decisions, such as what you eat, where you shop, and what kind of car you drive. I have a friend who drives a hybrid and eats only organic produce that she buys at the local farmer's market. She calls this voting with her pocketbook, spending her money in the way that supports what she believes in.

And you don't have to be wealthy to make donations that yield generous results. Even giving $10 or $20 to charitable organizations can feed a family for a week, buy a cow or goat, help fund a small business, or buy seeds to grow crops, making a huge difference in others' lives. Contributing to something greater than yourself doesn't have to involve money; it can be an exchange of your time, your interest, or your caring.

Research has consistently shown that giving of yourself to others—altruism—is associated with greater well-being, health, and happiness, as long as you don't "overgive." Giving of yourself doesn't mean being codependent, trying to fill an inner emptiness, or serving others at our own expense. The service I'm talking about comes from joy, inspiration, and purpose and supports more peace and well-being in your life.

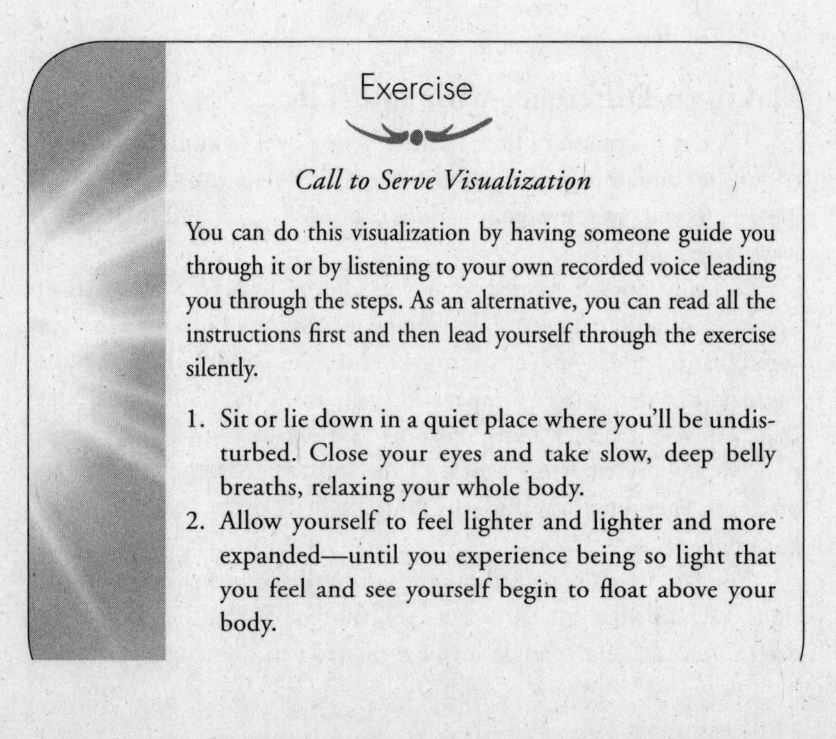

Exercise

Call to Serve Visualization

You can do this visualization by having someone guide you through it or by listening to your own recorded voice leading you through the steps. As an alternative, you can read all the instructions first and then lead yourself through the exercise silently.

1. Sit or lie down in a quiet place where you'll be undisturbed. Close your eyes and take slow, deep belly breaths, relaxing your whole body.
2. Allow yourself to feel lighter and lighter and more expanded—until you experience being so light that you feel and see yourself begin to float above your body.

3. Imagine now that you are high above your body, hovering over the earth. You look down at the planet beneath you—you see a beautiful, shimmering blue sphere. You can see the oceans and continents and vast cloud formations below. You look more closely and see the mountains, forests, valleys, and cities.
4. You see the billions of people and animals that all live interconnectedly on earth. You feel connected to all the life teeming beneath you. You feel you are a part of a bigger design. You put your attention on the question: *How am I being called to serve?*
5. You find yourself being drawn toward a place on the planet that holds a particular significance or fascination for you. You see a situation that moves you to serve. You may be shown someone, somewhere, or something that is familiar to you, or it may be completely new. (You may be drawn to things such as helping animals, working to cure a particular disease, preserving the oceans, or serving children in your area or in a developing nation.) Be curious and adventurous. See where you land, the kind of surroundings you find yourself in, and what's there for you to do. You may receive one or multiple glimpses of the opportunities that await you. Be open to all possibilities.
6. When you feel complete with your experience, express gratitude and gradually feel yourself returning to the room where you are sitting or lying down. Reflect on how you can use the images you received to be led to where you can be of service. See what unfolds in your life.

Summary and Happiness Action Steps

When you live inspired by purpose, you choose in favor of your passions, let the fire of inspiration light your path, and contribute to something greater than yourself in ways large and small. This puts the roof on your Home for Happiness. Use the following action steps to practice the Happiness Habits for a Life of Purpose:

1. Look for ways to turn your job into a career and your career into a calling. What can you change in your present circumstances to feel more inspired by your purpose?
2. Take the complete Passion Test every six months to stay aligned with what truly matters to you.
3. Begin each day by asking yourself, "What would be meaningful to do today?" Then be led by inspiration throughout the day.
4. Ask yourself, "How can I be of best service to others?" Take a step to volunteer locally: call your local nursing home, food bank, animal shelter, literacy program, Sierra Club chapter—the list is endless. Find out what you can do to help. Even an hour once or twice a month can make a difference in your life and the lives of others.

The Garden—Cultivate Nourishing Relationships

Whoever is happy will make others happy, too.

—Mark Twain, writer and humorist

I love sitting in my garden. My favorite spot is on a bench in a sunny corner where I have the perfect view of the flowers and trees in my yard. It's a wonderful way to unwind after a crazy day or just to spend a few minutes appreciating the beauty around me.

The people in your life are the garden surrounding your Home for Happiness. When you look around that garden, do you see beautiful roses and dahlias, or a neglected patch of weeds? Our relationships affect us in a similar way—either uplifting us, or dragging us down. Happy people cultivate relationships in their lives that nourish and support their happiness.

People Power

Scores of studies in the field of positive psychology demonstrate that having good social relationships is one of the strongest predictors of happiness. Large-scale surveys conducted by the University of Chicago's

National Opinion Research Center found that people with five or more close friends (not including family members) are 50 percent more likely to describe themselves as "very happy" than those with fewer strong relationships. Another survey of 800 people showed that those who valued wealth, success, and status over close friends and a loving relationship with a significant other were twice as likely to be "fairly" or "very" unhappy.

Edward Diener, the father of happiness research, and Martin Seligman, the father of positive psychology, conducted a study in 2002 focusing on two groups of people: those with the highest scores on a standard measure of happiness and those with the lowest. They discovered that the one trait the happy group had in common, which the unhappy group didn't share, was having close trusting relationships.

In my interviews, I found the same trait. Although the Happy 100 vary greatly in the number of relationships they have, each one of those relationships is a healthy one that supports their happiness. What sets the Happy 100 apart is that they don't depend on others to make them happy. When you're Happy for No Reason, you enjoy being with your friends and family, but you also enjoy spending time alone, in your own company. You bring your happiness *to* your relationships rather than trying to extract happiness *from* them.

Emotional Contagion

One of the most exciting discoveries that neuroscientists have made in the past decade is that our brains are actually wired to relate to others. Everyone with whom we interact, or even just nod to as we pass on the street, stimulates a "neural bridge" that connects us. Our brains contain "mirror neurons" that fire in or out of synch with the people around us.

Have you ever caught yourself unintentionally mimicking the facial expression, posture, body language, or speech rhythm of a person you're having a conversation with? Or yawning in response to someone else's yawn—even though you're not tired? When you observe someone else performing an action, these neurons "mirror" that action inside your brain as though you were performing it yourself!

Mirror neurons have also been linked to our ability to empathize with the emotions of others, explaining why, when a person who's angry or upset walks into a room, everyone in the room can feel it. Or why just seeing someone else overcome with emotion is enough to make our own eyes fill with tears. Some researchers now believe that autism, which causes an impaired ability to relate to others, may involve damaged mirror neurons.

Our emotions are contagious. According to the internationally known psychologist Daniel Goleman, the author of *Emotional Intelligence* and *Social Intelligence,* emotions spread from one person to another much like a cold. And while it can be good to "catch" an uplifting feeling, it can be damaging to take on others' feelings of anger, jealousy, anxiety, or hate.

"You probably came in contact with someone who has an infectious smile."

Dr. Goleman says that the more connected we are with someone emotionally, the greater the influence they have on us—especially over time. I've caught some great emotions from those closest to me, particularly Sergio. I didn't consciously have happiness on the checklist of qualities for my ideal mate, but I certainly feel blessed that Sergio is a deeply happy guy. He's earned his way into the Happy 100 fair and square, and in fact, is often bubbling over in song. At first, I thought he was just trying to impress me when, in the shower, he'd belt out beautiful Italian love songs I could hear all the way across the house. But even today, when he no longer needs to play the impressing game, singing joyfully and loudly in the shower is still part of his daily routine. And it doesn't stop there. Sergio sings when he's making breakfast, when he's doing the laundry (yes, he does the laundry), when he's returning emails—pretty much all day long. Sometimes I even have to come out of my office when I'm on a business call to ask him to turn down the volume. But I wouldn't trade being around his joyous influence for anything in the world. It has such a fabulous impact on my own happiness.

Think about the people in your life. Do you want to "catch their emotions"?

Hey, Girlfriend!

Our relationships have a biochemical effect on our bodies. When we make healthy connections with people, our brains flood our cells with happiness chemicals, and when we have unhealthy social interactions, harmful chemicals are released.

According to the latest research, women's biochemical wiring makes them more likely than men to seek out relationships with others. Though men and women both release adrenaline and cortisol when under stress, scientists found in a landmark UCLA study that in order to buffer those stress chemicals, women's brains release oxytocin, the bonding hormone I talked about in Chapter 6. This is why women who are going through a rough time often want to gather with other women or have a good, long yak-fest with a close girlfriend. Or why they may feel drawn to caring for their children or pets. Researchers call this behavior "tending and befriending." It is stimulated by oxytocin and in turn creates more oxytocin. The more women tend and befriend, the more oxytocin they release, producing a calming influence and further lowering their stress.

There's no question that friends help women to live happier and healthier lives. The famed Nurses' Health Study from Harvard Medical School found that the more friends a woman has, the less likely she is to develop physical problems as she ages and the better chance she has to lead a joyful life. In fact, the results were so significant that the researchers concluded that not having close friends or confidants was as detrimental to a woman's health as smoking cigarettes or being overweight.

My colleague John Gray, the author of *Men Are from Mars, Women Are from Venus,* whom I interviewed for this book, has reviewed extensive research about the relationship between stress, hormones, and gender. He told me that though women release oxytocin when faced with stress, men don't have this same biochemical response. According to the studies, when men are stressed and release cortisol, it lowers their dopamine and testosterone levels, causing frustration and depression. Dr. Gray says that men are biologically hardwired to seek out ways to stimulate the production of those neurochemicals by problem-solving, taking action, and overcoming risk and danger, rather than talking or taking care of others. The lower amount of oxytocin in their system makes them less interested in bonding with friends.

Relationships and Your Energy

Until you're firmly established in the state of Happy for No Reason, your happiness is affected by the energy of the people around you. When you surround yourself with relationships that support you, your energy expands. When you have a lot of toxic people in your life, your energy contracts.

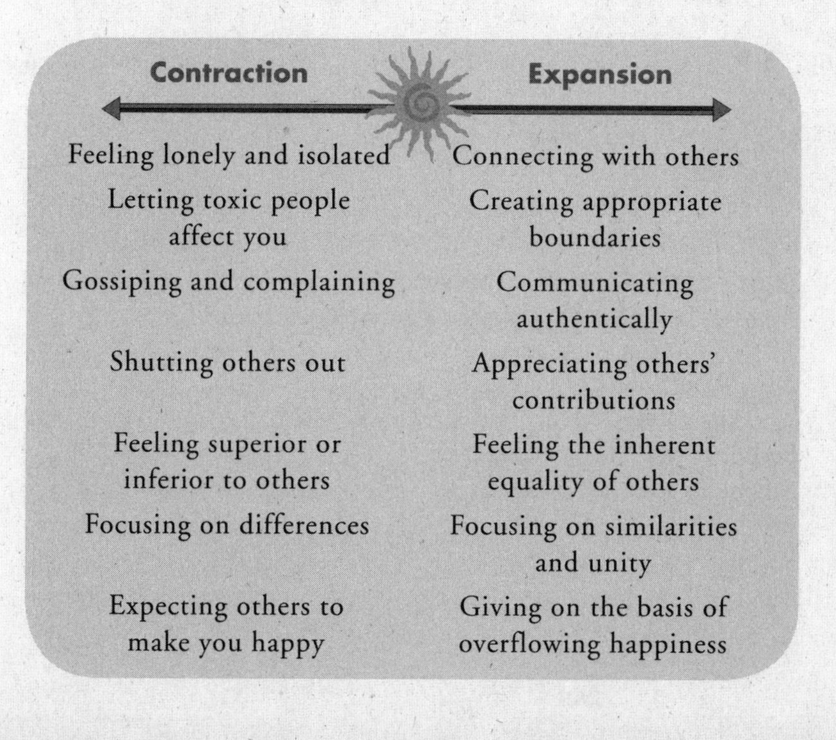

Practicing the following relationship habits will help raise your happiness set-point.

Happiness Habits for Relationships

1. Tend to Your Relationships
2. Surround Yourself with Support
3. See the World as Your Family

Happiness Habit for Relationships #1
Tend to Your Relationships

You become the average of the five people you associate with most.

—Jim Rohn, author and motivational speaker

We tend to our gardens by weeding, watering, and planting to make sure they flourish. We can tend to our relationships by spending more time with people who support our happiness and less time with those who erode it.

Of course, the happier you are inside, the less you're adversely influenced by your external environment. In my interviews with the Happy 100, I saw that they handle toxic people when they have to, but they also limit their interactions with them when they can.

Happy 100 member, author, and life coach Martha Beck, whom you met in Chapter 6, went through a profound personal transformation that brought her to a state of deep happiness. In the following story, she describes her experience learning to recognize the relationships in her life that support her.

Martha's Story

My Great Big Unrelated Family Reunion

I'd just moved to Phoenix, and, feeling isolated, I attended a book signing, hoping to meet other bookish people. The signing was about as interesting as mud, so I decided to leave. This turned out to be strangely difficult. As I walked away, I literally felt something trying to turn me around and push me back into the building. All the way home, I fought an intense impulse to turn the car around, go back, and *meet someone.*

A week later I walked into a coffee shop and saw Annette. I recognized her immediately, but not because she'd been at that book signing. She had been, but I hadn't seen her. I recognized Annette because *I just knew her.* It felt as though long ago, our souls had made an agreement to meet in Phoenix, Arizona, at that appointed time. This feeling was so strong it would have scared me—except that I'd felt it several times before, with different people, in different places.

I was about fifteen when I first got the feeling I'd met only a small percentage of the people I loved most. Unlike many teenagers, I found sex, drugs, and rock 'n' roll much less interesting than English literature and biology. I had lots of equally nerdy friends, a group of peers who pressured me only to study for the SATs. Still, I felt oddly misplaced. I'd walk the halls of my large public high school like a zebra separated from its herd, scanning for other striped creatures.

"There are more of us," I kept thinking. "Where are the others?"

Every now and then I'd meet someone—in class, at a debate meet, at the mall—who drew my attention like a magnet. These people fairly glowed in the dark; I couldn't take my eyes off them. They were of all ages and both genders. This wasn't about romantic attraction—I just . . . recognized them.

As I matured, these incidents grew even more noticeable. On my first day of college, feeling desperately scared and lonely, I walked into an art studio and instantly recognized the professor as one of my life's most important mentors. Later that day, I was sitting at a bus stop, drawing in a sketchbook, when a nicely dressed stranger glanced at my work.

"Listen," she said, "there's an art class you should be taking."

"I know," I said. "I'm already in it."

The stranger looked me in the eyes. There was no question we were talking about the same class. She nodded. Her bus arrived, and she got on. I never saw her again—though, of course, I knew and loved her. Still do. We'd kept our appointment.

If this is starting to sound weird to you, think how it felt to me. The longer I lived, the more intensely I "recognized" people I'd never met. What's more, I began to realize that the connection was often mutual: the strangers I knew, knew me. All of them had questions in their eyes, as though they were continually searching for lost loved ones in a crowd.

In my late twenties, I felt more and more at odds with my family and community of origin. Both were steeped in a particularly rigid religious orthodoxy that made my relationships with them feel increasingly unhealthy to me. I got therapy—good therapy—and the more diligently I looked within myself and learned to distinguish between what felt right to me and what felt wrong, the more I understood that spending less time with that family and community wasn't a failing on my part, but a necessary, healing, healthy choice.

And I realized why I'd felt a warm, living connection with people I barely knew or had only seen.

It was because *they* were my family.

Now, I'm so comfortable with the notion of family as a spiritually linked network of souls that it never surprises me to meet a new brother, sister, mother, father, daughter, or son. My nearest and dearest tend to enter my life in extravagantly miraculous ways.

Annette, for example, became my first writer friend, and soon thereafter, we invited two other writers, Dawn and Thora, to form a writing group. The night before our first meeting, I dreamed that a Navajo medicine woman handed me a blue stone butterfly and said, *"Dineh,"* which is Navajo for "the people." I didn't think about this much until I met Thora. Then I got gooseflesh; she looked exactly like the medicine woman in my dream. Then Dawn happened to mention her twin sister, Denae—which she pronounced exactly like the Navajo word *dineh.* At this point, I told the group about my odd dream. When I mentioned the blue stone butterfly, Annette burst out laughing. She opened her purse and pulled out a blue stone butterfly.

Without that writing group, I would never have finished a book at all. With their support, I finished a manuscript that eventually found an agent and a publisher. When I went to New York to meet my new editor, Betsy, I realized within about thirty seconds that she was my favorite sister.

After our first Manhattan lunch, I sent her a small ceramic turtle as a gift, along with a note explaining that turtles have always symbolized how we in the writing world need to go through life: sure, slow, steady, knowing when to pull our heads in. "I got the turtle," Betsy told me later, "and I thought, *she knows.*" Of course I knew. I'd been doing this long enough to recognize when I was keeping an appointment with one of my nearest and dearest.

My life seems to have turned into a long family reunion. These days, it's filled with so many loved ones, such a huge and varied tribe, that I sometimes find myself weeping helplessly with joy, wonder, and gratitude. When I meet someone I love, we rarely even bother to pretend we don't recognize one another.

At a conference, I meet another presenter who doesn't introduce himself. We simply fall into each other's arms, thrilled that we've both shown up for our appointment. "Hey," he says, beaming at me, "I have a book you need." I take the book, knowing that it contains exactly the information and inspiration for which I've been praying. I may never see him again, but we can feel one another's presence in the world.

On a book tour in Germany, a man I've never met grabs my hand and says, "*Du.*" I smile and say, "You." We both burst out laughing, thrilled to finally meet one another. "We don't speak the same language in our minds," he says in German, "but we do in our hearts." I don't speak German. I understand him perfectly.

In Africa, I walk into a one-room school, meet the teacher and several members of the small Shangaan village. I recognize literally everyone.

"I'm adopting this school," I say to the teacher. "I want to help you get anything you need."

She nods, matter-of-factly, and just says, "Yes."

Neither of us needs to add, "I'm so glad we kept this appointment."

Having reached a certain age, and lived through thousands of moments like these, I've learned to simply enjoy them without frantically wondering what it all means. Having a soul-family is more than enough reward in itself. But I still have a great many questions. Does everyone have a huge family of unrelated individuals, who may have nothing in common physically, but recognize one another by the texture of their souls? Is there some task each spiritual clan is meant to complete?

I don't know for sure, but I have a hunch the answer to each of these questions is "Yes." If I'm wrong, if my life history of recognizing family members proves to be nothing more than delusion, I won't mind. As delusions go, this one is wondrous, delightful, sweet, and harmless. But just in case I'm right—just in case this all sounds strangely familiar to you—the time may come when we see one another at a coffee shop, at a bookstore, in a tiny one-room school in some remote village, and feel that instantaneous thrill of recognition.

If this should come to pass, and you see me first, I have just one request: Don't be shy. I've been waiting to meet you for a very long time.

Building Up Emotional Immunity

Spending time with those you love—family, friends, or pets—can reset the balance of your biology toward greater happiness, so it's important to make wise choices about the company you keep.

Not everyone in our life will always nourish us. I'm sure you've had the experience of feeling good, until you're around a friend, relative, or coworker who drags you down. It's emotional contagion again: you're picking up their neuronal vibes. Staying out of range of emotional bullies and happiness vampires who suck the life out of you is the easiest way to avoid negative emotional contagion.

Usually it's obvious which people are toxic to be around: they're the complainers, the discouragers, the people whose criticism aims to wound. Some are harder to spot: they're self-absorbed, fearful, judgmental, and manipulative. They may even mean well; still, you come away from contact with them feeling drained and frustrated.

"It might help Skippy's feelings if you said he needed improvement instead of calling him a bad dog."

To populate your world with uplifting people and minimize your connection with people who are toxic, use your inner GPS. Close your eyes, take a deep breath, and imagine each person in your life. Who expands you and who contracts you?

Even when you've identified the toxic people in your life, the problem is that it's not always possible to stop spending time with them; you may work with happiness vampires or may even be related to them. What do you do then?

Learning to create appropriate boundaries is a must. As Dr. Phil says, "We teach people how to treat us"—by what we accept or don't accept from them. When you have to be around toxic people, here are some ways to bolster your immunity:

1. **Break the chain reaction:** Now that you know about mirror neurons, put them to work to your advantage. If you have to talk to an angry or negative person, consciously soften your gaze, keep your expression neutral, use body language that's the opposite of his or hers. Don't reflect the other person's tension, or your body will hijack you by mirroring that negativity.
2. **Put up an invisible barrier:** When you can't leave and you're being bombarded by toxic emotions, the author and UCLA psychiatrist Judith Orloff recommends imagining an invisible wall or a shield around yourself. This will give you a feeling of emotional protection and may help to buffer your desire to respond in kind.
3. **Stay on your side of the road:** Don't try to change the other person. It may be tempting to think that you can help others by trying to save them or pointing out the "error of their ways," but it rarely ever works. The most effective way to influence others is to model the behavior you'd like to see in them.

Shower the People You Love with Love

The best way to keep relationships happy, healthy, and supportive can be summed up in one word: appreciation. (What you appreciate, appreciates.) When we demonstrate our appreciation for the support we receive from others, it reinforces that behavior and deepens our connection to them.

Appreciation is a basic human need, both at home and at work. In fact, according to the U.S. Bureau of Labor, 40 percent of employees leave their job not because of salary or workload, but because they don't feel appreciated.

Too often, we take our closest personal relationships for granted as well, giving little energy and paying little attention to the people who mean the most to us. Psychologist John Gottman did a famous study of marital happiness using what he calls "the magic ratio" to predict whether 700 newly married couples would remain married or get divorced. Dr. Gottman said that couples who had a ratio of five positive interactions for every one negative interaction would stay together. In a follow-up done ten years later, a staggering 94 percent of the couples he had said would divorce were, in fact, no longer married.

Judith W. Umlas, author of *The Power of Acknowledgment,* says, "One of the most important things a person can do to raise his or her happiness level is to acknowledge those around them. According to a recent *Gallup Management Journal* article, when someone is acknowledged, dopamine is released—a neurochemical that's directly linked to being happy!"

In 2004, Dr. Donald O. Clifton and his grandson, Tom Rath, wrote *How Full Is Your Bucket?* based on over fifty years of comprehensive research done by social scientists and the Gallup Organization. Its message is easy to understand and apply: The most effective way to motivate, connect to, and inspire others, what the authors call "filling up a person's bucket," is through specific and sincere positive recognition. And when you fill someone else's bucket, it raises your own happiness level as well.

When I want to amp up the appreciation, I love using the following technique, called The Appreciation Practice. It's a wonderful way to enrich your relationship with anyone—spouse, child, friend, or coworker. Sergio and I practice this almost every night before going to sleep, and it always leaves me smiling.

Exercise

The Appreciation Practice

1. Begin by acknowledging something you appreciate about the other person (for example, "You make me laugh," "I feel supported by you," "You're kind"). When you're finished, switch roles. Go back and forth at least five times or as long as you like.
2. Now repeat the exercise, only this time acknowledge one thing you appreciate about yourself. Then let the other person have a turn. Go back and forth at least five times or as long as you like.

Happiness Habit for Relationships #2
Surround Yourself with Support

You have to do it by yourself,
And you can't do it alone.

—Martin Rutte, corporate consultant and speaker

We sometimes need more support than our friends and family can provide. When we're having a tough time or deciding to go for our dreams, the people closest to us may commiserate, take our side, or tell us we're fine the way we are, rather than offer us the strength and honesty we need to move forward.

Often, the best way to surround yourself with support is to join or form a group that meets regularly, whose sole purpose is to provide guidance and straight feedback—and keep you from sliding into your old patterns of victimhood.

During our research, Carol met the woman who told us the following story and was instantly impressed by her friendly, loving, and open manner. When Carol told her about the book we were writing on happiness, the woman said she had learned how to be truly happy many years ago and kindly agreed to be interviewed. Although Molly Baker is not her real name, her inner peace and well-being are the genuine article. Molly's story is a beautiful example of the role a support group can play in moving us toward greater experiences of happiness.

Molly's Story

That's What Friends Are For

John (a pseudonym) and I met in October and he proposed in December. I said yes on the spot. I didn't need to think about it. I was very attracted to him. Besides being an Ivy League graduate and having a good job, John was funny, popular, and a born leader—everything I felt I wasn't. Plus, I was twenty-one and ready to get married. This was the early 1950s, and I had no career goals except to be a wife and mother. Still, when John and I married ten months later, we really didn't know each other.

I soon discovered that my new husband drank—often and to excess.

That first year of marriage was a very unhappy time for me. John, a high-functioning alcoholic, was busy making a name for himself at his company. He worked late most nights, and then went out for business meetings, arriving home at all hours, almost always "under the influence." Yet, no matter how much he drank, he never seemed to have a hangover. He invariably got to the office on time and never missed a day of work. His boss had no idea of his problem.

I, on the other hand, was painfully aware of John's drinking. When John drank, his entire personality changed: he became wobbly, uproarious, sloppy, and stumbling. I was very uncomfortable being around him. There were car accidents—luckily only the cars were seriously damaged—and trips to the emergency room to stitch up his injuries. I was ashamed to tell my parents and sisters what was really going on in my life.

When I complained to John that he was drinking too much, he always denied it, claiming that I was being stupid or ridiculous. The sad thing was that I believed him. What's more, I saw that getting mad at John about his drinking just made him defensive and uncomfortable, which served only to make him drink more. I knew things were terribly wrong, but I didn't know what to do. What made it so hard was that at his core, John was such a good man. When he wasn't drunk, I loved being with him and respected him. My unhappiness and unexpressed anger grew steadily—as did my loneliness.

When our son, and then our daughter, arrived, things became more bearable. The years flew by as I hid on the hamster wheel of activity, keeping myself too busy to dwell on my situation. From the outside, we looked like a normal family, but in private, my relationship with John was steadily deteriorating.

When I complained to my two closest girlfriends about John, they always commiserated. It felt good to vent, but wallowing around with them in the same muck year after year never caused me to grow or change.

By the time we had been married twenty-three years, John's drinking was worse than I had ever imagined it could get, yet he still completely denied his illness. I felt so fundamentally empty, I didn't know how much longer I could take it.

One night I woke up and found that I was sobbing with fury and pounding on John's chest. All the anger I had been denying was spilling out in my sleep. John, snoring off the evening's drinking, never even woke. Afterward, I lay quiet for a long time, facing the fact that I was one sick cookie. I was drowning in resentment and despair, but the fear of being alone, of having to support myself, and of upsetting my parents and my children, even though they were already grown, paralyzed me.

Then one day, a few weeks later, a friend of mine told me about a support group for people who were involved with alcoholics. "We're both married to drunks. Let's go!" she said. I agreed eagerly.

We arrived at the church where the Al-Anon meeting was being held and walked into a room with folding chairs set up in a circle in the middle. Once everyone was settled, the meeting began.

I was immediately struck by everyone's openness. Each person seemed to be accepted as they were, and I felt an unconditional love flowing around the circle, enveloping the people I assumed were the regulars, as well as the newcomers. It was like coming in out of the cold; my whole body relaxed in the warmth of this gathering. Aside from introducing myself, I didn't have to say another word—unless I wanted to. I sat listening intently as people shared experiences that I knew all too well.

I began going to the meetings two or three times a week. I couldn't get enough of the love and acceptance that was given so freely. There was no criticism or judgment from anyone, and, equally important, they didn't allow me to stay stuck in self-pity. Ever so gently, the group helped me turn my focus away from John and his actions to finding the strength and confidence to turn my life around—whatever that meant for me. There was no advice given. I just heard story after story from people who had been where I was and had moved forward in their lives.

After each meeting, people always came up to me and hugged me, whispering words of encouragement into my ear. I was like a sponge, absorbing it all. Little by little, drop by drop, I began to feel whole.

It still wasn't easy at home. When John was drunk, I still felt victimized by his behavior and beaten down by his denial of any problem, but after each of our encounters, instead of stewing in my own helplessness, I shared my experience with my group and came away focused on my own worthiness and one step closer to finding serenity within myself.

Late one night, about a year and half after I first discovered my "circle of support," John came home at 2 o'clock in the morning, very drunk. He was fumbling around our bedroom, talking loudly, and being totally obnoxious.

I looked at this man who had been my husband for over twenty years and all I felt was compassion and a calm conviction that I didn't want to be in the room with him while he was in this state. I marveled at the complete peace I felt inside. I still well up with emotion remembering that moment: there was no more fear.

Clearly and evenly, I said, "John, I'm going to sleep in the other room tonight." And I got up and walked down the hall to the spare bedroom.

He followed me into the room and began arguing. "Oh, come on, what are you doing? Come back to the bedroom." His usual denial routine. I looked directly into his eyes. "No, John. I'm going to sleep here. I'll see you in the morning." There was not a trace of agitation or anger in my voice—which surprised me as much as it did him. He left the room and I went to sleep, feeling more strength and well-being than I'd ever felt before.

The next morning, I sat down with John and told him, "John, I can no longer accept your behavior. I want a separation." At this, all the color drained from his face, leaving him as white as the snowy starched shirt he was wearing.

I continued, "I am moving out today. I need to take some time to be quiet, and to figure out who I am and what I want."

I think John was in shock, because all he did was stand up and say, "Okay," before heading out the door for work.

That day I moved into a friend's house, which was empty since she was away on vacation. For three weeks, I reveled in my alone-ness and the newfound pleasure of my own company. As always, I continued to attend my Al-Anon meetings. Even outside the meetings, the people in the group were my "life-support system." If I got shaky, I'd call one or the other of them and they would remind me of how far I'd come and share their own experiences, strength, and hope.

At the end of the three weeks, John called me. Surprisingly accommodating, he offered to move to a friend's apartment and let me move back into our house. I accepted happily, and we went about our separate ways for another few weeks. I had finally decided that it was time to find a job and an apartment when John called and said he needed to talk to me.

When we met, John asked me, "Molly, what is it that you want?"

Having talked about this on many occasions in the presence of my group, I was completely clear about my answer. I smiled at him and said, "John, I know I love you. I know I respect you. I don't want a divorce, but I am not willing to accept your behavior when you are drunk."

He was silent for a moment, and then said, "That's all I wanted to know." Then he stood up and said good-bye.

Three days later, he called. I will never forget his words, "Molly, I am an alcoholic, I'm in AA, and I want to come home."

That was over thirty years ago.

Since that day, John hasn't had a drink and I haven't missed a meeting. Now, at more than five decades of marriage and counting, John and I are enjoying our life together—our separate interests and pursuits, as well as our deeply satisfying shared time. I love and respect my husband and feel his love and respect for me. I am grateful every day for the people in my life who were there for me. When they helped me take my eyes off John and others, and to concentrate on me—my attitudes and actions—miracles happened. I was able to find self-worth and serenity and become the empowered person I am today.

Except when I am ill or out of town, I still attend a local Al-Anon gathering once a week. The unconditional love and effective support I get there is as compelling now as it has ever been. As an elder in the Al-Anon community, I try to spend time with the newcomers, especially the shy and tentative people. I am well aware of how much courage it takes to come through that door for the first time—and I do all I can to put them at ease. I know deeply the magic of these rooms and the power of a support group to help people find their way through life.

The Wind beneath Your Wings

Though I've never attended a 12-step program myself, I know that, as Molly found, they are extraordinarily helpful for millions of people. Any group that reminds you of your soul's deepest truth when you forget is worth its weight in gold. I know this because I was a member of a women's support group for many years that was a godsend, keeping me on track on my search for true happiness.

In 1987 I took a life-changing seminar called Self-Empowerment Training, led by a wonderful therapist named Ali Najafi. At the end of the course, Ali recommended we form groups to keep the momentum of empowerment going in our lives. Five women—Holly, Jennifer, Sandy, Janice, and my dear friend and cowriter Carol—joined me in forming an extraordinary support group and quickly became my family. As the years passed, we welcomed new members Lane and Kami. Every week, we met at a different house—the host of the week provided treats—and we went around the circle twice, first talking about what we felt our "wins" were for the past week and then sharing our goals for the upcoming week. We asked for support for the changes we wanted to make and encouraged each other as much as we could. Everything said in our meetings was kept strictly confidential, and we were vigilant about giving each person an equal amount of time—though we'd bend the rules if someone had a crisis that needed more discussion. We went through many things together: marriages (including Holly's to my ex-boyfriend, the one who'd been the catalyst for my broken heart), births, and divorces. I saw how truly bonded we'd become when we had to face a shared tragedy: the sudden death of one of our members.

One cold snowy January afternoon, Sandy was killed in a car accident. Because she was single and had no other close family, it fell to us, her support group, to arrange her funeral. It turned out to be a celebration not only of a woman we all loved dearly, but also of the gratitude and love we felt for each other. When I moved away ten years later, I immediately found another women's group to join. This type of support has been so important in my life that I seek it out whenever I can.

The importance and power of support is the same all over the world. Zainab Salbi, whom you met in Chapter 3, told me a beautiful story that illustrates this. As part of her work with war survivors in Bosnia and Herzegovina, Zainab once met with a group of women in a very small village. One woman who was experiencing a lot of sadness confessed that she was being beaten regularly by her husband. She didn't want to leave her husband; she just wanted him to stop hitting her. The worst part was that she blamed herself for his abusive behavior. The other women in the group hugged her, cried with her, and admitted they were all going through the same thing. The group decided to take action. They told the woman to have her son alert them the next time her husband started to hit her.

The very next day, her husband started beating her. Her son went to the window, as instructed, and yelled out to all the other women in the group, "Help! My mother needs help!" Each woman dropped what she was doing. Dressed in their headscarves and sneakers, they all marched over, surrounded the house, and began shouting to the husband, "If you are going to hit her, you have to hit all of us! Are you going to beat us up too?" Astounded and ashamed, the man stopped. The other men, peeking from their windows, saw how the women banded together, and after that day, the incidence of domestic violence in that village dropped dramatically.

Creating Your Happiness Dream Team

Surrounding yourself with support can take many forms. Nancy Fursetzer, a member of the Happy 100, told me about her unique support group, which includes Albert Einstein, Helen Keller, Mother Teresa, Gandhi, Goethe, Abraham Lincoln, Lao-tzu, and many more great men and women of the past and present. Nancy has collected their quotes and posted them around her home and office, some displayed in frames, others written on notes stuck on mirrors, next to her computer, her phone, and the kitchen sink. Everywhere she turns, Nancy has inspiring reminders 24/7 from her personal Dream Team, proving that getting support doesn't have to be limited by time and space!

The value of a support group is that you create a TEAM, where Together Everyone Achieves More. This is based on the ancient principle that when two or more people gather for a common purpose or goal, they magnify their efforts and can more quickly and easily achieve the outcomes they desire. You can use the following exercise to hold your own support group meetings.

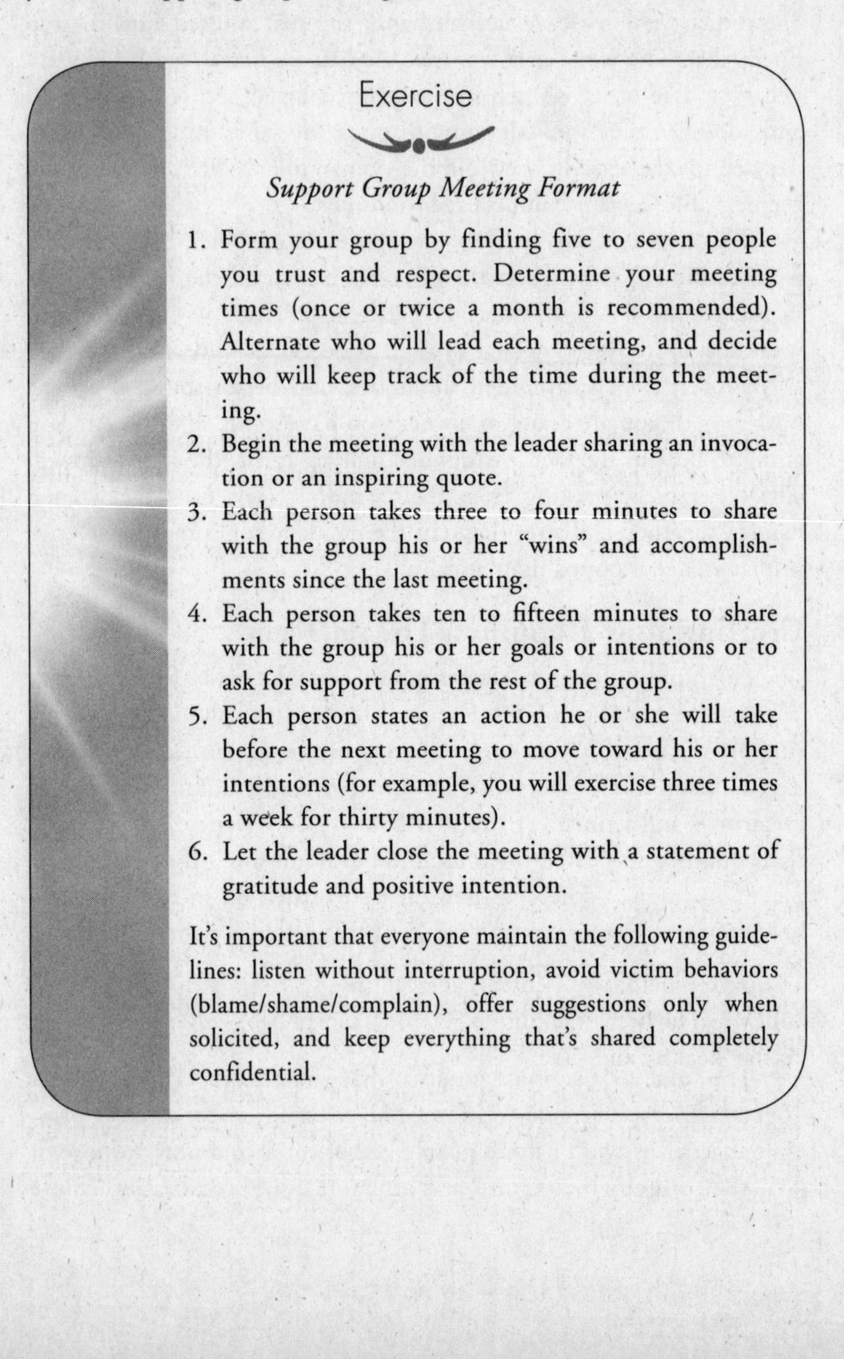

Exercise

Support Group Meeting Format

1. Form your group by finding five to seven people you trust and respect. Determine your meeting times (once or twice a month is recommended). Alternate who will lead each meeting, and decide who will keep track of the time during the meeting.
2. Begin the meeting with the leader sharing an invocation or an inspiring quote.
3. Each person takes three to four minutes to share with the group his or her "wins" and accomplishments since the last meeting.
4. Each person takes ten to fifteen minutes to share with the group his or her goals or intentions or to ask for support from the rest of the group.
5. Each person states an action he or she will take before the next meeting to move toward his or her intentions (for example, you will exercise three times a week for thirty minutes).
6. Let the leader close the meeting with a statement of gratitude and positive intention.

It's important that everyone maintain the following guidelines: listen without interruption, avoid victim behaviors (blame/shame/complain), offer suggestions only when solicited, and keep everything that's shared completely confidential.

Happiness Habit for Relationships #3

See the World as Your Family

Human beings are more alike than we are un-alike. . . . Try to spread your giving of yourself . . . to people who may not even look like you. You belong to everybody, and everybody belongs to you.

—Maya Angelou, author and poet

What I noticed in my interviews with the Happy 100 is that they see the whole world as their family. Their love, empathy, compassion, and caring, which are natural outgrowths of being Happy for No Reason, aren't limited to their relatives and friends, but extend to all of humanity. Nationality, race, religion—none of these creates a boundary. People who are Happy for No Reason see that people everywhere are just like them, and that we all want the same things: love and happiness. Because they always feel they're part of a larger family, happy people make it a habit to give whatever they can, wherever they are.

The Happy 100 believe that their happiness is one of the greatest gifts they can give to the world. In my interview with Liz Gilbert, whose story is in Chapter 7, she told me that after her book *Eat Pray Love* was published, she was often asked by reporters, "Don't you think it was a little selfish to travel around the world looking for yourself?" She always answered, "You know what? I actually think it would have been a little selfish to spend the rest of my life in narcissistic, depressive, anxious misery. That person adds nothing to society, adds nothing to any room that she enters, adds nothing to the people whom she touches. The best community service I can possibly offer the world is to stay healthy and sane."

During my search for the Happy 100, a business colleague told me about his friend, Happy Oasis. When I heard her name I was sure it would be an interesting interview. And it was. Happy truly lives up to her name. In the extraordinary story that follows, Happy describes an experience she had over twenty years ago while traveling in Asia that taught her what it truly means to see the world as your family and help others by sharing your own happiness.

Happy's Story

The Smiling Man

I've always been a free spirit. When I finished high school in 1983, instead of attending the Ivy League university my parents expected me to go to, I took off for Australia. I spent the next few years traveling and earning money, as I literally worked my way across Australia and Southeast Asia, pursuing my own course of study in anthropology.

When I left the United States, I was a naïve, sheltered eighteen-year-old. I considered myself a happy person, but looking back, it was more a case of ignorance being bliss. Until my travels in the Third World, I simply hadn't been aware of the extreme suffering of humanity.

I went to Bangladesh hoping to spend time with a group of tribal people who lived there. When I arrived in the capital city, Dhaka, I discovered that besides being monsoon season, there was a widespread famine that was causing a lot of illness and death all over the country.

One morning, I boarded a bus in Dhaka, heading for the more remote areas of the country. Looking around at the other passengers, I saw that I was the only Westerner on the bus. In addition, I was a blond, blue-eyed and very young-looking woman in a Muslim country where I had scarcely seen any women at all. I'd tried to dress in the Muslim style, wrapping a black sarong around my head and covering my arms and legs as much as I could, but I knew I was very conspicuous, and it made me a little uncomfortable.

We left the city and soon were driving through farmland and small villages. It had been raining heavily for days, and at one point, the bus had to pull off the rapidly flooding road onto a field to avoid disaster. As I watched, the road washed away and the small village nearby began to flood. The land the bus was parked on was quickly surrounded by water, and I saw crowds of people making their way toward our football-field-size island of higher ground. Soon there were hundreds of extremely skinny people, most of them children, barefoot and dressed in rags, lying on the ground outside the bus. I realized to my horror that they were dying; the dysentery and lack of food were taking their toll.

Soon I was the only one who had not disembarked to see what was going on or perhaps to help. I sat on the bus by myself, wondering what *I* could do to help. My first naïve impulse was to cash the $2,000 in traveler's checks I had in my money belt—meant to finance the next year or two of my traveling—and buy food for these people. But I quickly realized that there was no way to get to a bank.

Then I thought, *I can use the $150 in Bangladeshi currency I have to buy everyone a meal from the grocery store.* But looking at the flooded shanty village and rice paddies surrounding our little island, the reality dawned: there was no food to be bought anywhere.

My next desperate thought was, *Surely, the Red Cross will show up soon. They have to.* But the rain kept pouring down, and within an hour I had to accept that the Red Cross wasn't coming. Judging from what I had seen of the country so far, I doubted they ever came.

I started to cry, whimpering to myself. I wasn't concerned about my own survival; I was carrying a small knapsack with water, a little food, and a change of clothing. After my year traveling, I was used to living a very rugged life. But I felt so helpless, believing there was nothing I could do.

I heard something and looked up to see a man wearing only a loincloth stepping on to the bus. He was frail, skinny, and although he was probably only thirty-five, he looked very old. He hobbled toward me, gripping the tops of the wooden benches of the bus for support. When he reached me, he stood gazing at me, then stretched out his hand and touched what was showing of my hair under my head covering. Normally, I didn't let strange men touch my hair, but I was distracted by his eyes. They looked like the eyes of a ghost or an angel—of someone who had already died. Then, as he pulled his hand away, I noticed his fingers, or what was left of them. They were scaly and stubby, half the length of ordinary fingers. I froze: The man was a leper. Before I could react, he turned and hobbled off the bus, disappearing into the crowd outside. Shaken by the encounter, I sat in silence, feeling even more helpless and out of my element than before.

I was still upset when, a few minutes later, another man came up beside the bus and stood outside my window, gazing in at me. He looked like everybody else I'd met in Bangladesh—scantily clad, very skinny, barefoot—except he was smiling broadly.

It suddenly seemed horribly inappropriate to me that this man was smiling under these circumstances. Through my tears, I snapped at him, "How can you smile in such a situation?"

To my surprise, he answered me in perfect Queen's English, "A smile is all I have to give, madam."

I was shocked at the power of these nine simple words. They turned my world—and all my ideas about helping others—upside down. But before I could respond, he motioned to me, saying, "Come. Come with me."

I got off the bus and went with him into the rain. We spent the next ten hours walking through the field, singing to one person after the other as they lay dying. Kneeling beside each person, the Smiling Man, as I called him, sang beautiful, soul-stirring Muslim chants while I sang Christian songs I had learned at summer camp.

Our singing—well, mostly the Smiling Man's, as he was so much better at this than I was—calmed people and seemed to give them peace. Sometimes he would stroke their foreheads; at other times he would touch their shoulders and encourage me to do the same. I was shy about this when it was a man in front of us, since in Muslim countries a woman isn't supposed to touch men she is not related to, but under the circumstances it seemed okay. We would do this until there was a sign the person felt better, such as the slight curve of a smile, or some response that showed relaxation. Then we'd leave them to journey into the other realm called death by themselves, or stay beside them until they were gone. As the hours ticked by, we went around and around that field, singing to dozens and dozens of people.

At one point, as we picked our careful way through the maze of bodies, I recognized the man from the bus—the leper who had touched my hair—lying motionless on the ground. I stopped and took a closer look. With his eyes closed, he seemed to blend in with the earth beneath him. Then, with a jolt, I realized he was dead. I felt a pang of sorrow; I wished we had found him sooner. Sending up a silent prayer, I turned away and hurried to catch up with the Smiling Man, who was already kneeling next to a child and beginning to sing.

The Smiling Man and I talked on and off throughout the day. There were times when I felt overwhelmed by the scene around me and began to cry. Mostly he ignored my tears, but at one point he said to me, "We have a reason to cry and we aren't crying. You have nothing to cry about. Why are you crying?" It was said kindly, but with a touch of fatherly sternness. It was his way of asking me to take on the role of leadership, as if saying, "Gather yourself. Let's do what we can."

The rain finally subsided. The driver called out and people began to board the bus. I said good-bye to the Smiling Man and went back to my seat. As I sat there, waiting to leave, I knew I'd probably never see him again. Still, he'd become my hero. I admired his wisdom and what I can only describe as gumption. Without a penny, without a dollar—without any material item—he'd eased the suffering of hundreds of people by offering his love and joy. I made a silent vow to be like that smiling man.

In the years since then, I have made it a priority in my life to be as happy as I can, to share that happiness with as many people as possible, and to treat everyone I meet as family. Even here in America, at the grocery store, at the bank, wherever you go, you often don't know what's going on with the people you see. Somebody could be terribly depressed, and by just smiling, opening up, and reaching out—giving of myself the way the Smiling Man did—I've found I really can offer some relief and light. That's the reason I changed my name to Happy Oasis: to be an oasis of happiness for everyone. And the wonderful side effect is that I get to carry that oasis inside myself wherever I go. It's the basis of the high level of happiness I enjoy today.

The Smiling Man showed me that giving love to others isn't complicated or difficult. I know firsthand that when a smile is all you have to give—it can be enough.

The Power of Connection

Smiles are universally recognized signs of friendliness and loving intention. Even a brief smile can have an enormous impact. I heard Caroline Myss tell a story from her book *Invisible Acts of Power* that illustrates this perfectly. The story is about a young man who'd become so despondent that he'd decided to return to his apartment to commit suicide. As he stood on a street corner waiting for a car to pass, the woman behind the wheel looked directly at him and flashed him a huge smile. The smile was so warm and caring that it convinced him there was still goodness in the world, and he turned away from ending his life. No matter who or where you are, a sincere smile bridges even the largest age and cultural differences and creates a sense of connection.

Robert Biswas-Diener, often referred to as the Indiana Jones of positive psychology because he's traveled to remote regions around the world studying happiness, has found that connection is a powerful influence on happiness, among even the poorest citizens of the world. Biswas-Diener, in collaboration with his father, Edward Diener, examined the life satisfaction of homeless people and slum dwellers in Calcutta. The results were fascinating. Good social relationships and healthy bonds with family made residents of the Calcutta slums more resilient and better able to withstand the negative effects of dire poverty.

It was Robert who introduced me to Happy 100 member Roko Belic, a young documentary filmmaker whose first documentary, *Genghis Blues,* made with his brother, Adrian, was nominated for an Oscar in 2000 and won many awards. Roko's current project is a film on happiness called *Happiness Revolution* that's taken him to many countries including Brazil, India, Namibia, and Japan, to document how people around the world experience—or don't experience—happiness. Based on what he's found on his travels, Roko also believes that a sense of belongingness is vital for sustaining well-being and happiness.

Roko told me in our interview that he'd gone to Japan because he'd heard from many sources that, though a materially wealthy country, Japan wasn't doing so well emotionally. Riding the subway in Tokyo, he was shocked to see that 80 percent of the commuters were actually asleep or trying to sleep. Because work is the highest priority in most people's lives there, they tend to work outrageously long hours, sometimes as many as twenty hours a day. This dedication to productivity has taken its toll, not only in sleep deprivation, but in the amount of connection people feel with each other.

But Roko had also heard that some of the world's oldest people live in Japan, specifically Okinawa. Familiar with the research showing that happy people live longer, he and his crew left Tokyo and went to a small village on the island of Okinawa to see if the Okinawans' longevity had anything to do with being happy.

There, Roko found a small pocket of happiness. Many people he met were in their nineties, and although they spent their days farming in the hot sun and living what we Westerners would consider a rudimentary lifestyle, the joy in their lives was palpable. What made this even more striking is that a large number of the residents were older women who'd lost their husbands and children when Okinawa was razed during World War II. But far from being bitter or sad about their losses, these women radiated good humor and happiness.

The key was the strong sense of connectedness that seemed to include all the generations. Every Friday night, the villagers got together and had a dance. While a band played, everyone, from the young children to the old ladies, danced together to traditional music. Roko said that everyone had a good time, even the teenagers whose American counterparts would be too "cool" for gatherings like these. The Okinawans' high level of joy shows how powerful a sense of community is for supporting individual happiness.

What if that sense of community included the whole world? Imagine feeling as comfortable with anyone, anywhere, as you do hanging out with your closest friends or family. That's really what it means to see the world as your family. Palestinian American Naomi Shihab Nye, celebrated poet and essayist, shares an experience of this she had in the Albuquerque airport terminal:

> After learning my flight had been detained four hours, I heard the announcement: "If anyone in the vicinity of Gate 4-A understands any Arabic, please come to the gate immediately."

Well, one pauses these days. But Gate 4-A was my own gate, so I went there. An older woman in full traditional Palestinian dress, just like my grandmother wore, was crumpled on the floor, wailing loudly.

"Please help," said the flight service person. "Talk to her. What is her problem? We told her the flight was going to be four hours late, and she did this!"

I stooped to put my arm around the woman and spoke to her haltingly: *"Shu dow-a, shu-biduck habibti, stani stani schway, min fadlick, sho bit se-wee?"*

The minute she heard my words, however poorly used, she stopped crying. It turned out she thought our flight had been canceled entirely, and she needed to be in El Paso for a major medical treatment the following day. I said, "No, no, we're fine, you'll get there, just late. Who is picking you up? Let's call him."

We called her son and I spoke with him in English. I told him I would stay with his mother till we got on the plane and, once aboard, would ride next to her. Then, while we were waiting to board, we called her other sons. Then we called my dad, and he and she spoke for a while in Arabic. They found out, of course, they had ten shared friends.

Then I thought—*just for the heck of it*—why not call some Palestinian poets I know and let them chat with her? This all took up about two hours. She was laughing a lot by then, telling about her life, patting my knee, answering questions. She had pulled a sack of homemade *mamool* cookies—little powdered sugar crumbly mounds stuffed with dates and nuts—out of her bag and was offering them to all the women at the gate.

To my amazement, not a single woman declined one. It was like a sacrament. The traveler from Argentina, the mom from California, the lovely woman from Laredo—we were all covered with the same powdered sugar. And smiling. There is no better cookie.

And then the airline broke out free beverages from huge coolers, and two little girls from our flight, one African American, one Mexican American, ran around serving us all apple juice and lemonade. They were covered with powdered sugar too.

I noticed that my new best friend—by now we were holding hands—had a potted plant poking out of her bag, some medicinal thing with green furry leaves. Such an old country traveling tradition. Always carry a plant. Always stay rooted to somewhere.

And I looked around that gate of late and weary ones, and thought, *This is the world I want to live in. The shared world.* Not a single person in this gate—once the crying of confusion stopped—seemed apprehensive about any other person. They took the cookies. I wanted to hug all those other women too.

This can still happen anywhere. Not everything is lost.

The more we experience even total strangers as our family, the happier we'll all be. The following exercise will help you get in the habit of seeing the whole world as your family.

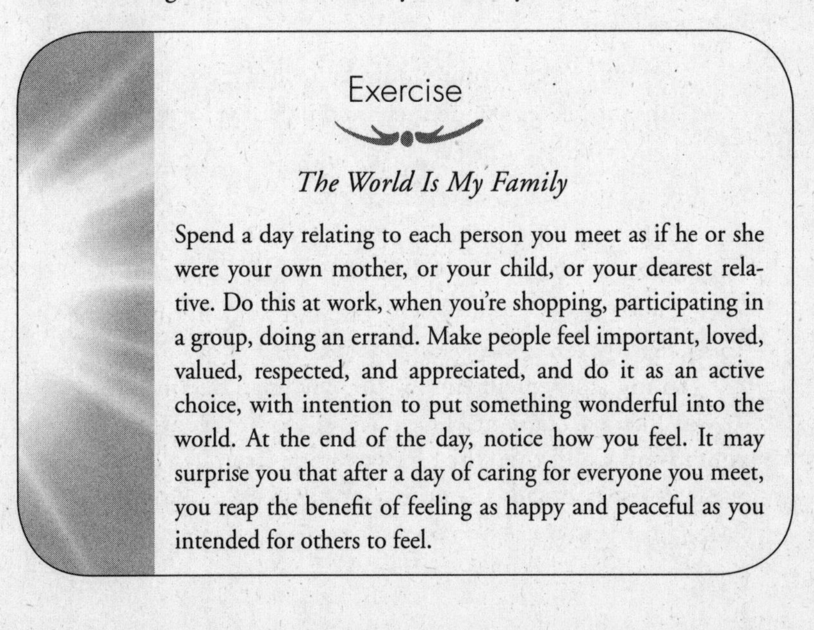

Exercise

The World Is My Family

Spend a day relating to each person you meet as if he or she were your own mother, or your child, or your dearest relative. Do this at work, when you're shopping, participating in a group, doing an errand. Make people feel important, loved, valued, respected, and appreciated, and do it as an active choice, with intention to put something wonderful into the world. At the end of the day, notice how you feel. It may surprise you that after a day of caring for everyone you meet, you reap the benefit of feeling as happy and peaceful as you intended for others to feel.

Summary and Happiness Action Steps

When you cultivate nourishing relationships, you use emotional contagion to your advantage, surround yourself with support, and see the world as your family. This creates a beautiful garden around your Home for Happiness. Use the following action steps to practice the Happiness Habits for Relationships:

1. Use your inner GPS to identify your nourishing and toxic relationships, the "roses and weeds" in your garden.
2. Use the emotional immunity boosters when you need to interact with toxic people.
3. Do the Appreciation Practice daily for one week.
4. If appropriate, check out a 12-step program that can help you with your situation.
5. Create a support group and set up a schedule of regular meetings.
6. See the world as your family by focusing on the ways we are more alike than different and radiating lovingkindness to everyone you meet.

PART III

Happy for No Reason Ever After

Our business is to be happy.

—His Holiness the Dalai Lama

The Happy for No Reason Plan for Life

It is only possible to live happily ever after on a day-to-day basis.

—Margaret Bonnano, writer

By now you know that "happily ever after" isn't just for fairy tales or for only the lucky few. From reading the compelling research and the experiences of truly happy people—perhaps even trying some of the exercises—you know that when you practice the 21 Happiness Habits, you too can join the Happy 100 and experience inner peace and well-being as the backdrop for everything else in your life.

Here's a summary of the seven steps you've just taken to build your Home for Happiness, along with the habits that go along with them.

Happiness Habits

The Foundation—Take Ownership of Your Happiness

1. *Focus on Solutions*: To become more empowered, build on what's already working to improve any situation in your life.
2. *Look for the Lesson and the Gift*: Instead of blaming others or making excuses, find the lesson and the blessing in each circumstance.
3. *Make Peace with Yourself*: Lighten your load by accepting the past and moving forward.

The Pillar of the Mind—Don't Believe Everything You Think

4. *Question Your Thoughts*: Examine your beliefs to determine if your mind is telling you the truth.
5. *Go Beyond the Mind and Let Go*: Free yourself from your negative thoughts and feelings.
6. *Incline Your Mind toward Joy*: Lean into the thoughts that support your happiness.

The Pillar of the Heart—Let Love Lead

7. *Focus on Gratitude*: Put your attention on what you appreciate to expand the energy of your heart.
8. *Practice Forgiveness*: Release your resentment and anger toward others to free your heart.
9. *Spread Lovingkindness*: Practice "beaming" love and good wishes to everyone you encounter.

The Pillar of the Body—Make Your Cells Happy

10. *Nourish Your Body*: Balance your brain and body chemistry through optimal nutrition and supplementation.
11. *Energize Your Body*: Use movement, breath, and proper rest to increase the vital life force in your body.

12. *Tune In to Your Body's Wisdom*: Love and honor your body and listen to its needs.

The Pillar of the Soul—Plug Yourself In to Spirit

13. *Invite Connection with Your Higher Power*: Find silence through prayer, meditation, or time in nature to experience your relationship to your Higher Power.
14. *Listen to Your Inner Voice*: Make connection with your soul's wisdom to guide you in life.
15. *Trust Life's Unfolding*: Open to grace and put yourself in the flow of life.

The Roof—Live a Life Inspired by Purpose

16. *Find Your Passion*: Discover what truly matters to you and align yourself with what makes your heart sing.
17. *Follow the Inspiration of the Moment*: Focus on *what* you want and allow yourself to be led to *how* it will unfold.
18. *Contribute to Something Greater Than Yourself*: Respond to your inner calling to serve others in ways great and small.

The Garden—Cultivate Nourishing Relationships

19. *Tend to Your Relationships*: Appreciate the people in your life and use emotional contagion to enhance your happiness.
20. *Surround Yourself with Support*: Create a support system that helps you stay focused on living your best life.
21. *See the World as Your Family*: Feel a sense of love and connection to all of humanity.

To download a free Happiness Habits miniposter, *go to www.HappyforNoReason.com/bookgifts.*

Making the Happiness Habits second nature requires practice. It takes time and repetition for your brain to create the neural pathways that will support a higher level of happiness. Here are some tips to help you on the way:

1. Remember the Guiding Three.
2. Take baby steps.
3. Set up a support system.

Remember the Guiding Three

You can employ the first principle of the Guiding Three—*Whatever expands you makes you happier*—by using your inner GPS to inform your choices in life every day.

Engage the second principle—*The universe is out to support you*—by asking yourself whenever necessary, "If there were a higher purpose to what's happening, what would it be?"

The best way to use the third principle—*Whatever you appreciate, appreciates*—is my Secret Formula that you learned in Chapter 2: intention, attention, and no tension.

Intention: Keep your intention to be Happy for No Reason clear and lively in your awareness. Put your written Happy for No Reason intention from Chapter 2 in a place where you'll see it on a regular basis.

Attention: Keep the momentum going by regularly putting your attention on developing the Happiness Habits and doing the action steps at the end of each chapter designed to help you practice them.

No Tension: The state of peace and well-being you want is already there inside you. Relax, let go, and trust that it's all unfolding.

The process is like planting a flower: you plant it (your intention), you water and fertilize it (your attention), and then you relax (no tension), knowing that over time you'll begin seeing the blooms. You can let go—the process is happening.

Take Baby Steps: Overcoming Your Resistance to Change

To make the quickest progress, you don't have to take huge leaps. You just have to take baby steps—and keep on taking them. In Japan, they call this approach *kaizen,* which translates literally as "continual improvement." Using kaizen, great and lasting success is achieved through small, consistent steps. It turns out that slow and steady is the best way to overcome your resistance to change.

Most of us resist change—even when it's good for us! It's the reason that so many people have exercise bikes stuck in their garages, rarely used gym memberships, and that case of low-carb, low-calorie, low-fat canned diet shake gathering dust in the pantry. This resistance is based in our physiology. Our brain often views change with suspicion, if not downright fear. To overcome that resistance, keep the changes you make small and gradual enough to fly under your brain's "fear radar." When you set goals that are easily achievable, your brain's fear response isn't activated.

What's more, as you continue to take small steps, the brain begins creating new neural pathways that support each new Happiness Habit. Soon your new habits become hardwired and you find yourself easily and automatically practicing your desired behaviors.

Set Up a Support System: Happiness Loves Company

To make this process even more effortless and enjoyable, you can invite other people to join you. Enlist the support of a coach, mentor, friend, or group of friends. Practicing the Happiness Habits with others helps us *own* them on a deeper level.

The psychiatrist Dr. William Glasser, the author of many books, including *Every Student Can Succeed,* has spent years studying how people learn. Expanding on the theories of the twentieth-century educator Edgar Dale, he says:

We Learn . . .

10% of what we read
20% of what we hear
30% of what we see
50% of what we see *and* hear

70% of what we discuss with others
80% of what we experience personally
95% of what we teach to someone else

This means you can increase the impact of reading *Happy for No Reason sevenfold* by simply discussing the information you've learned in this book with other people. Here are some great ways to get support from others:

1. **Find a Happy for No Reason Buddy:** Like an exercise partner, another person who's practicing the Happiness Habits can help keep you on track. When someone else is cheering you on and depending on you for help to stay focused, it makes your goal of being Happy for No Reason a priority in your life. Besides, having a buddy always makes everything more fun.
2. **Form a Happy for No Reason Support Group:** Multiply the buddy effect by starting a Happiness Habit support group, where you gather regularly—face to face, online, or by phone—to advise, listen, and encourage each other as you all raise your happiness set-points. You can spend each meeting focusing on a different habit. Your group will add their attention to your Happy for No Reason intention, increasing its power exponentially. My prediction is that you'll end each meeting feeling uplifted and blessed to find fellow travelers who share your goal of increasing the level of joy in the world. (Visit www.happyfornoreason.com to locate a support group near you.)
3. **Consult with a Happy for No Reason Life Coach:** Many people are using life coaches and finding them very helpful in supporting the achievement of their goals. Contact a Happy for No Reason life coach who is specially trained to guide you in raising your happiness set-point. (Visit www.happyfornoreason.com to find out more about Happy for No Reason life coaches.)
4. **Seek Out Happy for No Reason Mentors:** I consider the Happy 100 my Happy for No Reason mentors and know how incredibly valuable their influence is in my life. Being around people who already experience a deep inner state of happiness will help you build your Home for Happiness more quickly and easily. In some

traditions, "being in the company of the wise" is considered one of the most powerful steps you can take to enhance happiness in life.

The World Is as You Are

How the world appears to you is determined by the color of the glasses you look through. When you're happy, you see happiness all around you. When you're unhappy, you find unhappiness everywhere. I love the following fable which illustrates this beautifully.

> Long ago in a faraway village, there was a place known as The House of a Thousand Mirrors. A happy little dog learned of this place and decided to visit. When he arrived, he bounced happily up the stairs to the doorway of the house. He looked through the doorway with his ears lifted high and his tail wagging as fast as it could. To his great surprise, he found himself staring at a thousand other happy little dogs with their tails wagging just as fast as his. He smiled a great smile, and was answered with a thousand great smiles just as warm and friendly. As he left the house, he thought to himself, "This is a wonderful place. I will come back and visit it often."
>
> In this same village, another little dog, who was not happy like the first one, decided to visit the house. He slowly climbed the stairs and hung his head low as he looked into the door. When he saw the thousand unfriendly-looking dogs staring back at him, he growled at them and was horrified to see a thousand little dogs growling back at him. As he left, he thought to himself, "This is a horrible place, and I will never come back here again."

Everyone in the world is your mirror. When you're Happy for No Reason, the world reflects that happiness back to you.

Be Part of the Happiness Revolution

As you build your Home for Happiness, it won't be hard to find others to join you—there's a happiness revolution going on. Happiness is showing up everywhere, in magazines, newspapers, books, and on TV. There are even ad campaigns and huge billboards touting phrases like "Dare to Be Happy." More and more people want to discover how to be truly happy in their lives now. I read recently that happiness today is what self-esteem was for the 1990s and self-actualization was for the 1970s. This is good news because the more people who have their attention on happiness, the more momentum is created for everyone.

The entire world doesn't have to be happy for there to be a fundamental shift in the happiness level on the planet. There have been numerous studies conducted that indicate that when even just 1 percent of a population experiences greater peace, well-being, and coherence by meditating together regularly, it has an effect on the entire community, lowering the crime rate, number of accidents, acts of violence, and incidents of disease.

Learning to be Happy for No Reason puts you on the leading edge of the happiness revolution and is a powerful way to contribute to the world. You become like a beacon, lighting up your own life and the lives of everyone around you. This idea is beautifully expressed by an ancient Chinese proverb that still holds true today:

When there is light in the soul, there is beauty in the person.
When there is beauty in the person, there is harmony in the house.
When there is harmony in the house, there is order in the nation.
When there is order in the nation, there is peace in the world.

Happy for No Reason—Our Personal Fulfillment

In the introduction, I mentioned how blessed both Carol and I feel to have been able to write this book. Spending time interviewing the Happy 100 and focusing all of our attention on the subject of happiness has made us both happier, healthier, and kinder people (at least according to our spouses!). The perspective of Happy for No Reason permeates our interactions with people, our perception of the world around us—everything! I'm amazed at the power of those four little words, Happy for No Reason, to uplift and remind people of the happiness they already have inside.

This was confirmed for me recently during a conversation I had when I was ordering a lamp over the phone. While the woman processed my information, we started talking about happiness. When I mentioned the title of my book, the woman became very animated, saying, "Happy for No Reason! I love that! Sometimes I feel happy and I don't know why, but I've never known what to call it. Happy for No Reason is the perfect description." The next day I received a surprise email from her that included this paragraph:

> At the end of the day as I drove home after speaking with you, I kept hearing "Happy for No Reason" in my head. I couldn't help but smile—and found myself smiling for miles.

The ripple effect of Happy for No Reason continued: reading her email made me smile too.

For Carol, this idea of being happy from the inside had been percolating for many years. When the title *Happy for No Reason* came to me and I told Carol about it, she instantly agreed that it was the perfect way to describe that state beyond ordinary happiness.

The next day she called me, very excited, and said that she had been going through some old journals of hers and had come across the lyrics to a song she'd written in 1984. She had completely forgotten about the song, but when she read it again that day, it had given her goose bumps. When she told me the lyrics, I too was blown away by the synchronicity:

> Driving my car, yellow lines flashing by,
> New York winter and a New York sky
> Then for no reason special that I can see,
> Suddenly I'm happy as a person can be.
>
> Hot soapy water, doing the dishes,
> Staring at the clouds and making wishes.
> Then for no reason special that I can see,
> Suddenly I'm happy as a person can be.

Joy inside me blossoms like a rose,
Something sweet and warm flows.
Then for no reason special that I can see,
Suddenly I'm happy as a person can be.

Cue the *Twilight Zone* theme song: Doo-doo-DOO-doo. Doo-doo-DOO-doo. We laughed, but both of us knew it was no accident we were doing this book together!

Working on *Happy for No Reason* has totally transformed Carol's life. She says that although she considered herself pretty happy before, the knowledge of Happy for No Reason has given her a level of everyday peace and joy she'd had only glimpses of earlier. She feels a new confidence knowing that no matter what happens to her, she has a great toolbox full of Happiness Habits that can help her find her way back to the happiness she has inside.

For me, writing *Happy for No Reason* has been the fulfillment of my childhood longing: to find deep happiness and to share it with others. Building my Home for Happiness has erased the angst and emptiness that weighed me down for so many years. I feel extraordinary gratitude for the steadily growing experience of Happy for No Reason in my life.

In his last days, my dad, my original Happy for No Reason role model and the inspiration for this book, gave me one final gift.

Celebrating his ninety-first birthday at a dinner at home with the entire family, my father ate what turned out to be his last meal. It was also the last time he was up and about before he passed away, peacefully, a week later. Though we didn't realize what he was doing at the time, that evening he made a very specific and deliberate point to take each one of his children—my sister, my brother, and me—one by one over to the Tree of Life needlepoint, his final masterpiece, which was hanging on the living room wall.

As he smiled lovingly and pointed at the framed needlepoint, I knew he was trying to convey something important. He could barely talk, but now I believe that with this final gesture he was trying to communicate to me, "You're the next generation in the Tree of Life, and I want you to pass on the message of my life. I have lived a deeply happy life. Please live that happiness yourself and help others to live it too."

This book is my way of passing on my dad's message.

My deepest desire is that each one of us becomes full of light, love, and happiness in our own life and through that we create a world of peace.

May we all be Happy for No Reason!

RECOMMENDED RESOURCES

Programs to Help You Be Happy for No Reason . . . Now!

Now that you know it's possible to be Happy for No Reason, you've set your sights on experiencing it more and more in your life—and the sooner the better. To help speed your progress, I created the following programs that provide greater support than you can get from a book alone.

Happy for No Reason *Seminar*

In the Happy for No Reason Seminar I will personally guide you in applying the principles, habits, and tools in this book to immediately transform your life and lay the foundation for lasting happiness. You will put into practice the seven steps of building your inner Home for Happiness and raise your happiness set-point so that peace and well-being are established as your everyday reality.

Happy for No Reason *Coaching*

However grounded we are in the principles we've learned, life has a way of throwing curveballs that continually challenge us. My coaching program is designed to assist you in integrating the Happiness Habits into your everyday life to make your happiness truly unshakable. Coaching will help you develop new strategies for thinking, feeling, and acting that support your happiness. It is the fastest and surest way to overcome old habits and begin living the life of your dreams.

Happy for No Reason *Paraliminal CD*

The Happy for No Reason Paraliminal CD is like an automatic, perpetual happiness generator. Based on the breakthrough technologies of neurolinguistic programming and whole-brain learning, Paraliminal CDs help you acquire new behaviors and more positive feelings in minutes. I cocreated the CD with my friend Paul R. Scheele, the world leader in this technology and truly the master of the mental makeover. Just put on the stereo headphones and sit back and listen to the words and music, and you'll be guided from the inside out to experience more happiness in your life.

Happy for No Reason *Interview Series*

The knowledge in this book won't change your life until you make it an integral part of your daily reality. My in-depth interviews with the Happy 100 and other happiness experts will show you these concepts, habits, and tools in action and bring them vividly to life. Seeing them applied in the context of people's varied real-life experiences will help you integrate them and inspire you with a vision of possibilities.

Happy for No Reason *CD Course*

I've created a CD course—a personal learning program—that you can use in your home or office. As you listen, you will go step-by-step through life-changing processes that will shift your awareness, change your habits, and lead you to a richly happy life.

Happy for No Reason *Keynote Presentations*

In my twenty years of delivering keynote addresses to countless corporations, associations, and professional and nonprofit organizations, I have learned that a keynote presentation can transform and galvanize individuals and organizations with measurable and often startlingly powerful results. It is my joy to offer my services in the inspiration and transformation of your audience or organization. Where individuals are happy and productive, any level of success is possible.

***For more information on these and other programs, please visit* www.HappyForNoReason.com/Programs.**

General Happiness Books

The Art of Happiness, by His Holiness the Dalai Lama (New English Library, 1999).
Authentic Happiness: Using the New Positive Psychology to Realize Your Potential for Lasting Fulfillment, by Martin Seligman (Free Press, 2004).
Feel Happy Now!, by Michael Neill (Hay House, 2008).
Happier: Learn the Secrets to Daily Joy and Lasting Fulfillment, by Tal Ben Shahar (McGraw-Hill, 2007).
Happiness: Developing Life's Most Important Skill, by Matthieu Ricard (Little, Brown, 2006).
Happiness Makeover: How to Teach Yourself to Be Happy and Enjoy Every Day, by M. J. Ryan (Broadway, 2005).
How We Choose to Be Happy: The 9 Choices of Extremely Happy People—Their Secrets, Their Stories, by Rick Foster and Greg Hicks (Perigee Trade, 2004).
The Joy Diet: 10 Daily Practices for a Happier Life, by Martha Beck (Crown, 2003).
Positivity Psychology Coaching: Putting the Science of Happiness to Work for Your Clients, by Robert Biswas-Diener and Ben Dean (Wiley, 2007).
Stumbling on Happiness, by Dan Gilbert (Vintage, 2007).
What Happy People Know: How the New Science of Happiness Can Change Your Life for the Better, by Dan Baker and Cameron Stauth (St. Martin's Griffin, 2004).

Building Your Home for Happiness Books

Chapter 3 (Personal Power)

The Game of Life (Hay House Classics), by Florence Scovel Shinn (Hay House, 2006).
How Did I Get Here? Finding Your Way to Renewed Hope and Happiness When Life and Love Take Unexpected Turns, by Barbara DeAngelis (St. Martin's Griffin, 2006).
The Power of Now: A Guide to Spiritual Enlightenment, by Eckhart Tolle (New World Library, 2004).
The Secret, by Rhonda Byrne (Atria Books/Beyond Words, 2006).
The Solutions Focus: Making Coaching and Change Simple, by Paul Z. Jackson and Mark McKergow (Nicholas Brealey Publishing, 2007).

Chapter 4 (Mind)

Biology of Belief: Unleashing the Power of Consciousness, Matter, and Miracles, by Bruce H. Lipton (Mountain of Love, 2005).
Loving What Is: Four Questions That Can Change Your Life, by Byron Katie and Stephen Mitchell (Three Rivers Press, 2003).
The Sedona Method: Your Key to Lasting Happiness, Success, Peace and Emotional Well-Being, by Hale Dwoskin (Sedona Press, 2003).

Chapter 5 (Heart)

Count Your Blessings: The Healing Power of Gratitude and Love, by John Demartini (Hay House, 2006).
Forgive for Good, by Frederic Luskin (HarperSanFrancisco, 2003).

The HeartMath Solution: The Institute of HeartMath's Revolutionary Program for Engaging the Power of the Heart's Intelligence, by Doc Lew Childre and Howard Martin (HarperSanFrancisco, 2000).

The Hidden Messages in Water, by Masaru Emoto and David A. Thayne (Atria, 2005).

Chapter 6 (Body)

The Diet Cure, by Julia Ross (Penguin, 2000).

Essential Cleansing for Perfect Health, by Brenda Watson (Renew Life Press, 2006).

Everything You Need to Know to Feel Go(o)d, by Candace Pert and Nancy Marriott (Hay House, 2006).

The Four-Day Win: End Your Diet War and Achieve Thinner Peace, by Martha Beck, PhD (Rodale, 2007).

Good Night: The Sleep Doctor's 4-Week Program to Better Sleep and Better Health, by Michael Breus, PhD (Dutton Adult, 2006).

Hormones, Health, and Happiness: A Natural Medical Formula for Rediscovering Youth with Bioidentical Hormones, by Steven F. Hotze, MD (Wellness Central, 2007).

Mars and Venus Diet and Exercise Solution: Create the Brain Chemistry of Health, Happiness, and Lasting Romance, by John Gray (St. Martin's Press, 2003).

The Mood Cure: The 4-Step Program to Take Charge of Your Emotions—Today, by Julia Ross (Penguin, 2003).

Natural Highs: Supplements, Nutrition, and Mind-Body Techniques to Help You Feel Good All the Time, by Hyla Cass, MD, and Patrick Holford (Avery, 2003).

Women's Bodies, Women's Wisdom: Creating Physical and Emotional Health and Healing, by Christiane Northrup, MD (Bantam, 2006).

Chapter 7 (Soul)

Awakening into Oneness: The Power of Blessing in the Evolution of Consciousness by Arjuna Ardagh (Sounds True, 2007).

How to Know God: The Soul's Journey into the Mystery of Mysteries, by Deepak Chopra (Three Rivers Press, 2001).

Inspiration: Your Ultimate Calling, by Wayne Dyer (Hay House, 2007).

No Self, No Problem, by Anan Thubten (Dharmata Press, 2006).

A Return to Love: Reflections on the Principles of "A Course in Miracles," by Marianne Williamson (Harper Paperbacks, 1996).

Chapter 8 (Purpose)

Beneath a Vedic Sun: Discover Your Life Purpose with Vedic Astrology, by William Levacy (Hay House, 2006)

The Better World Shopping Guide, by Ellis Jones (New Society Publishers, Canada, 2006).

Finding Your Own North Star: Claiming the Life You Were Meant to Live, by Martha Beck (Three Rivers Press, 2002).

The Passion Test: The Effortless Path to Discovering Your Destiny, by Janet Bray Attwood and Chris Attwood (Hudson Street Press, 2007).

The Power of Full Engagement: Managing Energy, Not Time, Is the Key to High Performance and Personal Renewal, by Jim Loehr and Tony Schwartz (Free Press, 2004).

Success Built to Last: Creating a Life That Matters, by Jerry Porras, Stewart Emery, and Mark Thompson (Plume, 2007).

The Success Principles: How to Get from Where You Are to Where You Want to Be, by Jack Canfield and Janet Switzer (Collins, 2006).

Chapter 9 (Relationships)

Getting the Love You Want: A Guide for Couples, by Harville Hendrix (Pocket Books, 2005).

Lasting Love: The 5 Secrets of Growing a Vital, Conscious Relationship, by Gay Hendricks and Kathlyn Hendricks (Rodale, 2004).

Men Are from Mars, Women Are from Venus: The Classic Guide to Understanding the Opposite Sex, by John Gray (Harper Paperbacks, 2004).

Chapter 10

One Small Step Can Change Your Life: The Kaizen Way, by Robert Maurer, PhD (Workman, 2004).

Tools and Techniques

Agape International Spiritual Center—Rev. Dr. Michael Beckwith
www.agapelive.com
The Agape International Spiritual Center is a transdenominational spiritual community whose doors are open to all seekers in search of authentic spirituality, personal transformation, and selfless service to humankind.

AIM Program of Energetic Balancing (AIM)
www.aimprogram.com
Developed by Stephen Lewis, AIM uses sophisticated computers to assist people in removing energy blockages and in raising their happiness thermostat. The AIM Program is free to any person with autism or Down syndrome.

The Art of Living Foundation
www.artofliving.org
This international nonprofit educational and humanitarian organization offers workshops teaching meditation and breathing techniques that calm the mind, release stress, clear the body of toxins, and energize the whole system in minutes.

B.E.S.T.—Morter HealthSystem
www.morter.com
Morter HealthSystem developed and teaches the Bio Energetic Synchronization Technique—B.E.S.T.—a physical energy-balancing procedure to reestablish the full healing potential of the body using its natural healing abilities. B.E.S.T. helps balance the autonomic nervous system and supports true, vibrant health.

The Biocybernaut Institute—Dr. James Hardt
www.biocybernaut.com
The Biocybernaut Institute offers Advanced Brian Wave Neurofeedback training. People are gently guided to their own self-discovery through programs that train them how to open their hearts and do deep forgiveness work that will enhance their life experiences and alpha brain waves.

The Canfield Training Group—Jack Canfield
www.jackcanfield.com
The Canfield Training Group offers life-changing programs that focus on living *The Success Principles,* raising self-esteem, and optimizing peak performance. Jack Canfield, America's Success Coach, helps you get from where you are to where you want to be.

Center for Soulful Living—Bill Bauman
aboutcsl.com
The Center for Soulful Living is a worldwide community of people dedicated to living in soul-centered and grace-filled ways. Their primary intention is to help people connect with their own inner wisdom, power, and brilliance.

Cortical Field Re-Education
www.corticalfieldreeducation.com
Cortical Field Re-Education (CFR), developed by Harriet Goslins, is a revolutionary approach to improving health and well-being by enhancing communication between the brain and the body. It is an integrative program that encompasses not only physical healing, but the emotional, spiritual, and energetic levels that accompany healing.

The Demartini Method
www.drdemartini.com
Derived from quantum physics, The Demartini Method is a predetermined set of questions and actions that neutralizes emotional charges and brings balance to your mind and body. The process allows you to break through to new levels of inspiration, creativity, and performance.

Emotional Freedom Technique (EFT)
www.emofree.com
EFT uses gentle tapping on key meridian points on the body to release just about every emotional, health, and performance issue you can name. At www.emofree.com you can download a free manual that will teach you how to use this technique as well as watch a video demonstration of EFT.

Hanna Somatics
www.livingsomatics.com
Hanna Somatics is a program consisting of slow, gentle movements that improve the function of the nervous system. The benefits include a significant reduction of pain and an increase of ease and happiness in the body.

Healthy Wealthy nWise
www.healthywealthynwise.com
Healthy Wealthy nWise is one of the largest online transformational magazines in the world. Their Passion interview live teleconferences are free. Past interviews have included Stephen R. Covey, Wayne Dyer, Marci Shimoff, David Lynch, John Gray, Byron Katie, Paula Abdul, Neale Donald Walsch, Rhonda Byrne, and Willie Nelson

The Hendricks Institute—Gay and Kathlyn Hendricks
www.hendricks.com
The Hendricks Institute teaches core skills for conscious living. Its focus is on assisting people in opening to more creativity, love, and vitality through the power of conscious relationship and whole-person learning.

Holosync
www.centerpointe.com
Holosync is a sophisticated form of neuro-audio technology that easily and effortlessly produces the electrical brain wave patterns of deep meditation every time. It is a scientifically proven brain technology that gives you all the benefits of meditation.

The Institute of HeartMath
www.heartmath.com
The mission of HeartMath is to establish heart-based living and global coherence by inspiring people to connect with the intelligence and guidence of their own hearts. The HeartMath system is composed of research, programs, products, and technologies to improve health, well-being, and personal fulfillment.

Intentional Living Program—Dr. Sue Morter
www.drsuemorter.com
Dr. Morter's Intentional Living Program is a unique mind/body approach and method that empowers people to break through limiting blocks to live the life of their dreams. This experiential and educational program works on the level of repatterning the brain and body to achieve optimal functioning and success.

John Douillard's Life Spa
www.lifespa.com
Life Spa is a Boulder, Colorado, center for Ayurveda and Panchakarma, designed to rejuvenate, detoxify, and balance the deeper tissues of the body. Their programs transform the body at the cellular level.

Lefkoe Institute: Making Change Easier—Morty Lefkoe
www.lefkoeinstitute.com
The Lefkoe Institute helps individuals who want to make lasting changes in their behavior and/or emotions in a gentle yet effective way. Using the Lefkoe Method unwanted beliefs are literally unwired for good.

Lindwall Foundation—Freedom through Releasing
www.lindwallreleasing.org
The Lindwall Releasing Process is a powerful process for letting go of negative memories or limiting thoughts. The process involves allowing a past disturbance

to surface, confronting the situation as needed, then releasing the negative impact and emotional content by speaking affirmations.

The Mood Cure Website—Julia Ross
www.moodcure.com
The Mood Cure is based on the pioneering work done at Julia's California clinic, Recovery Systems, since 1988. This comprehensive, natural approach uses targeted brain-fueling amino acids, combined with a high-protein, healthy fat, veggie-rich diet, to produce improved mood in days.

Nancy Fursetzer
www.Positician.com
Certified Positician® coach. Positicians look for the best in everything and teach others to do the same. Positician certification available.

Network for Grateful Living—Brother David Steindl-Rast
www.gratefulness.org
A Network for Grateful Living (ANG*L) is a nonprofit organization dedicated to gratefulness as the core inspiration for personal change, international cooperation, and sustainable activism in areas of universal concern.

Option Method—Lenora Boyle
www.changelimitingbeliefs.com
Lenora Boyle has been helping people to be happier since 1991 through her interactive seminars, private coaching practice, and teleclasses. She teaches seminars using the Option Method that specializes in going to the root of the problem: the limiting belief or past conditioning.

Paraliminals—Learning Strategies
www.learningstrategies.com/Paraliminal/Home.asp
Paraliminals are a neurolinguistic programming and whole-brain learning technology that increase your personal power by activating your "whole mind" with a precise blend of music and words. Each session is carefully scripted to give you life-changing results.

The Passion Test
www.thepassiontest.com
Janet and Chris Attwood's Passion Test is an incredibly simple yet profound tool

that has been given to thousands of people all over the world. The Passion Test is the perfect way to align yourself with those things that you are most passionate about so that you can share your special gifts.

Patanjali Kundalini Yoga Care
www.kundalinicare.com
Patanjali Kundalini Yoga Care is a spiritual guidence service for sincere seekers based on traditional kundalini science. Provides assessments, individual recommendations for spiritual practice, and follow-up support and guidence.

Positive Psychology Services—Robert Biswas-Diener
www.intentionalhappiness.com
Positive Psychology Services offers a wide range of coaching, training, and speaking services based on the new science of positive psychology.

Psych-K
www.psych-k.com
Psych-K helps you rewrite the software of your mind by changing self-limiting beliefs into beliefs that support you. Psych-K develops whole-brain communication, which quickly and easily changes subconscious beliefs.

Releasing the Inner Magician (RIM)—Dr. Deborah Sandella
www.innermagician.com
The RIM method is an advanced mind-body method for releasing the past and rewiring sabotaging thoughts and feelings. RIM helps you tap your Inner Magician, the divine intuitive power within, that dissolves pain to reveal the natural strength and passion of your spirit.

The Sedona Method—Hale Dwoskin
www.sedona.com
The Sedona Method is a unique program for making lasting, positive changes in your life. The technique supports you in quickly shifting your state of consciousness from one of contraction, stress, and resistance to one of expansion, relaxation, and acceptance.

Solutions Focus—Paul Z. Jackson and Mark McKergow
www.thesolutionsfocus.com
Solutions Focus is the new wave of positive, minimal change for people and organizations—the proven way to find what works as simply and gently as possible. They offer trainings, books, articles, speeches, consultations, and much more.

The Soulmate Kit—Arielle Ford
www.soulmatekit.com
The Soulmate Kit is a step-by-step guide comprising a DVD, three CDs, and a 104-page workbook designed for both men and women. It guides users through a deep and detailed program for clearing out the emotional baggage of the past while creating and magnetizing Mr. or Ms. Right into your life.

Soul Medicine Institute—Dawson Church
www.soulmedicineinstitute.org
Soul Medicine Institute is dedicated to encouraging the understanding that a vibrant spiritual connection is essential to wellness. Soul Medicine Institute facilitates training, education, and research into the role of intention, consciousness, and energy in healing.

Soulwave Institute—Katie Darling
www.soulwave.org
Katie Darling's work explores the scientific and spiritual idea that everything is a wave, including you and me, existing within an oceanic field. Soulwave trainings offer a direct experience of this that clears the way for powerful healing, joy, aliveness, and a new kind of wisdom called dynamic intelligence.

Spring Forest Qigong—Chunyi Lin
www.springforestqigong.com
Spring Forest Qigong is a revolutionary technique based on a healing practice that is thousands of years old, revised and enhanced for a twenty-first-century world. Qigong Master Chunyi Lin created Spring Forest Qigong with one goal in mind: putting the power in your hands to fully realize that you were born a healer.

Switched-On Seminars: Brain Performance Optimization—Jerry Teplitz
www.teplitz.com
Switched-On Seminars focus on rewiring the circuitry of your brain to create new levels of success. Seminars in Selling, Network Marketing, Golf, and Management integrate the left and right hemispheres of your brain to help stop your brain from being triggered by unpleasant past experiences and allow you to easily adapt to new opportunities and changes.

Tapas Acupressure Technique (TAT)
www.tatlife.com
TAT is a leading-edge energy meridian healing technique to end stress, create vibrant good health, and live a happy life. On the www.tatlife.com website you can download a free booklet on how to do TAT for yourself.

Vedic Behavior and Trend Analysis Systems—William R. Levacy
www.vedicsky.com
Vedic Behavior and Trend Analysis Systems helps analyze behavior and forecast events so you can anticipate good outcomes for your actions. It provides a road map for effective living, in tune with the laws of nature.

The Work—Byron Katie
www.thework.com
The Work is a simple yet powerful process of inquiry that teaches you to identify and question the stressful thoughts that cause all the suffering in the world. People who do The Work faithfully report life-changing results.

Yes To Success Seminars—Debra Halperin Poneman
www.yestosuccess.com
This is the seminar that launched the careers of many top transformational leaders including Deepak Chopra, Janet Attwood, and Marci Shimoff! Founded in 1981, Yes to Success, Inc., provides a system for uncovering your true purpose and then gives you the tools you need to realize that purpose. Learn how to live each and every day joyfully and profoundly.

Additional Happiness Resources

Happiness Websites, Newsletters, E-zines, Blogs, and Films

www.goodmorningworld.org

Receive Good Morning World's Idea Dream daily email messages for a better world. The daily email includes one idea dream from over 64,000 *Ideas and Dreams for a Better World* collected since October 2004.

www.happinessclub.com

The Happiness Club's mission is to promote the benefits of being happy through meetings, newsletters, and an informative website to the people in your community and around the world.

www.thehappinessshow.com

The Happiness Show is a website offering free happiness information, resources, and over 130 twenty-eight-minute episodes in streaming audio and video for all Internet connections.

www.happinessproject.typepad.com

The Happiness Project website is the blog of author Gretchen Rubin, who spent a year test-driving every principle, tip, theory, and scientific study she could find on happiness. On this daily blog, she recounts some of her adventures and insights as she grapples with the challenge of being happier.

www.happinessfilm.com

The Happiness Revolution. Academy Award–winning filmmaker Roko Belic presents a full-length documentary on happiness filmed in more than fourteen countries, in such locations as the Louisiana bayou, the desert of Namibia, the beaches of Brazil, and the gardens of Findhorn. This film showcases amazing findings about happiness from a variety of sources, from a scientist performing brain scans in his lab to a rickshaw puller in the streets of Calcutta.

www.reflectivehappiness.com

The Reflective Happiness Program gives you direct access to the minds that founded positive psychology. The program consists of Happiness Building

Exercises, Happiness Tests and Questionnaires, access to the Positive Psychology Community Forum, Newsletter, and Book Club, as well as Questions and Answers with Dr. Martin Seligman, the father of positive psychology.

www.wisebrain.org
The Wise Brain website developed by Rick Hanson, PhD, and Rick Mendius, MD, provides information about the neuroscience of psychological well-being and spiritual growth. You can subscribe to the free *Wise Brain Bulletin,* a twice-monthly e-zine that features happiness tools and methods and contemplative wisdom.

Happiness Classes and Conferences

Awakening Joy
www.awakeningjoy.info
Awakening Joy is a ten-month experiential course led by James Baraz, founding teacher of Spirit Rock Meditation Center, designed to develop your natural capacity for well-being and happiness.

University of Pennsylvania Positive Psychology Center
www.authentichappiness.sas.upenn.edu
The Positive Psychology Center offers questionnaires, resources, articles, and a master's degree in applied positive psychology.

Annual Positive Psychology Summit
www.gallupippi.com
The Gallup Institute for Global Well-Being offers an annual global well-being forum featuring the International Positive Psychology Summit and New Insights from the Gallup World Poll.

ACKNOWLEDGMENTS

This book was a collaborative effort in so many ways. I feel deeply grateful for the extraordinary support I received and for the invaluable contributions of friends, family, colleagues, the Happy 100, and experts in a variety of fields. Carol and I would like to thank many wonderful and generous people who have shared in this journey with us.

From Marci:

Carol, for giving your heart, mind, and soul to this project with total devotion and working tirelessly to create the best book possible. Thank you for being there for me as a gifted writer, a brilliant collaborator, and a loving friend. I couldn't have done this book without you, nor would I have wanted to.

Sergio, for being my rock, my hero, and my love. Thank you for your unwavering support, your profound insights, and for continually showing me in many ways, big and small, that love is always most important. I am so blessed to share my life with a man who is truly Happy for No Reason!

My extraordinary family: Mom and Dad, the two best parents in the world, for their unconditional love and for always believing in me. My sister, Lynda, for being the other "spiritual one." My brother, Paul, who taught me everything I know (at least that's what he tells me). My wonderful Aunt Marian, fabulous sister-in-law, Susan, and great nephews and niece, Aaron, Vickie, Jared, and Tony. Maija Snepste, who's a loving addition to our family. Leah Basch for being such an awesome "little sister." And to Francesca, Max, and Silvia Baroni, for sustaining me with your love and those superb Sunday night Italian dinners at your home.

Bonnie Solow, my literary agent and dear friend, who has seen us through this entire book-writing process with love, grace, encouragement, incredible patience, and consummate skill. Thank you for holding my hand and nourishing my heart. You are the best literary agent in the world and a most extraordinary friend. And to Lulu for spreading joy everywhere.

Jack Canfield, my phenomenal mentor and *Chicken Soup* "soul" brother, for guiding me, inspiring me, and so generously sharing with me all your extraordinary wisdom and knowledge. I wouldn't be where I am today without you. I love you and deeply value our friendship and the tremendous impact you've had on my life. Inga Canfield, my "fun fairy" and wise sage all in one package: thank you for being a great friend. Mark Victor Hansen, Patty Aubery, Russ Kamalski, Patty Hansen, and the entire *Chicken Soup for the Soul* family for always being there for me with wisdom, love, and support. Jennifer Hawthorne, for starting on this writing path with me. May bluebirds always surround you with happiness.

Pete Bissonette, Paul Scheele, and Learning Strategies for being my wonderful partners in bringing a new level of happiness to the world. I love working with you and feel fortunate to be on the same team with you. My colleagues on the Transformational Leadership Council, I am constantly awed by your individual and collective brilliance, sheer goodness, and commitment to make a difference in the world. I so deeply appreciate your support. Deborah Rozman, Howard Martin, Doc Childre, and my other great friends at the Institute of HeartMath for your contribution in the sphere of human development and for generously assisting me in my work.

Maharishi Mahesh Yogi, my first spiritual teacher, for giving me the gift of meditation, life-changing knowledge, and profound, ageless wisdom.

Janet (Jani) Attwood for being my best cheerleader, dear friend, and favorite person to laugh with. Your loving heart is as big as the universe. Chris Attwood, thank you for your great wisdom and your open heart. You nailed it every time I called for help. Jani and Chris, it has been so much fun playing in the book world with you at the same time—you are my family.

Bill Bauman, for being my personal guardian angel and spiritual mentor. Your expanded vision, deep love, and unique sense of humor are just a few of the reasons you are a constant blessing in my life. Bill Levacy, for always inspiring me in the right direction and at the right time. You've guided me impeccably for the past fifteen years—you're a star! Nandu, for helping me stay on course and keeping the energy high.

Catherine Oxenberg, my dear soul sister, your spiritual perspective and loving friendship bring so much joy and peace in my life. I love you. Debra Poneman for being my first mentor, my great friend, and for helping me say *Yes to Success*.

Marianne Williamson, for being an exquisite role model. I love how you contribute to the world, and your magnificence as a leader, a visionary, and a friend. Hale Dwoskin and Amy Edwards, for encouraging me to remember the truth and always being available with your love and wisdom. Arielle Ford and Brian Hilliard, for sharing your love and skill in living. Gayatri Schiffer and Brian Siddhartha Ingle, for keeping joy, order, and spirit in our home. Jill Lublin and Steve Lillo, for being so willing to jump in to help. Your fantastic skills, insights, and care saved the day many times. Stephen M. R. Covey, for our conversation that encouraged me more than you know.

Swami Chandrasekharanand Saraswati and Joan Shivarpita Harrigan for your brilliant teachings and practices that have made such a difference in my life.

My phenomenal friends who have given me love and support throughout this journey: Lenora Boyle, AlexSandra Leslie, Suzanne Lawlor, Mary Weiss, Stewart and Joan Emery, Peggy O'Neill, Barbara Stanny, Elinor Hall, Ron Hall, Jeddah Mali, Robert Kenyon, Renee Skop, Lynn Robertson, Cindy Buck, John and Bonnie Gray, Yakov Smirnoff, Donna Bauman, Diane Alabaster, Suelena Pamplin, Bruce Allen, Master George Yau, Michael Laughrin, Janet Switzer. My women's groups: Holly Moore, Lane Cole, Janice Peterson, Sandy Kopff (smiling down), Kami Mailloux, Terri Tate, Elyn Kopeck, Katherine Revoir, and my Monday morning visions group. And to all my friends who saw articles on happiness and sent them to me (you know who you are).

From Carol:

Marci, for inviting me to join you on this life-changing project. You've added to my life in so many ways and I will always be deeply grateful. My wonderful husband, Larry Kline, who cheered me on every step of the way, patiently accepting month after month of nonstop work. Your love and support mean more to me than you can ever know. My stepchildren, Lorin and McKenna—your sense of self and spirit of adventure continually inspire me. My mother, Selma, who is always so loving and encouraging. My sister, Bobbie, the other author in the family, who listened understandingly and was always willing to help me with grammar questions. My "sensible" brother, Burt, for giving me wise counsel whenever I called. My other sibs and their spouses, Jim and Di, Wilbur, Pam, Holly and Charlie, who took up the slack. I owe you—and love you all. Cindy Buck, for being my loving friend, cheerleader, and confidante. I couldn't have done it without you, Cindala. My women's group: Karen Joost, my serene heart-sister, and Toni D'Orr, the embodiment of kindness, for so freely sharing your insights and affection. I love you more with each passing year. My adored friends: Debbie Pogel—the other Shaina Rivkah, Josie Batorski, Peggy O'Neill, Ceci Balmer, Nina Falk, Lane Cole, Holly Moore, Betsy Dockhorn, Georgia Nemkov, Christian Wolfbrandt, Stephanie Hewitt, the Woolfs, Marcy Luikart, Kathy Bennett, Laurie Edgcomb, and Wilma Melville; your friendship and support keep me going and make life so sweet.

From Both of Us:

Our amazing editors: Betsy Rapoport, who's not only superbly talented at what she does, but is funny, kind, and oh so wise. You were a joy to work with! Cindy Buck, whose editorial brilliance and valuable input improved this book tremendously, and whose friendship we prize deeply. We love you, Cin. Nancy Marriott, your hard work, unflagging enthusiasm, and positivity were a blessing to us. And Kristin Loberg, your skill, good humor, and steadiness were matched only by your vast experience and competence.

Katina Griffin, Marci's executive assistant, for kindheartedly going above and beyond the call of duty to support us and this book. Sue Penberthy, Marci's loyal assistant and bookkeeper, who for eleven years has nourished her with "mother" energy and always kept the money flowing. Suzanna Gratz, for your dedication and persistence juggling a multitude of balls in such a loving fashion. Laurie Kalter and Megan

Woolever, for your great support, thorough research, and crackerjack project management. And D'ette Corona, who kept our permissions process in order and whose remarkably even keel continues to amaze us. You are a gem.

Sarah Clarehart, for your wholehearted dedication, saintly patience, and graphic design genius. Randall Heath and Liz Howard, for your skillful artistry. Joe Burull and Jerry Downs, for your keen photographic eye and your hard work making Marci look her best! Aylene Rhiger, for your website wizardry. Jerry Teplitz, for your muscle-testing mastery. Paul Hoffman, for making our message sing! Scott de Moulin and Dallyce Brisbin, for your generous and brilliant coaching.

Our publishing "dream team," the fabulous and talented people at Free Press: Dominick Anfuso, for being the most easygoing, charming, reassuring, and positive editor on the planet. We feel so lucky to have worked with you on this project. Martha Levin, for your confidence in this book. Maria Auperin, for your kindness, patience, and competence helping us every step of the way. Leah Miller, for your joyful care in coordinating so many details for this book. Eric Fuentecilla, for your excellent work on the cover. Eleni Caminis, for your printing heroism. And the wonderful marketing and publicity team, including Suzanne Donahue, Carisa Hays, and Heidi Metcalfe, for helping get this book in the hands of so many readers.

The Happy 100, for giving so freely of your time and experience to help others find the same happiness you radiate so beautifully. The many people who responded to the Happy for No Reason survey. We read each and every one, and they provided us such valuable information.

The subject matter experts in the various fields who patiently answered our many questions. In addition to the many experts already quoted in the book, we're grateful to the following people: Arjuna Ardagh, Jim Bunch, Katie Darling, Dr. John Demartini, Amy Edwards, Pralaya Gordon, Joan Shivarpita Harrigan, Dr. Steven Hotze, the late Isa Lindwall, Dr. Elena Loboda, Sue Morter, Christian Opitz, George Ortega, Swami Chandrasekharanand Saraswati, Susan Seifert, Mark and Bonita Thompson, and Jerry White. Thank you for explaining complex scientific processes in a way that we nonscientists could easily understand and for sharing brilliant insights in the field of happiness. Your contributions provide the objective framework for the concept of Happy for No Reason and the steps of building your Home for Happiness.

Robert Biswas-Diener, one of the kindest men ever, who shared his time and expertise with us whenever we called on him.

Our guinea pigs, those people who took the time to read and give us feedback on our manuscript: Chris Attwood, Janet Attwood, Sergio Baroni, Lane Cole, Oriana Green, Lisa Hotchkiss, Katrina Hunt, Brian Siddhartha Ingle, Suzanne Lawlor, Peggy O'Neill, Gayatri Schiffer, Barbara Stanny, and Kevin Twohy. Your input was immensely useful.

Because of the size and scope of this project, we may have left out the names of some people who contributed along the way. If so, please forgive us, and know that we really do appreciate you very much.

We are so grateful and love you all!

GIVING BACK

In the spirit of giving back, we are delighted to donate a portion of the author proceeds from *Happy for No Reason* to the following two worthy causes:

Operation Smile. Founded in 1982, Operation Smile is a worldwide children's medical charity whose network of global volunteers are dedicated to helping improve the health and lives of children and young adults. Since its founding, Operation Smile has treated more than 100,000 children born with cleft lips, cleft palates, and other facial deformities. In addition to contributing free medical treatment, Operation Smile trains local medical professionals in its twenty-five partner countries and leaves behind crucial equipment to lay the groundwork for long-term self-sufficiency.

Operation Smile, Inc.
6435 Tidewater Drive, Norfolk, VA 23509
Phone: (888) OPSMILE, Fax: (757) 321-7660
Website: *www.operationsmile.org*

The Pachamama Alliance. The Pachamama Alliance is dedicated to empowering indigenous people to preserve their territories and way of life, and thereby protect the natural world for the entire human family. Their main strategy includes supplying rainforest peoples with the tools and resources necessary to support the continued strength and vitality of their communities and culture. The indigenous people offer a new way of seeing and living in the world that is inherently interconnected and sustainable. Together, this reciprocal partnership is working to bring forth an environmentally sustainable, spiritually fulfilling, and socially just human presence on this planet.

The Pachamama Alliance
1009 General Kennedy Avenue, PO Box 29191, San Francisco, CA 94129
Phone: (415) 561-4522
Web site: *www.pachamama.org*

ABOUT MARCI SHIMOFF

Marci Shimoff is a celebrated transformational leader and happiness expert who has inspired millions of people around the world with her message of the infinite possibilities that life holds. One of the nation's foremost motivational experts and a top-rated professional speaker, she has delivered programs for a large variety of audiences and organizations, including numerous Fortune 500 companies. For over twenty years, she has received wide acclaim for sharing her breakthrough methods for personal fulfillment and professional success.

Marci is also one of the best-selling nonfiction authors of all time and the woman's face of the biggest self-help book phenomenon in history, *Chicken Soup for the Soul,* which has reached more than 150 million people. She is the coauthor of six of the top-selling titles in the series, including *Chicken Soup for the Woman's Soul* and *Chicken Soup for the Mother's Soul.* Her books have sold more than 13 million copies worldwide, in thirty-three languages, and have been on the *New York Times* best-seller list for a total of 108 weeks, with four titles reaching #1 for a total of twelve weeks. Her books have also topped the *USA Today* and *Publishers Weekly* best-seller lists.

In addition, Marci is a featured teacher in the international movie and book phenomenon *The Secret,* offering her insights on the key principles to creating lasting success and fulfillment. A popular and engaging media personality, Marci has appeared on more than 500 national and regional television and radio shows and has been interviewed for more than 100 newspaper articles throughout North America. Her work has been published in national women's magazines, including *Ladies' Home Journal* and *Woman's World.*

President and cofounder of The Esteem Group, Marci delivers keynote addresses and seminars on self-empowerment and peak performance to corporations, women's associations, and professional and nonprofit organizations. She received her MBA in organizational behavior from UCLA and also completed a one-year advanced certification program to become a stress management consultant.

Marci is a founding member and serves on the Executive Committee of the Transformational Leadership Council, a group of 100 top leaders serving over 10 million people in the self-development market. Marci is dedicated to fulfilling her vision and life's purpose of helping people to live more empowered and joy-filled lives.

To find out more about Marci's keynote presentations, books, or seminar programs, you can contact her at:

The Esteem Group
369-B Third Street #314
San Rafael, CA 94901
Phone: 415-789-1300
Fax: 415-789-1309
www.marcishimoff.com
www.happyfornoreason.com

ABOUT CAROL KLINE

Carol Kline is the coauthor of five books with over 5 million sold, in the best-selling *Chicken Soup for the Soul* series, including *Chicken Soup for the Dog Lover's Soul* and *Chicken Soup for the Cat Lover's Soul,* and the #1 *New York Times* best-selling *Chicken Soup for the Mother's Soul 2.* In 2006, she cowrote *You've Got to Read This Book: 55 People Tell the Story of the Book That Changed Their Life,* with Jack Canfield and Gay Hendricks.

A freelance writer and editor since 1980, Carol, who has a BA in literature, specializes in narrative nonfiction and self-help. She has written for newspapers, newsletters, and magazines, and, in addition to her own *Chicken Soup* books, has also contributed stories and her editing talents to many other books in the *Chicken Soup for the Soul* series.

Carol is also a speaker, self-esteem facilitator, and animal welfare advocate. In addition, she has taught stress-management systems to the general public since 1975. At present, she is at work on several writing projects on a variety of topics.

To write to Carol or to inquire about her writing or speaking services, please use the following contact information:

Carol Kline
Carol Kline, Inc.
P.O. Box 521
Ojai, CA 93024

E-mail: ckline@happyfornoreason.com

BIOGRAPHIES OF THE HAPPY 100 WHOSE STORIES APPEAR IN *HAPPY FOR NO REASON*

Janet Attwood is the coauthor of the #1 national best-selling book, *The Passion Test,* coauthor of *From Sad to Glad,* and the cofounder of the #1 online transformational magazine, *Healthy Wealthy n Wise*. An expert on passion, she presents her Passion Test programs all over the world. Janet's "Empowered Women CD Series" is now being broadcast in women's homeless shelters across the United States. www.janetattwood.com

Martha Beck is a *New York Times* best-selling author and a monthly columnist at *O: The Oprah Magazine*. Called by NPR "the best-known life coach in America," her books include *The Four-Day Win: End Your Diet War and Achieve Thinner Peace* and *Expecting Adam*. www.liveyournorthstar.com

Michael Bernard Beckwith is the founder of the Agape International Spiritual Center in Los Angeles. Dr. Beckwith conducts retreats and is a teacher of meditation, a seminar leader, and the originator of the Life Visioning Process, which he teaches throughout the country. His books include *Inspirations of the Heart, Forty Day Mind Fast Soul Feast, A Manifesto of Peace,* and *Living from the Overflow*. www.agapelive.com

Rhonda Byrne is the producer and creator of the worldwide book and film phenomenon *The Secret* and was listed among *Time* magazine's 100 Most Influential People in the World in 2007. Originally from Australia, Rhonda is currently in the United States, where she is continuing her work on projects that will uplift, inspire, and bring joy to the world. www.thesecret.tv

Chellie Campbell is the author of *The Wealthy Spirit* and *Zero to Zillionaire,* and created the popular Financial Stress Reduction® Workshop to help people become successful at producing more income, managing their money, and having more time off for fun! A professional speaker, seminar leader, and poker champion, Chellie teaches her workshops in the Los Angeles area and gives programs throughout the country. www.chellie.com

Aerial Gilbert is the outreach manager at Guide Dogs for the Blind and is also an avid athlete. She rows regularly on San Francisco Bay and has competed successfully in numerous rowing events. Aerial shares her personal experiences in public presentations to fraternal organizations, businesses, schools, and other groups. www.guidedogs.com

Elizabeth Gilbert is the author of numerous books, including the best-selling *Eat Pray Love,* which has recently been optioned by Paramount Pictures for a film starring Julia Roberts. She has also written for the *New York Times Magazine, Real Simple,* and *O: The Oprah Magazine.* Liz currently lives in New Jersey and is at work on a new book. www.elizabethgilbert.com

Mariel Hemingway is an actress who has been pursuing her passion for yoga and health for more than twenty-two years and is now seen as a voice of holistic and balanced living. Her latest book, *Mariel Hemingway's Healthy Living from the Inside Out,* is a how-to guide to finding one's balance and health through self-empowering lifestyle techniques. www.marielhemingway.com

Gay Hendricks, PhD, has served for more than thirty years as one of the major contributors to the fields of relationship transformation and body-mind therapies. Along with his wife, Dr. Kathlyn Hendricks, Gay is the author of many best-sellers, including *Conscious Loving, Spirit-Centered Relationships,* and *The Corporate Mystic,* as well as the founder of the Hendricks Institute, which offers seminars in North America, Asia, and Europe. www.hendricks.com

Chunyi Lin is a certified international Qigong Master, founder of Spring Forest Qigong, and the coauthor of #1 Amazon.com best-seller, *Born a Healer*. In addition, Master Lin has created a series of home learning materials for students, including videos, guided audio meditations, and reference manuals. His vision is "a healer in every family and a world without pain." www.springforestqigong.com

Mary G. Lodge is a mother to five children, eleven grandchildren, and five great-grandchildren. Her hobbies include writing, painting, and gardening and she enjoys speaking on the subject of forgiveness. Contact her at LodgeDoor@aol.com

Lisa Nichols, featured teacher in *The Secret,* is a dynamic international motivational speaker and powerful advocate of personal empowerment. Coauthor of the *Chicken Soup for the African American Soul* series, Lisa is the founder and CEO of Motivating the Teen Spirit, LLC, which is recognized by many as the most comprehensive empowerment skills program available today for teen self-development. www.lisa-nichols.com

Happy Oasis is the founder and CVO, Chief Visionary Officer, of Raw Spirit Festival, Earth's largest raw health, ecosustainability, and world peace festival in Sedona, Arizona. Traveling abroad for decades as an adventure anthropologist and adopted by tribes, Happy authored *Uncivilized Ecstasies* and *Bliss Conscious Communication.* www.RawSpiritFest.com

Catherine Oxenberg is a European princess and an award-winning actress who has appeared in numerous films and television programs and is best known for her role in the popular television series *Dynasty*. In 2006, she and her husband, actor Casper Van Dien, starred in the TV series *Watch Over Me.* She is also the proud mother of five beautiful children. www.catherineoxenberg.com

Rico Provasoli is a retired chiropractor, now full-time writer. His recent titles include *Golf between the Ears* and *Please Don't Tell My Guru*. He lives in northern California. He continues to sail, laugh, and give living thanks for everything. He travels as a public speaker leading seminars on Relief from the Inner Critic. www.ricoprovasoli.com

Zainab Salbi is the founder and CEO of Women for Women International, the 2006 recipient of the Conrad N. Hilton Humanitarian Prize. Zainab is also the author of *Between Two Worlds: Escape from Tyranny: Growing Up in the Shadow of Saddam* and *The Other Side of War: Women's Stories of Survival and Hope.* www.womenforwomen.org

CJ Scarlet, having triumphed over a life-threatening illness, is now an author, motivational speaker, and personal coach dedicated to helping others achieve the happiness and prosperity they deserve. CJ's first inspirational book, *Neptune's Gift,* is now available online at www.cjscarlet.com

Lynne Twist, author of the best-selling book *The Soul of Money,* is a global activist, fund-raiser, speaker, and consultant who has dedicated her life to global initiatives that serve the best instincts in all of us, including ending world hunger, protecting the world's rainforests, and creating a sustainable future for all life. www.soulofmoney.org

PERMISSIONS

We are grateful to the various people who shared with us their compelling and uplifting stories for inclusion in this book. In addition, we thank the following individuals and organizations who have given us permission to reprint their material:

pg. 18 Grumpy Gene cartoon. Printed by permission of Hagen Cartoons.
pg. 32 Money cartoon. Printed by permission of Patrick Hardin.
pg. 35 Dog cartoon. Printed by permission of Mike Twohy; © 1992 *The New Yorker Magazine.*
pg. 54 Pumpkin cartoon. Printed by permission of Mark Anderson.
pg. 63 *The Solutions Focus Technique.* Printed by permission of Paul Z. Jackson and Mark McKergow.
pg. 64 Blaming cartoon. Printed by permission of Martha Campbell.
pg. 78 *M-Power March.* Printed by permission of Morter HealthSystems.
pg. 86 Bad programming cartoon. Copyright 2001 by Randy Glasbergen. www.glasbergen.com
pg. 97 *The Work Mini-Worksheet.* Printed by permission of Byron Katie.
pg. 105 *The Letting Go Exercise.* Printed by permission of The Sedona Method®.
pg. 108 Dear Diary cartoon. Printed by permission of Mike Twohy; © 1996 *The New Yorker Magazine.*
pg. 118 Heart Rhythm graphs. Printed by permission of the Institute of HeartMath.
pg. 119 Good beat cartoon. Printed by permission of Jonny Hawkins.
pg. 127 Dr. Emoto's water photos. Printed by permission of I.H.M. Co., LTD.
pg. 132 *The Quick Coherence® Technique.* Printed by permission of the Institute of HeartMath. Quick Coherence is a registered trademark of the Institute of HeartMath.
pg. 150 Smile transplant cartoon. Copyright 2001 by Randy Glasbergen. www.glasbergen.com
pg. 159 Ziggy ©2005 Ziggy and Friends, Inc. Reprinted with permission of Universal Press Syndicate. All rights reserved.
pg. 161 "Your Brain's True and False Emotional Chemistry" from *The Mood Cure* by Julia Ross, copyright © 2002 by Julia Ross. Used by permission of Viking Penguin, a division of Penguin Group (USA) Inc.
pg. 163 "The Four-Part Mood Type Questionnaire" from *The Mood Cure* by Julia Ross, copyright © 2002 by Julia Ross. Used by permission of Viking Penguin, a division of Penguin Group (USA) Inc.

pg. 175 *Breathing the Universe Exercise*. Printed by permission of Spring Forest Qigong.

pg. 187 Cell phone cartoon. Copyright 2001 by Randy Glasbergen. www.glasbergen.com

pg. 190 *Postcard.* From *A Lotus Grows in the Mud* by Goldie Hawn, with Wendy Holden, © 2005 by Illume, LLC. Used by permission of G. P. Putnam's Sons, a division of Penguin Group (USA) Inc.

pg. 196 Dr. Emoto's water photos. Printed by permission of I.H.M. Co., LTD.

pg. 198 *Hello, God. I'm Liz.* Adapted from *Eat, Pray, Love* by Elizabeth Gilbert, ©2006 by Elizabeth Gilbert. Used by permission of Viking Penguin, a division of Penguin Group (USA) Inc. Additional material is from an interview with the author.

pg. 227 The *Identifying Your Passions Exercise* used by permission of Janet Attwood and Chris Attwood.

pg. 245 Infectious smile cartoon. Copyright 2001 by Randy Glasbergen. www.glasbergen.com

pg. 253 Skippy cartoon. Printed by permission of Jonny Hawkins.

pg. 271 Gate 4-A Albuquerque Airport story. Printed by permission of Naomi Shihab Nye.